THREE MEDIEVAL RHETORICAL ARTS

# Three Medieval
# Rhetorical Arts

EDITED BY

## JAMES J. MURPHY

University of California Press
Berkeley, Los Angeles, and London

1971

# Contents

Introduction      JAMES J. MURPHY       vii

Anonymous of Bologna:
*The Principles of Letter-Writing*
(1135 A.D.)      JAMES J. MURPHY       1

Geoffrey of Vinsauf:
*The New Poetics*
(C. 1210 A.D.)      JANE BALTZELL KOPP       27

Robert of Basevorn:
*The Form of Preaching*
(1322 A.D.)      LEOPOLD KRUL O.S.B.       109

Appendix: Excerpts from Two University
Textbooks on Dialectic: Aristotle's
*Topics* and *On Sophistical Refutations*

      W. A. PICKARD-CAMBRIDGE       217

Bibliography       231

# Introduction: The Medieval Background

This volume presents three medieval treatises on speaking and writing—three "Arts" (books) designed by their authors to assist their colleagues in the preparation of poems, letters, hymns, sermons, or any other kind of composition.

The authors are of various nationalities, being Italian, French, or English, and their immediate subjects may appear equally varied to a modern reader. The three Arts also a considerable span of time, from 1135 to 1322, yet there is remarkable agreement among them, especially in terms of their respect for order and for plan. All are, in other words, *preceptive* in nature—that is, they were written to give specific advice to future writers and speakers. As one might expect, each was written by a school master. Their underlying respect for planning, which is a heritage of ancient grammar and rhetoric, is perhaps best expressed by Geoffrey or Vinsauf in the opening passage of his *New Poetics*:

> If a man has a house to build, he does not rush with a hasty hand into the act itself: the work is first measured out with his heart's inward plumb-line, and the inner man marks out the design beforehand, according to a definite plan; his heart's hand shapes the whole before his body's hand does so, and his building is a plan before it is a reality.

Robert of Basevorn, author of *The Form of Preaching*, castigates the theologians who attempt to preach without order "when they do not even know the form of preaching." And the anonymous author of the twelfth century *Rationes dictandi* stresses the importance of knowing the "Approved Format" of the five-part formal letter.[1]

If one defines "rhetoric" as a set of precepts that provide a definite method or plan for speaking and writing, then each of these medieval arts can be called "rhetorical." One of the authors called himself a grammarian, a second was a theologian, and the third was *dictator* in a Bolognese school. Nevertheless each one, in his own way, shared in the Greco-Roman preceptive tradition begun by Isocrates and Aristotle and continued by Cicero, Horace, Quintilian, and Donatus.

Since the long history of this Western preceptive tradition has some bearing on the nature of the three Arts included here, it might be useful at this point to describe briefly the manner in which the ancient precepts reached the writers of the middle ages.

The ancient world—which for this purpose ends about A.D. 426 with the publication of the final book of the *De doctrina christiana* of Saint Augustine—produced four separate traditions within the general framework. First of these is the Aristotelian tradition.[2] The chief works are his *Rhetoric,* and two dialectical works titled *Topics,* and *On Sophistical Refutations.* (The *Poetics* plays an insignificant role in Europe prior to the fifteenth century and thus falls outside the scope of our remarks here.) The Aristotelian approach to discourse is philosophical, with a close interrelation proposed between the various modes of discourse. Aristotelian dialectic, or the art of reasoning about opinion, became extremely important in the medieval universities as a base for the Disputation (*dis-*

1. For further bibliographic details of works treated in this section, see James J. Murphy, *Medieval Rhetoric: A Select Bibliography* (Toronto, 1971); or Murphy, "Rhetoric in Fourteenth Century Oxford," *Medium Aevum* 34 (1965), 1–20; or Murphy, "The Medieval Arts of Discourse: An Introductory Bibliography," *Speech Monographs* 29 (1962), 71–78.
2. For a resume of the major elements in this tradition, see Friedrich Solmsen, "The Aristotelian Tradition in Ancient Rhetoric," *American Journal of Philology* 62 (1941), 35–50, 169–190. The *Rhetoric* is available in several useful translations, especially by Lane Cooper (New York, 1932) and by Friedrich Solmsen (New York, 1954). The two dialectical works may be found in *The Works of Aristotle Translated into English,* Ed. W. D. Ross (twelve volumes: Oxford, 1924–1928), Vol. 1.

*putatio*); Paris and Oxford, for instance, made the *Topics* and *On Sophistical Refutations* required reading for several centuries.

The second tradition, the Ciceronian, is based on concepts first stated by Isocrates;[3] it includes the Pseudo-Ciceronian *Rhetorica ad Herennium*,[4] the *Institutio Oratoria* of Quintilian,[5] and the seven rhetorical works of Cicero himself:[6] his youthful *De inventione* in particular was widely copied and disseminated in the middle ages. Cicero's own favorite work, *De Oratore*, is markedly different from his earlier treatises and is closer in spirit to the twelfth and last book of Quintilian's work. But the Ciceronian tradition as it was transmitted to the middle ages consisted primarily of *De inventione*, the *Rhetorica ad Herennium*, and a mutilated text of Quintilian. Here the approach is frankly pragmatic, with heavy emphasis on legal argumentation using the complex doctrine of *Constitutio* (*or status*) borrowed from a Hellenistic theorist named Hermagoras of Temnos.

According to Cicero, rhetoric's five parts are *inventio* (finding of material), *dispositio* (arranging of it), *elocutio* (putting words to invented material), *pronuntiatio* (physical delivery), and finally *memoria* (retention of ideas, words, and their order).[7] During the third and fourth Christian centuries Roman writers like Fortunatianus reduced the whole Ciceronian corpus to an abbreviated form in a series of compendia or abstracts. It is the compendium, then, which is taken up by Martianus Capella, copied by Cassiodorus and Isidore of Seville, and ultimately taken into the heart of the middle

3. A concise summary of the Ciceronian tradition may be found in Martin L. Clarke, *Rhetoric at Rome* (London, 1953); for the influence of Isocrates see Harry M. Hubbell, *The Influence of Isocrates on Cicero, Dionysius, and Aristides* (New Haven, Connecticut, 1913).
4. "Cicero" (*i.e.* Pseudo-Cicero), *Rhetorica ad Herennium*, ed. and trans. Harry Caplan (Cambridge, Mass., Loeb Classical Library, 1954).
5. Quintilian. *Institutio oratoria*, trans. H. E. Butler, 4 vols. (Loeb Classical Library, 1953); and also Quintilian, *On The Early Education of the Citizen-Orator*, trans. the Reverend John Selby Watson and James J. Murphy, Introduction by James J. Murphy (Indianapolis, New York and Kansas City, 1965).
6. All seven of Cicero's rhetorical works are available in Loeb Library editions: *De inventione, Topica, Orator, De optimo genera oratorum, De partitione oratoria, Brutus, and De oratore*; for their medieval use, however, see Murphy, "Cicero's Rhetoric in the Middle Ages," *Quarterly Journal of Speech* 53 (1967), 334–341.
7. An abstract of Ciceronian doctrines also occurs in Donald Lemen Clark, *Rhetoric in the Greco-Roman Tradition* (New York, 1957), pp. 67–142.

ages by other encyclopedists.[8] Consequently, medieval libraries often contained both Cicero, in the form of *De inventione*, and Cicero capsulized,in the form of a book like Isidore's *Etymologia*. Cicero remains the great apostle of discourse, but it is not always his own testament that is quoted.

Still a third ancient development can best be described as "The Grammatical Tradition." [9] The grammarian Aelius Donatus and the poet Horace are its chief authors. Its chief sponsor was the Roman school system which flourished for half a thousand years in the Mediterranean world; in places like Gaul and Germany the Roman schools lasted for some time after Rome itself was conquered by the barbarians in 410 A.D. The Roman rhetorical schools systematically introduced their young students to grammatical matters through the study of individual words, of model poems or speeches, by the careful reworking (*imitatio*) of poems and other models in the classroom, and by paraphrasing the models in the students' own words. Quintilian in his *Institutio oratoria* (95 A.D), for instance, defines grammar as having a double function: "the art of speaking correctly and the interpretation of the poets." [10] This was to be a basic definition for most of the middle ages. There was no commonly accepted textbook on Latin grammar, however, until the appearance of the *Ars maior* of Donatus about 350 A.D.; Donatus set out the standard "eight parts of speech" and other basic syntactical rules so definitely that his name became a medieval byword for a primer or elementary textbook.[11] This syntactical emphasis was continued later by the grammarian Priscian (fl. 525 A.D.) whose lengthy *Ars grammatica* became the standard advanced textbook

8. The full history of this early encyclopedic movement is as yet unwritten. For texts, see Martianus Capella, *De Nuptiis Philologiae et Mercurii* in *Martianus Capella*, ed. [Wilhelm] Adolfus Dick (Leipzig, 1925); Cassiodorus Senator, *An Introduction to Divine and Human Readings*, trans. with intro. by Leslie Webber Jones (New York, 1946); and Isidorus, *Etymologiarum sive Originum Libri –XX*, 2 vols., ed. W. M. Lindsay (Oxford, 1911).
9. There is no satisfactory single history of this subject. Some very brief yet revealing remarks may be found in R. H. Robins, *Ancient and Medieval Grammatical Theory in Europe* (London, 1951).
10. Quintilian, *On the Early Education of the Citizen-Orator* ed. James J. Murphy (New York: Library of Liberal Arts 220), Book One, Chap. Four (p. 28).
11. When the fourteenth-century English writer Reginald Pecock wrote a survey of religious doctrine, for instance, he called it the *Donet of Christian Religion*. More than a thousand manuscript copies of Donatus still exist.

for much of the middle ages despite the appearance of rival works around 1200 A.D. (Medieval users frequently divided Priscian's 18-book work into two unequal parts, treating the last two books separately under the title *On Constructions* (*De constructionibus*); our author of *The Principles of Letter-writing*, for example, uses this section of Priscian's work to discuss ways of varying the grammatical form of letters.)

But the *Ars Maior* of Donatus is also important for its expansion of grammar into the stylistic matter of the tropes and figures. The *Rhetorica ad Herennium* had treated thirty-five figures of diction, nineteen figures of thought, and then ten tropes in discussing the ways to add "ornament" to language. Donatus, as a grammarian, discussed seventeen figures of speech, fourteen of which are different from those of the *ad Herennium;* moveover, Donatus expanded the list of tropes from ten to twenty-eight. The history of *figurae, exornationes,* and *scema* has not yet been written, despite some attempts to begin the task, consequently this enlargement of grammatical concern into the realm of figures and tropes represents a still-uncharted movement.[12]

The so-called *Art of Poetry* (*Ars poetica*) of the poet Horace (65–8 B.C.) is also important in the ancient grammatical tradition.[13] It is the one classical discussion of poetry that attempts to be *preceptive*—that is, it lays down specific advice to writers about how to go about the composition of poetry. (Aristotle's *Poetics* of course deals primarily with drama.) Horace thus laid down precepts for writers, just as the rhetorical texts of the time laid down precepts for speakers. There is in fact a high correlation between the ideas of Horace and the rhetorical precepts of Cicero.[14] Horace therefore marks a bridge between ancient grammar and rhetoric because of this preceptive emphasis. When Geoffrey of Vinsauf wrote a new

---

12. See, however, Leonid Arbusow, *Colores Rhetorici: Eine Auswahl rhetorischer Figuren und Gemeinplätze als Hilfsmittel für akademische Übungen an mittelalterlichen Texten* (Göttingen, 1948); and Heinrich Lausberg, *Handbuch der literarischen Rhetorik,* 2 vols. (Munich, 1960).

13. The usual title of this brief work has been added by critics since Horace wrote it in the form of a letter to one Piso and did not give it a title. For text see Horace, *Satires, Epistles and Ars Poetica,* ed. and trans. H. Rushton Fairclough (Cambridge, Mass.: Loeb Classical Library, 1955).

14. For instance, George C. Fiske and Mary Grant, *Cicero's De Oratore and Horace's Ars Poetica* (Madison, Wisconsin, 1929).

preceptive treatise on poetry in the early thirteenth century, it was only natural that his title (*The New Poetics*) should indicate that he intended his book to supplant the 'Old Poetics' of Horace.

Finally, a fourth and less important ancient tradition of discourse deserves mention.[15] It is almost a contradiction of terms to call this a "sophistic rhetoric," because sophistry is by definition inimical to rhetoric, and yet some note should be paid to the perpetuation of the two types of schoolroom exercises—*declamatio* and *progymnasmata*—which flourished in a special way during that period usually known as the Second Sophistic (A.D. 50–400). Declamations were exercises in fictitious speech-making. One kind, the *suasoria*, asked the student to prepare and deliver fictitious political speeches; the second, the *controversia*, called for fictitious legal speeches. Seneca the Elder's collection was popular in the middle ages, but was used as a collection of *exempla* rather than a preceptive guide to preparing for future discourse; Nicholas Trevet, in fact, wrote a moralizing commentary on Seneca. A second result of of the Second Sophistic was the popularization of the *progymnasmata* of Hermogenes, a second-century sophist, transmitted directly into the middle ages by Priscian. *Progymnasmata* were short exercises in composition, the most influential of which proved to be those dealing with ways to describe persons and places. This is another unexplored chapter in medieval culture.

At the end of the classical period, then, a fully equipped library of treatises on the arts of discourse might have included works in all four traditions: Aristotelian, Ciceronian, Grammatical, and Sophistic.

Significantly, though, the middle ages opened with a major debate about the very principle of preceptive tradition itself. The Church, faced with the massive general problem of delineating the rightful relation between sacred and secular, also faced this problem in relation to discourse. "My preaching," Saint Paul had said, "was not in the persuasive words of human wisdom, but in the showing of the Spirit and the Power" (I Cor 2:3–4). And the Greek preacher Origen had wondered whether God's grace was perhaps not the

15. The characteristics of the Second Sophistic are summarized briefly in the opening chapter of Charles Sears Baldwin, *Medieval Rhetoric and Poetic* (New York, 1928).

only true means of moving man's mind. It is interesting to note the dilemma of Saint Jerome, to whom God appeared in a dream after he had been reading the Latin classics: "Thou art not a Christian," God thundered, "but a Ciceronian." And even Saint Augustine was, in a sense, converted from rhetoric to Christianity. The debate involved virtually every major ecclesiastical figure of the second to the fourth century, but it was ended by Augustine, himself a former teacher of rhetoric and an admirer of Cicero. Augustine's *De doctrina christiana* (426 A.D.) is therefore one of the most significant works of the early middle ages.[16]

The *De doctrina* begins by pointing out that the means of finding material for understanding Scripture (the *modus inveniendi*) is different from the means of expressing the ideas found (the *modus proferendi*). Augustine urged the Church to study the human arts of discourse—in particular, rhetoric—either through formal schooling or through study of great models. Cicero was of course Augustine's ideal as a theorist, but he turned to Holy Scripture to show that the sacred writings do indeed contain all three levels of style described by the Roman rhetoricians. This was both a defense of the style of Scripture and, in turn, a plea for study of Scripture as a guide to style. It was an effective argument, both in terms of the immediate debate within the Church, and in terms of example to later writers. When the early English writer Bede (673–735 A.D.) wished to write his little Latin treatise on the schemes and tropes of Donatus, for instance, he was able to find 122 Scriptural examples to substitute for the classical ones.[17]

After Saint Augustine, the next important step was taken in the 9th century by Rabanus Maurus in his *De clericorum institutione*.[18] It was a germinal step, a slight one, but important nevertheless because it marked a change in attitude towards the corpus of the old profane learning. The encyclopedists—Capella, Isidore, Cassiodorus —had transmited mere compendia. Alcuin, the teacher of Rabanus, returned directly to Cicero for his doctrine of communication. But

16. See Murphy, "Saint Augustine and the Debate about a Christian Rhetoric," *Quarterly Journal of Speech* 46 (1960), 400–410.
17. Bede, *De scematibus et tropis*. It has been translated by Gussie Hecht Tanenhaus, "Bede's *De schematibus et tropis*—A Translation," *QJS* 48 (1962), 237–253.
18. James J. Murphy," Saint Augustine and Rabanus Maurus: The Genesis of Medieval Rhetoric," *Western Speech* 31 (1967), 97–110.

Rabanus foreshadowed the developments of the central middle ages
by the deliberate pragmatic selection of only the pertinent doctrines he wished to use. He did not take all of Cicero, or even all of
Isidore, but picked and chose, fitting the old to the new. "We turn
everything to our use," he said—*ad nostrum dogma convertimus*.
He was thus a half step beyond the predecessors who accepted as
an indivisible whole the entire lore of the old disciplines. Rabanus
thus foreshadowed the pragmatism of Alberic of Monte Cassino,
who converted the ancient Ciceronian precepts into the new *ars
dictaminis* in the eleventh century, and of Geoffrey of Vinsauf
who wrote a "New Poetics" in the thirteenth. Rabanus, was, as a
matter of fact, equally predictive of the development of the *ars
praedicandi* in the fourteenth century and was therefore the intellectual forebear of writers like Robert of Basevorn.

From the middle of the ninth century, then, some different element can be seen in the attitude toward the Western preceptive
tradition. It is clear that after Rabanus Maurus the development of
the medieval theories of discourse took a well-defined turn toward
pragmatic selection. Thus medieval rhetoric has a diverse rather
than a unified history: the writers of letters fastened upon certain
rhetorical doctrines: preachers of sermons selected still others, and
even the grammarians compounded the original expansion of Donatus by broadening their field of studies. The basic principle of
medieval rhetoric is a frank pragmatism, making highly-selective
use of ideas from the past for the needs of the present.

For this reason it is necessary at this point to say something about
the various forms in which this prescriptive tradition appeared between 1050 and about 1350.

First of all, it might be noted that the ancient rhetoric itself continued to appear in the middle ages. The Ciceronian tradition was
clearly dominant, especially Cicero's *De inventione* and the Pseudo-
Ciceronian *Rhetorica ad Herennium*, which can be found both in
their original forms copied into medieval books, and also in the form
of commentaries written up to about the end of the thirteenth century. Thierry of Chartres, for instance, wrote a commentary on *De
inventione*. Quintilian, on the other hand, generally is found to be
absent except for occasional references, after some popularity at
Chartres and Bec in the middle of the twelfth century; as a matter of

fact, it was the reappearance of the complete text of Quintilian's *Institutio* in 1416, found by Poggio Bracciolini at St. Gall that marked the end of the "medieval" phase of this subject and pointed the way to the classical rhetorical revival of the Renaissance. In connection with the Ciceronian texts, it is also significant that vernacular translations of Cicero appeared in France and Italy as early as the 1260's

The *Rhetoric* of Aristotle, as contrasted to that of Cicero, seems to have been used very rarely in the middle ages as a rhetorical text.[19] It was translated into Latin twice, the second time by William of Moerbeke, and the famous Parisian scholastic Giles of Rome among others wrote a full commentary for it. On the face of things it would have seemed likely that the general popularity of Aristotle would have made this particular book popular too; on the contrary, medieval rhetoric remained essentially Ciceronian and what Aristotelian influences there were entered the arts of discourse through the so-called "scholastic method" rather than through the book itself. Aristotle's *Rhetoric*, in fact, found medieval use as a book of moral philosophy—linked with his *Ethics* and *Politics*— and not as a preceptive manual.[20]

The truly medieval forms of the arts of discourse, however, fall into three major categories: *ars dictaminis*, the letter writing art; *ars praedicandi*, the art of the thematic sermon; and *ars grammatica*, which is itself divided into several categories.

The *ars dictaminis*, the art of letter writing, was the first of these medieval arts to appear in Western Europe.[21] It is now clear that

19. Nearly three fourths of the nearly 100 surviving manuscripts of the medieval Latin version of the *Rhetoric*, for instance, are bound in with copies of Aristotle's *Ethica or Politica*. See Murphy, *Quarterly Journal of Speech* 52 (1966), 109–115; also: Murphy, "Cicero's Rhetoric in the Middle Ages," *Quarterly Journal of Speech* 53 (1967), 334–341.
20. Murphy "Aristotle's *Rhetoric* in the Middle Ages," *Quarterly Journal of Speech* 52 (1966), 109–115. Also: Murphy, "The Scholastic Condemnation of Rhetoric in the Commentary of Giles of Rome on the *Rhetoric* of Aristotle," in *Arts libéraux et philosophie au moyen âge* (Montreal-Paris, 1969), pp. 833–841.
21. For a brief survey of early developments see Charles H. Haskins, "The Early *Artes dictandi* in Italy," in *Studies in Medieval Culture* (Oxford, 1929), 170–192; for lists of English manuscripts see Noel Denholm-Young, "The *cursus* in England," in *Collected Papers on Mediaeval Subjects* (Oxford, 1946), 26–55. The standard collection of texts is Ludwig Rockinger, *Briefsteller und formelbücher des eilften bis vierzehnten Jahrhunderts*, Quellen und Erörterungen zur bayerischen und deutschen Geschichte, 9 (Munich, 1863).

the first major *ars* on this subject was that of Alberic of Monte Cassino, who wrote his *Radium dictaminis* (sometimes known as *Flores rhetorici*) about 1087. The center of dictaminal activity quickly shifted from Monte Cassino to the city of Bologna, however, where several major works on the subject appeared in rapid succession in the early 1100's Significant authors include Adalbertus Samaritanus, Hugh of Bologna, and Bernard of Romagna. The anonymous *Rationes dictandi* (1135 A.D.), included in this volume, was the first to set forth what became the standard medieval doctrine of five parts for a letter. By 1200 the great mass of popular manuals were written—most of them in Italy—by such masters as Bernard of Bologna, Bernard de Meung, Guido Faba, Boncompagno, Bene of Lucca, Lawrence of Acquilegia, Pons of Provence, and Thomas of Capua. The doctrine was simple enough: basically it depended upon an analogy to the Ciceronian parts of speech. Cicero named six major parts of a speech: *exordium*, or introduction; *narratio*, or background, *divisio*, or statement of parts; *confirmatio*, or proof; *refutatio*, or attack against an opponent's argument; and finally, *peroratio* or conclusion. The *dictamen* writers divided the Ciceronian *exordium* into two separate parts: first, the *salutatio*, or formal greeting of the addresses by his titles and praises, and second, the *captatio benevolentiae*, or introduction proper in which goodwill was sought. The *dictamen* doctrine goes on to make *narratio* the next part, explaining background. Then there is, in place of Ciceronian *confirmatio*, the petition—*petitio* and, finally, *conclusio*—but there is very little theory about conclusions in medieval dictamen treatises. So we have as a consequence the "approved format" of a five-part letter—salutation, introduction, narration, petition and conclusion. It is evident from an examination of these manuals that the writer's chief problems are solved once he decides on an appropriate greeting to his addressee. This is further borne out by the large number of model letter collections which abounded everywhere in medieval Europe.

The history of dictamen theory, especially in its relation to the collection of model letters, throws an interesting light on the literary practices of medievel Europe. Dictamen flourished first in Italy, then for a while in France, especially at Orléans, but by about 1250 the *ars notaria* replaced it in Italy, and in France it was absorbed by the grammarians. Very little new was written in the field after the early thirteenth century, although the old masters were, of course, copied and used.[22]

A second branch of the medieval arts of discourse is the *ars praedicandi*, or art of preparing a "thematic" or "university style" sermon.[23] Nearly three hundred authors of such manuals have been identified (of which, incidentally, only about twenty-five have been edited in some form). It should be recognized at once that the medieval preacher had five separate types of aids available to him: 1) the Scriptures themselves, furnishing both material and even wording for his sermons; 2) collections of *exempla* and other bits of information about man or the universe; 3) concordances, alphabetical lists, etc., designed to *find* materials for him; 4) collections of sermons; and finally, 5) the preaching manual itself, which corresponded to the type of rhetorical treatise written by Cicero or Aristotle. It cannot be emphasized too strongly that this fifth type of preaching aid is fundamentally different in kind from the other four. Each of the other four supplies *materia* rather than *forma*.

Very little is known of the immediate antecedents of the formal *ars praedicandi* as a preceptive form. Charland sees as considerable the influence of the "scholastic method" of the universities, with its emphasis on dialectical divisions and the amplification of ideas through Topic (*loci*) derived from Aristotelian teaching. Caplan, on the other hand, stresses the influence of classical rhetoric.[24] Despite the clear injunctions of Jesus Christ concerning the Christian duty to "Preach to all nations," and despite the enthusiasm of influential theorists like Augustine, there was no major attempt during the first 1200 years of the Christian era to produce a special-

22. However, Italian authors and Italian theories continued to dominate the field down into the fifteenth century. The Englishman Thomas Sampson, who made his living as a private teacher of *dictamen* in Oxford around 1380, based his *Modus dictandi* (British Museum MS. 17 B XLVII, ff. 42–48) on Bolognese doctrines, for instance, as did John de Blakeney in the 1430's.

23. The basic work in this field—with biographies of authors, a sketch of the movement, and two key Latin texts—is Th.-M. Charland, *Artes Praedicandi. Contribution A l'Histoire de la Rhétorique au Moyen Age*. Publications de l'institut d'études médiévales d'Ottawa, 7 (Paris and Ottawa, 1936); Charles Smyth, *The Art of Preaching 747–1939* (London, 1940), presents a rapid overview of these developments.

24. Charland, *Artes praedicandi*, pp. 9–10; Harry Caplan, "Classical Rhetoric and the Mediaeval Theory of Preaching," *Classical Philology* 28 (1933), 73–96.

ized body of rhetorical precepts to aid preachers. Certainly sermon-izing was a major feature of the Church, especially after the ecumenical Council of Nicea in 325 A.D., when the world was divided into "dioceses" with a bishop over each to be responsible for such Christian efforts as preaching in each area. The continuing popularity of Cicero's rhetoric during all those centuries perhaps accounts for the lack of more specialized preaching manuals—and after all, Augustine himself recommended studying good preachers as being better than studying books—but for some reason not yet entirely clear to us this situation changed dramatically at Paris in the early part of the thirteenth century. During the academic year 1230–1231 a number of Latin sermons were preached at the University of Paris using a new and remarkably standardized format employing a "theme" (Scriptural quotation) and a complex process of division and amplification worked out from the opening quotation.[25] Be-cause of the association of this thematic sermon with universities, it has come to be known also as the "University-style sermon." Within a few years, specialized preaching manuals outlining this thematic process began to appear in northern Europe, and continued to be written all over the continent as late as the sixteenth century.

This peculiarly medieval rhetorical form is quite distinct from the comparatively unshaped and less formal "homily" style of ser-mon which was characterized by a direct, almost conversational style of speaking. (John Chrysostom's famous sermon *On the Statues* is a typical example of a sermon constructed without sys-tematic progression of ideas, no doubt relying primarily on the per-sonality of the preacher and his rapport with his congregation. Very probably the popular sermons of the Franciscans and others were also "homilies" in this sense, and did not follow a prescribed for-mat.) The rapid spread of the specialized manuals of the new *ars praedicandi* during the thirteenth and fourteenth centuries, on the other hand, indicates a truly medieval contribution to the history of rhetorical forms.

The typical *ars praedicandi* outlines six parts for a sermon, speci-fying methods of division, and providing a large number of methods to be used in amplifying the Scriptural theme:

25. Texts in M. M. Davy, *Les sermons universitaires Parisiens, 1230–1231* (Paris, 1931).

1. Theme: a Scriptural quotation
2. Protheme: Exordium for the theme itself; usually followed by a prayer.
3. Introduction of theme (antetheme): Explanation of the purpose of the sermon.
4. Division of theme: usually into three or multiples of threes, with *auctoritates* to "prove" each division.
5. Subdivision of theme.
6. Amplification or diliation of each of the divisions, and subdivisions.

While this organizational plan is analogous to the Ciceronian parts of an oration, it differs markedly from the practice common among *dictamen* manuals. The dominant features of the *ars praedicandi* are two: *divisio* and *amplificatio*. It might be noted also that there is seldom much discussion of methods for concluding a sermon. This may not mean that medieval sermons were endless—although perhaps some members of the audience had their doubts about this; instead it reflects a medieval concern with the basic subject matter itself, with the very Scripture itself. Even more important, however, is that this unconcern for the conclusion gives us some clue both to the origins of the genre and to its proper place in the history of the arts of discourse.

Coming as it does out of the scholastic milieu of thirteenth century Paris it might well be expected that the *ars praedicandi* would be scholastic itself, especially since preaching of this type was required of Masters of Theology. Given the dialectical environment, then, it would not be surprising if this characteristic sermon form had followed the form of an epicheireme, or a syllogism with Scriptural tags for proofs of each premise. The history of the subject demonstrates that this was not so. Even though the thematic sermon looks at first glance like a *spoken gloss*—i.e., a stated passage is divided, and then commented upon—the whole emphasis of the early portions is upon audience preparation, in the psychological sense of Cicero's theory. And more important, the writer of a thematic sermon proposes no progression of ideas, nor is there usually a summary or recapitulation at the end of the sermon. The one or two attempts at "syllogizing"—for instance, by Jean de

Chalons, a fourteenth century author—were not widely copied. But it is the general tone of concern about the rhetorical situation— the fact of a living audience which sets the *ars praedicandi* off from *dictamen* and from more "scholastic" written forms of discourse.

English authors, incidentally, are prominent in this field. In the thirteenth century there were Alexander Ashby, Richard de Thetford (one of the most influential in Europe), Hugh Sneyth, and Jean de Galles. Then, in the fourteenth century there were Robert of Basevorn, Thomas Waleys, Robert Holcott, and Ranulph Higden, author of *Polychronicon*. In the fifteenth century were Geoffrey Schale, Simon Alcock, Thomas Penketh, and Thomas of Salisbury. Robert of Basevorn's *Forma praedicandi*, included in this volume, is particularly interesting: writing in 1322, apparently at Oxford, he provides so "typical" an *ars* that his *Forma praedicandi* is sometimes seen as the exemplar of the whole theory, and he found numerous imitators both in England and on the continent.

It now remains to describe the various forms of *ars grammatica* which appeared during the middle ages.[26] The twelfth century is usually regarded as the dividing point between ancient and medieval grammar. The ancient domination of Donatus and Priscian was then challenged by the appearance of Alexander de Villa Dei's *Doctrinale* (1199) [27] and the composition of specialized works in the fields of *rithmus* and *metricum*. The *Doctrinale* and the popular *Graecismus* by Evrard of Bethune [28] both deal with syntactical matters— the *ars recte loquendi* of ancient grammar—but the *Doctrinale* discusses a total of eighty tropes and figures, while the *Graecismus* treats one hundred and four. In terms of relationship with rhetoric, then, even the grammarian's *ars recte loquendi* expands vigorously in the area of style.

Besides these two very popular textbooks, moreover, there are treatises written in each of the other three subdivisions of medieval

26. The standard work in this area is still M. Charles Thurot, "Notices et extraits de divers manuscrits latins pour servir a l'histoire des doctrines grammaticales au moyen age," *Notices et extraits* 22 (1868) [Now reprinted, Frankfurt, 1964], especially pp. 59–148. There is, however, no comprehensive history of medieval grammar.
27. Alexander de Villa Dei, *Doctrinale des Alexander de Villa Dei*, *Monumenta Germaniae Paedogogica*, 12 (Berlin, 1893).
28. Evrard of Bethune, *Eberhardi Bethuniensis Graecismus*, ed. Ioh. Wrobel, Corpus grammaticorum medii aevi, I (Vratislaviae, 1887).

grammar. The definition of Thomas of Capua is often quoted to explain the three subdivisions:

> There are three kinds of writing known from of old: prosaic, as in Cassiodorus; metrical, as in Virgil; and rhythmical, as in Primatis . . . (Dictaminum . . . tria sunt genera a veteribus diffinita, prosaicum, ut Cassiodori, metricum, ut Virgilii, et rithmicum, ut Primatis . . .)

The *ars prosaicum*, first of these, is often joined with the *ars dictaminis*, although in France (and especially with John of Garland) the subject of prose writing is kept as a separate sub-topic. The second subdivision, the *ars rithmica*, deals with rhythmical composition for either letters or for hymns: "Rithmus," says John of Garland, "is a consonance of clause endings ordered with a certain measure but without metrical feet." The most common form of the epistolary *rithmus*, of course, is the so-called *cursus*, the system of rhythmical *clausulae* which spread over Europe after the time of Pope Gelasius II (1118–1119). The medieval *cursus* borrows for prose some of the compositional principles usually employed in writing verse. It might be noted here that this is a subject claimed by grammarians as well as by the more politically minded writers of *artes dictaminis*.

On the other hand, the third subdivision of the grammatical art, that is, the *ars metrica* or *ars poetria*, is more familiar to the student of the middle ages. Since 1926, with the publication of John M. Manly's *Chaucer and the Rhetoricians*, it has been popular to refer to their authors as "rhetoricians." [29]

The medieval *artes poetriae* are themselves divided into two types. First there is the short, specialized type of treatise dealing with *figurae*, *colores*, *tropi*, and other verbal ornaments. They appeared separately all over Europe, often without mention either of an author's name or of their reason for being. But a glance at the common grammatical lore of the day will show that even in those cases where they derived their definitions and examples from *Rhetorica ad Herennium* rather than Donatus—and even this is difficult to

29. The definitive treatment, with some Latin texts, is Edmond Faral, *Les arts poétiques du XII° et du XIII° siècles* (Paris, 1924). And also see John M. Manley, "Chaucer and the Rhetoricians," *Proceedings of the British Academy* 12 (1926), 95–113.

ascertain after about 1250—it is possible to visualize their use in elementary schooling, as adjuncts to ordinary grammar instruction.

The second type of *ars poetriae,* consisting of major preceptive arts, includes such works as the *Ars versificatoria* of Mathew of Vendome, the *Laborintus* of Evrardus Allemanus, the *Ars versificaria* of Gervais de Melkley, and of course the *Poetria nova* of Geoffrey of Vinsauf which is included in this volume.[30] Vinsauf's treatise, composed in hexameter verse between 1208 and 1213, falls into seven sections: Preface, general remarks, disposition, amplifications and abbreviation, ornaments of style, memory and delivery, and an epilogue. It is by far the most famous, and partly because its repertoire of rhetorical figures and tropes is derived ultimately from the Pseudo-Ciceronian *Rhetorica ad Herennium,* it has often been singled out as the chief representative of the "rhetorical" element in medieval poetic theory.[31]

The three *Artes* translated in this volume, therefore, represent major streams of medieval thought about writing and speaking. Each one speaks for itself, of course, and for the medieval tradition that produced it; but beyond that there is an evident sharing of a common cultural heritage. Both ancient grammar and ancient rhetoric contribute to this heritage, the proportions varying from work to work, while ancient logic or dialectic has little apparent influence. Consequently it is not really fair to assume—as is so often done—that the so-called *trivium* of grammar, rhetoric, and dialectic maintained an unbroken sway throughout the whole medieval period. The authors of these three Arts clearly owed very little to dialec-

30. Faral, *Les arts poetiques,* includes the texts of Matthew of Vendôme (pp. 109–193), Evrard Allemanus (pp. 337–377), and Geoffrey of Vinsauf (pp. 197–262) as well as the text of Vinsauf's *Documentum* covering much the same ground (pp. 265–320). For text of Gervais de Melkley see Gervais von Melkley, *Ars poetica,* ed. Hans-Jurgen Grabener, *Forschungen zur romanischen Philologie,* 17 (Munster, 1965).

31. John of Garland's *De arte prosayca metrica et rithmica* (before 1249) belongs in one sense to the same category as Vinsauf's work, but it branches out to include all three modes of the medieval *ars grammatica*—the prosaic, metrical, and rhythmical aspects of language. Garland's *Ars,* then, is noteworthy as one of the most ambitious medieval attempts to provide a correlation among these three main streams of "grammatical" art. For text see *Romanische forschungen* 13 (1902), 885–950 (prose and metrics section) and Giovanni Mari (ed.), *Il trattati medievali di ritmica latina* (Milan, 1899). The sections on prose and metrics have been translated by Traugott Lawler (unpublished dissertation, Harvard University, 1966).

tic, turning instead to rhetorical and grammatical sources for their precepts. (To provide the reader with an idea of the training in language which the university course in *dialectica* did afford medieval students, however, the Appendix to this volume includes excerpts from the two Aristotelian works used as textbooks: the *Topics* and *On Sophistical Refutations*.) [32]

The modern reader may also wonder at the absence of works dealing with secular speaking. The answer is plain: the middle ages did not produce any major original works on secular speaking, for the simple reason that the political climate which had encouraged such writing in ancient Greece and Rome simply did not exist in medieval Europe. Only with the rise of Italian communes, late in the period, do we see the re-establishment of what might be called a popular oratory, and when this did occur, the well-established rhetoric of Cicero was already available to meet the need.

For the student of medieval culture, then, these three translated works may provide insights into such varied facets of the middle ages as education, literature, diplomacy, and religion—into every sphere, in fact, in which the use of language played a part. Brunetto Latini, teacher of Dante, noted in his *Tresor* (1266) that while the "Masters" teach two kinds of rhetoric (oral and written), "the precepts are common to both" (*li enseignment sont commun*). The manner in which these three medieval theorists applied this commonality to their own special areas can only be seen by reading their works, and it is to that end that this volume is dedicated.

32. See Murphy, "Two Medieval Textbooks in Debate," *Journal of the American Forensic Association* 1 (1964), 1–6.

Anonymous of Bologna

# The Principles of Letter-Writing
## (*Rationes dictandi*)

Translated by James J. Murphy

One of the major medieval developments in the realm of discourse was the *ars dictaminis*, or art of letter writing. In the ancient world there was no separate theory for letter writers, since it was assumed that any person educated with standard rhetorical training would be able to master this task without difficulty. But after the collapse of the Roman empire in the fifth century, and the later invasions of barbarian tribes, there was no longer a widespread system of education in Western Europe. Nevertheless the communication needs of both church and state continued to increase during the tenth and eleventh centuries, and a new approach was needed to solve this problem. A Benedictine monk, Alberic, is generally credited with the first systematic application of Ciceronian rhetoric to the matter of letter writing, which he wrote at the monastery of Monte Cassino in central Italy in the year 1087.[1]

The work translated here is the anonymous *Rationes dictandi*, written in 1135 in the northern Italian city of Bologna.[2] It is evidence of the rapidity with which that city became the center of the new *ars dictaminis*, where the new art was usually taught in a Bolognese *studio*, or lower school, rather than in a university. The treatise also indicates how rapidly the basic doctrines became stabilized, since by 1135 the anonymous author was already writing about the "Approved Format" for letters. When he did discuss

1. Alberic of Monte Cassino, *Flores rhetorici*, ed. D. M. Inguanez and H. M. Willard, Miscellanea Cassinese, 14 (Monte Cassino, 1938).
2. Latin text in Ludwig Rockinger, *Briefsteller und Formelbücher des eilften bis vierzehnten Jahrhunderts*. Quellen und Erörterungen zur bayerischen und deutschen Geschichte, Neunter Band (Munchen, 1863; reprinted New York, 1961), I, 9–28. Rockinger mistakenly attributes the treatise to Alberic of Monte Cassino; but see Charles H. Haskins, "The Early *Artes dictandi* in Italy," in *Studies in Medieval Culture* (Oxford, 1929), 181–182. The assistance of Brian Reddick in this translation is gratefully acknowledged.

variations in letters it was clearly in terms of deviation from that standardized format. Although the *artes dictaminis* continued to be written all over Europe down into the sixteenth century, they were generally on the Bolognese model and they almost always specified the five-part letter construction which our author here termed the "Approved" mode.

*The Principles of Letter Writing* is divided into thirteen sections, the longest of which treats the Salutation or greeting to the intended recipient. This involves a complex discussion of social levels, with their consequences for the letter writer and his language, providing an interesting view of the various strata of medieval society. The length of the treatment is of course further indication of the important attached to Salutations.

It is clear from the tone of the work that by 1135 the *ars dictaminis* was already accepted as a *genre* in its own right. While in 1087 Alberic of Monte Cassino had discussed the traditional *trivium* of Grammar, Rhetoric, and Dialectic, and used Cicero for some examples, the anonymous author of the *Principles* took it for granted that his readers were concerned only with letters and not with any broader studies. He did not explain or justify the "Approved Format"—he simply stated it as an evident fact. The matter was evidently beyond the need for proof or justification. The tone is pragmatic, the doctrine already securely fixed.

Nothing is known about the author of the book. He was probably a lay teacher in a Bolognese *studio,* and would no doubt have merited the title of *dictator* because of his subject. He mentioned his desire to provide knowledge for those ignorant in the art, but was conscious of the possibility of criticism by other teachers. In its present form the treatise may represent a schematic summary designed to be amplified by a teacher in a classroom.

# The Principles of
# Letter-Writing

## I
### PREFACE

We are urged by the persistent requests of teachers to draw together in a brief space some certain points about the principles of
letter writing. But we ask that the expert should not laugh, that
the spiteful tooth of the envious should not bite, and that the un-
skilled in the art should not back away—for after all, even if the
fulness of the moon is wanting, this undertaking is not on that
account useless in every part.[1] Therefore let honest men hear
honestly what is here honestly set forth, and by hearing understand, and lock what they understand securely in the treasure box
of the heart. And even let those who are advanced in this art
add in some other points, just as grain is thrown by the handful on
the threshing floor for the sake of separating it out.

1. This type of flamboyant opening, often using multiple metaphors, is common
to the authors of the *ars dictaminis*. Note for instance the "treasure box" and
"threshing floor" metaphors later in the same paragraph. Nevertheless the actual
text of the treatise is quite sober and businesslike. For an interesting study of
this phenomenon see Ernst Kantorowicz, "An 'Autobiography' of Guido Faba,"
*Medieval and Renaissance Studies* I (1941), 253–280. The medieval tradition goes
back at least to the fifth century writer Martianus Capella, who introduces a dry
compendium of rhetorical theory with a fanciful account of "Lady Rhetoric" in
his encyclopedic *The Marriage of Philology and Mercury* (Latin text, *De nuptiis
philologiae et Mercurii*, ed. Wilhelm Dick, Leipsiz, 1925).

## II
### What a Written Composition Should Be

A written composition is a setting-forth of some matter in writing, proceeding in a suitable order. Or, a written composition is a suitable and fitting treatment of some matter, adapted to the matter itself. Or a written composition is a suitable and fitting written statement about something, either memorized or declared by speech or in writing.

Now, some written compositions are metrical, others rhythmic, others prosaic.[2]

A metrical composition is a written presentation which is properly distinguished by prescribed measures of feet and duration.

A rhythmic composition is one which is bound together syllabically according to a fixed numerical rule.

But since it is our intention to treat only prose composition, let us describe more carefully what it is and how it should be written.

A prose composition is a written presentation ignoring the measures of meter, and proceeding in a continuous and suitable order. Now, here let us describe the proper meaning of this first term, for, in Greek, *proson* is said to be "continuous." Then, we say that a written statement is "suitable" in which we treat the subject under discussion in words ordered according to the grammatical rules for prose or poetry.

Let us now examine particularly how to fashion this kind of composition, either in an approved and basic format or in accordance with circumstances.

The terms "approved and basic" (*recta et simplici*) are used at this point because the words of the writer might reach even the least educated or the most ignorant persons; for example, for this purpose I might say: "O loyal one and most beloved, I well believe that it is known to you what great trust I have in you concerning all my affairs."

---

2. This three-part division was to become standard in the middle ages. Another Italian writer, Thomas of Capua (d. 1239), added the names of writers as examples to set up a widely-used statement on the subject: "There are three kinds of writing known from of old: prosaic as in Cassiodorus, metrical as in Virgil, rhythmical as in Primatis." Thomas's text is edited by Emmy Heller, in *Die Ars dictandi des Thomas von Capua* (Heidelberg, 1929).

By the term "accordance with circumstances" we mean a method for the more experienced writers. It is an apt accordance, a set of words ordered in a way different from ordinary syntax; it must by all means be made harmonius and clear, that is, like a flowing current.

Although we could discuss a correct arrangement of words at this point, even though that will be decided more by the ear than anyone's teaching could explain, nevertheless we have enough to do here simply to provide some form of introduction to those untrained in this art.

## III
### The Definition of a Letter

An epistle or letter, then, is a suitable arrangement of words set forth to express the intended meaning of its sender. Or in other words, a letter is a discourse composed of coherent yet distinct parts signifying fully the sentiments of its sender.

## IV
### The Parts of a Letter

There are, in fact, five parts of a letter: the Salutation, the Securing of Good-will, the Narration, the Petition, and the Conclusion.

## V
### What the Salutation Is

The Salutation is an expression of greeting conveying a friendly sentiment not inconsistent with the social rank of the persons involved.

Now, every salutation is said to be either "prescribed," "subscribed," or "circumscribed."

It is said to be "prescribed" if the name of the recipient is written first, followed by those things which are joined with that person's name, in this manner: "To G—, the most intimate of friends and the most eminent in the glory of all worthiness, F—, the student of letters who is ever so slow yet is also persistent, expresses greetings and the feeling of warm affection."

Next, a salutation is called "subscribed" if the name of the recipient is placed at the end, with those things which are joined with it coming before in such a way that the name is as clearly revealed in the preceding salutation as it would be if the whole were written in the opposite order.

A salutation is said to be "circumscribed" if the name of the recipient is written in several places in this way: "To Innocentius, revered in Christ our Lord, by the grace of God the highest Pontiff and universal Pope of all the holy church, *R*—, the bishop of Verona conveys due reverence in Christ."

### What Should be Included in a Salutation

Next, we must consider carefully how somewhere in the Salutation we want some additions to be made to the names of the recipients; above all, these additions should be selected so that they point to some aspect of the recipient's renown and good character.

Now, if we want to add something to the names of the senders, let it at least be made suitable, since it should be chosen to indicate humility and certainly not pride. It is therefore necessary for us to be guided by the ranks of the persons involved in such a way that, as often as names of ecclesiastical ranks or professional status are joined with the names of the senders, they will be qualified by added phrases so that through them no pride whatsoever is displayed; for example, if it is a clerk or someone of ecclesiastical status, he should always be titled thus: "Johannes, clerk" or "deacon" or "bishop" or "abbot," . . . "although unworthy" or "undeserving" or "sinful." In secular positions or offices, of course, it is not necessary for it to be done in this way, if we say for instance: "*N*—, friend of the Tuscans," or "*N*—, Duke of Venice," or "Marshall of Tusca" and the like.[3]

Next, it should be noted in regard to salutations that the names of the recipients should always be placed before the names of the senders, whether with all their adjectives in the dative case or, likewise

3. The author frequently uses the letter "N" to stand for "Name" (*nomen*) indicating that the letter writer can fill in whatever name suits his particular purpose when writing.

with all their adjectives in the accusative, unless—and only when—
a more important man is writing to a less important man. For then
the name of the sender should be placed first, so that his distinction
is demonstrated by the very position of the names.[4]

Now, when the name of the recipient is written with its adjectives in the dative case, then without fail we should end the salutation with declined words; that is, they should be added in the
accusative or genitive or in a strong ablative, according to the discretion of the writer. A salutation is concluded in the accusative
when we say: *salutem et intime dilectionis affectum* ("greeting,
and of profound pleasure the feeling"). If, on the other hand, we
should change the order, the salutation is concluded in the genitive,
as we would say: *affectum intime dilectionis* ("feeling *of* profound
pleasure"). It will conclude in the ablative if we add: *cum salute
perenni* ("*with* continuing greeting") or something similar.

But if we write the names of the recipients with all their adjectives in the accusative case, it is absolutely necessary that we close
the salutation itself with infinitives or in some way in which its
words are related to the infinitive construction; for instance:
"Gregorius, by divine grace, resplendent in the splendors of universal wisdom, *N*— wishes to live in happy prosperity and to
abound always in success in the future," or "to carry on with continued success"—implying in this salutation, of course, the word
"hopes" or "wishes" or "desires," just as in another salutation the
word "sends" or directs" or "entrusts" would be implied.

Next, let us show briefly what is proper in salutations sent to all
sorts of persons.

Of course, among all people some are oustanding; others are inferior, and still others just in between. Now, people are said to be
"outstanding' to whom no superiors are found, like the Pope or the
Emperor.

Therefore, when a letter-writer (*dictator*) undertakes to write,

4. While the complex matter of case endings is difficult to understand because of
the differences between Latin and English, it is important as a further indication
of the great stress placed on the exact shadings of meaning used to point out the
social relationships between recipient and writer. The gist of the admonition is
that if you address someone in the dative case (English: "*to* John"), then you are
obliged to end the whole Salutation with a declined word of either objective case,
possessive case, or case of agency.

and the difference between the ranks of the persons involved is known, he must take into consideration from the first whether the purpose is for one man to write to one other man, or for one to write to several, or several to one, or several to several; and whether equal is writing to equal, inferior to superior, or superior to inferior.

Next, the kind of subject must be considered, so that the writer may fashion the salutation with words suitable and prescribed according to it.

Next, the writer should know what is fitting to be attached to the names of the persons involved, as for instance the proper ending of any salutation.

If one man is writing to one or several or several to one or several, and the writing happens to be among equals, or from inferiors to superiors, the names of the recipients should be placed first, in the order of the salutation, in the dative or accusative case with their adjectives. The names of the senders, on the other hand, with their corresponding adjectives, should be placed last, in the nominative case. But if superiors are writing to inferiors, the names of the senders should be placed first so that their rank may be indicated by the sequence of the writing itself.

### The Salutations of a Ruler to the Pope, and of every Subject to the Prelates.

Furthermore, if the salutation is ever directed to the Pope from the Emperor himself, or from some man of ecclesiastical rank, it is best for it to be sent in the following form or one like it: "To the venerable in the Lord and Christ N—, by the grace of God highest and universal Bishop of all the Holy Church, N— by the grace of God august ruler of the Romans," or "N—, priest of the Ravenna church, although unworthy, expresses due reverence in Christ," or "steadfastness of due obedience," "stewardship of due reverence," "allegiance of due servitude" or "obedience of due allegiance."

Now, these salutations or ones similar to them are fittingly sent among ecclesiastics, at least from subordinates to prelates, and "in Christ" or "in the Lord Jesus Christ" must always be added.

In fact, there are particular terms which we are accustomed to put in salutations of this kind: "reverence," "allegiance," "devotion," "obedience," "servitude," and "servanthood."

And from these nouns adjectives should be developed which are similar to the nouns, and should be included in the salutation in the manner written above.[5]

### The Pope's Universal Salutation

"Bishop Innocentius, servant of the servants of God [6] in His beloved son Christ, to *N*—, august emperor of the Romans, sends greetings and papal blessings."

### The Emperor's Salutations to All Men

"*N*—, august emperor of the Romans by the grace of God, expresses friendship and good wishes to the Bishop of Faventia," or "to the Earl of Pictava," or "to the people of Pisa."

But when any bishop or duke or people of any city writes to the emperor, the following things or ones like them should be added in conjunction with the name of the ruler: "To the renowned, most excellent, most invincible, most eminent conqueror and always august emperor of the Romans, *C*—, *N*—, archbishop of Pisa, though unworthy, expresses his due obedience in Christ," or something similar to the forms above.

### Salutations of Ecclesiastical Among Themselves

"*N*—, by the grace of God bishop of the holy church of Bologna, although unworthy, sends unceasing good wishes in Christ," or "greeting in Christ eternal," "fraternal greetings and prayers in the Lord," "desires an increase of fraternal good-will and love," "expresses a feeling of brotherly affection," or "sends greetings and heartfelt prayers in the Lord."

Now, it may happen that prelates have reverend persons under their authority to whom not "blessings" but "greetings and an increase of true" or "sincere" or "pure piety" should be written.

### Principally to Monks

". . . An increase of true piety in Christ," "the reward of holy conversation," "the reward of eternal bliss."

---

5. This idea is taken from medieval grammar which developed the ancient idea of word-change (*metaplasmus*) into a highly complex pattern of word-variation called Transsumption (*transsumptio*). For an example of its use in verse-writing see Geoffrey of Vinsauf's *New Poetics*, p. 89ff.
6. This standard formula "servant of the servants of God" (*servus servorum dei*) is still used by the Pope.

For truly, in writing to monks we are accustomed to make mention always of "piety" or "holy conversation."

### Salutations of Prelates to their Subordinates

"N—, by the grace of God bishop of the holy church of Bologna, although unworthy, sends to P—, servant of the church of Holy Mary, greetings and blessings," "greetings and an increase of blessings," or "blessings in the Lord with good-wishes."

For, indeed, it is always customary for ecclesiastical prelates in their salutations to their subordinates to pronounce a blessing.

And it should also be noted that the same prelates of churches, even if they are writing to subordinates who are under their own authority, do not send "blessings" to them unless they are priests; "greetings with a feeling of friendship" or whatever is appropriate are sent between friends. If, on the other hand, they are not priests, they should be sent "greetings with a feeling of esteem."

In a letter of suspension, excommunication, or harsh reproof, they should write simply as follows: "N—, by the grace of God bishop of Faventia, to N—, an elder"—and nothing else, as "writes this letter" will be understood. If, however, it is necessary to convey a warning, the salutation should say "greetings according to merit," or "favor where it is considered deserved," or "friendship which is deserved by worthiness," or "greetings as they can be deservedly bestowed."

Whoever would wish to know the salutations suitable from subordinates to prelates, would learn that there are six words appropriate to the composition of these: "allegiance," "reverence," "obedience," "devotion," "servitude," and "servanthood." And to whichever of these we could use, we would add an adjective which suits it: adding "due allegiance," or "veneration," or inserting "in Christ," or "in the Lord," or "in Jesus Christ," or "in the Lord Jesus Christ" in this way: "due veneration in Christ," or "due allegiance in Christ Jesus."

Now if we should want to vary the form, the accusatives should be changed to genitives, and whichever of the things mentioned above that would be suitable should be added on, so that we would say: "the servitude," or "allegiance of due veneration in Christ," or "the veneration of due servitude in the Lord."

We may make these as humble as we might suitably wish, as in "the most devoted veneration in Christ," or "the servitude of the most devoted veneration"; moreover, "in Christ Jesus," or "in those who are of Christ" might also be added.

### Salutations among Noblemen, Princes, and Secular Clergy

"To the vigorous soldier and noble friend, Earl *N*—, *P*—, the Duke of Venice, sends greetings and wishes for every good fortune," "greetings and warm affection," or "uninterrupted affection with unceasing good-wishes," if perhaps one of these forms is suitable to be sent between these men. The following passage will show which forms are clearly appropriate to be sent between comrades and friends.

### Salutations of Close Friends or Associates

"To *N*—, the closest of friends," or "the most beloved of comrades," or "the dearest of favorites," or "bound to one another by a mutual union of affection," or "linked together by an indissoluble chain of affection," or "*N*—, devoted to the study of letters, sends greetings and a feeling of warm affection," "the affection of warm feeling with unceasing good-wishes," "steadfastness of personal fellowship," "the sweetness of the dearest friendship," "the constancy of sincere good-will," or "the sweetness of imperishable love."

Another example of uniting in friendship: "Guido, already bound by a sincere bond of affection, *N*—, follower of the profession of logician, wishes to be bound further to him by a mutual chain of affection and to be disturbed by no hostility, wishes him to live forever and to abound in all good things, to live always honorably and never to cease in his affection, to possess always wisely a happy life, and to hold always more firmly to the rightful ways."

These salutations are also sent appropriately to comrades or close friends, since the different ranks of these persons can be indicated by a rather easy variation. For where "Guido, already bound by a sincere bond of affection" is writiten, "friendship" or "fellowship" or "brotherhood" could be written where "of affection" is written, in whichever way the truth of the matter will require.

## Salutations of Subjects to their Secular Lords

When secular subordinates write a salutation to their lords, they should not under any circumstances say "veneration" or "allegiance," but should say instead "service," "compliance," "servitude," "loyalty" "subordination," and the like.

"To his most beloved lord" or else "to his most pre-eminently esteemed and most worthy excellency," "N—, his loyal servant" or "his devoted follower" or "subject to him in all things," "declares his loyal servitude," "earnestness in the highest loyalty," "obedience of due servitude," "servanthood of due obedience," "loyalty and all manner of servitude," "servitude in the warmest loyalty," and the like.

## Salutations of These Same Lords to their Subordinates

"N—, son of Guido, N—, loyal servant" or "devoted follower," "sends greetings and good-will," "greetings and enduring good wishes," "good-will and every support," "unceasing assistance, with greetings," and the like.

## Salutations of Lords to Blamable and Offending Subordinates

"N—, bishop of Faventia although unworthy, to John, presbyter of the church of Holy Mary, sends greetings and pardon according to merit," "greetings as they have been deserved," "pardon insofar as it is considered deserved," or "greetings proportionate to his iniquity" and the like.

## The Salutation of a Teacher to his Pupil

"N—, promoter of the scholastic profession, wishes N—, his most dear friend and companion, to acquire the teachings of all literature, to possess fully all the diligence of the philosophical profession, to pursue not folly but the wisdom of Socrates and Plato."

## The Salutation of a Pupil to his Teacher

"To N—, by divine grace resplendent in Ciceronian charm,[7] N—, inferior to his devoted learning, expresses the servitude of a

---

7. Cicero was popularly acknowledged in the Latin middle ages as "Master of Eloquence" (*magister eloquentiae*) even by those who had never read his rhetorical works or seen the widely distributed collections of his speeches. See James J. Murphy, "Cicero's Rhetoric in the Middle Ages," *Quarterly Journal of Speech* 53 (1967), 334-341.

sincere heart," or "always obedient honorable service," or some other phrase corresponding to those suitable to be sent from subordinates to prelates.

### What Should be Included in Parents' Salutations to their Sons

In salutations which are sent out of a feeling of love from parents to their sons, we are accustomed always to put the term "blessings"; this is stipulated since it is written: "The obedience of sons gladdens their parents, and the sons are always enriched by their blessings."

### Salutations of Parents to their Sons

"Peter the father and Mary the mother, to John their most beloved son, send parental blessings with their greetings," or "fresh greetings and eternal blessings."

### Salutations of Sons to their Parents

On the other hand, a salutation of a son to his parents should by all means be one which is described above as appropriate to be sent to superiors by subordinates, as for example, "filial veneration with love," "servitude of filial veneration," and the like.

### Salutations of Delinquent Sons to the Same Parents

"To Peter and Mary his parents, N—, once their son but now deprived of filial affection," "once dear to them but now without cause become worthless, does whatever he can though he seems to be able to do nothing."

Another example: "To N—, most beloved lord," or "dearest father" or "relation" or "brother" or "comrade," "N—, shackled by iron chains" or "subjected to the harshest confinement of prison" or "tied by heavy bonds," "sends wishes for all manner of good fortune which he himself utterly lacks," "sends wishes with his greetings for all the prosperity he does not have," and the like.

### Considerations in Salutations

It is necessary to reflect carefully at this point so that we may apply ourselves to preparing several such letter salutations as will be appropriate to the subject we are going to take up later in the letter.

For instance, if someone wanted to chide someone else who seemed to have deserted good customs and devoted himself to vicious ones, he should express his greetings thus: "Alderic, indecently devoting himself to vicious conduct and presenting himself otherwise than is proper, N—his brother" or "once his close friend," "advises him to abandon vices altogether and to return to the pursuit of honor."

## Another Consideration

Furthermore it is a custom to take the material of the salutation from the name of the recipient in such a way that we urge him to greater good-will.[8] In this way, for example, if he is called Benedictus or Gratianus or Johannes (which means "grace of God"), or Benignus or Amatus or some similar names, we can begin in someone's salutation as follows:

To Benedictus by name: "To the man of all wisdom by divine grace, Benedictus by grace, Benedictus by name, Benedictus even by deed, N— offers loyal service and wishes the protection of divine blessings."

To Gratianus by name: "Gratianus, resplendent by divine grace both in deeds and in honors, N—wishes to be uplifted always by divine grace and not ever to be disturbed by any evil."

To any whatsoever: "Maximus" or "Honorius" or "Odorius, blessed with invigorating spirits," or "Desiderius, desirable according to the meaning of his name itself, *N*— wishes to flourish in prosperous successes and to shine forth in the fame of all honor."


# VI
### The Securing of Good Will

Now that these things have been explained, especially the varieties of salutations, let us turn to the Securing of Goodwill. The Securing of Goodwill (*benivolentiae captatio*) in a letter is a certain fit ordering of words effectively influencing the mind of the recipient.

---

8. Note that Geoffrey of Vinsauf begins his Preface to the *New Poetics* with a play on the name of Pope Innocent III.

Now this may be secured in a letter in five ways: from the person sending the letter, or from the person receiving it, or by both at once, or from the effect of circumstances, or from the matter at hand.

Goodwill will be secured by the person sending the letter if he mentions humbly something about his achievements or his duties or his motives.

On the other hand, it will be secured according to the person receiving the letter when not only the humility of the sender but also the praises of the recipient are duly indicated.

Goodwill will be secured also from the effect of circumstances if something is added which would be appropriate to both persons involved, or which would be in the purpose of things, or could be suitably or reasonably connected to goodwill, such as "intimacy," "affection," "fellowship," "familiarity," "lordship and service," "fatherly feeling and filial feeling," and the like.

In any case, goodwill will be secured from the matter at hand if the extent of its future importance is openly set forth. That kind of securing of goodwill is also used in the conclusion of a letter.

If however the situation arises for a combative letter to be written, that is, for enemies or opponents, the goodwill could in fact be sought in it according to the persons of the adversaries, namely in that fashion which Cicero introduces in his *Books on Rhetoric;* [9] this method should be used, by all means, if we would lead our opponents into hatred, jealousy, or contention. If the matter at hand is honorable, or if the auditor is known to be friendly, we should seek goodwill immediately and clearly; if it is not honorable, we should use indirection and dissimulation. As a matter of fact, opponents are led into hatred if their disgraceful deeds are cited with cruel pride; into jealousy if their bearing is said to be insolent and insupportable; and into contention if their cowardice or debauchery is exposed.

Besides, very often the largest part of the securing of goodwill is in the course of the salutation itself. For that reason we should devise

9. Probably Cicero's *De inventione*, which includes a discussion of means for countering prejudice or hostility in an audience (I. xvii). However, the same material appears in the Pseudo-Ciceronian *Rhetorica ad Herennium* (I. v.). Both works were readily available in twelfth century Bologna.

our letters in such a way that whenever the humility of the sender
or the merits of the recipient are advanced at large in the salutation,
we should either begin the rest of the letter immediately with the
narration or with the petition, or we should point out our own goodwill rather briefly and modestly.

Also, in the remaining parts of the letter a not inconsiderable
goodwill is expressed again and again—such as in certain names
indicating the honor or glory of the recipient's office or rank. The
recipient himself would be called many times "father" or "lord" or
"eminent pontiff" or "noble duke" or "closest of comrades" according to the principles of variation noted earlier.


# VII
## The Narration

The Narration is the orderly account of the matter under discus-
cussion, or, even better, a presentation in such a way that the materials seem to present themselves. We should by all means run
through such a Narration quickly and clearly for the advantage of
the sender's cause.

Some Narrations are simple, others complex. A Narration is simple that is completed by the narration of only one matter. A Narration is complex, on the other hand, in which several matters are
recounted.

Furthermore, some Narrations are written about the past, others
about the present, and still others about the future. The subject of
handling these various forms will be taken up later in its proper
place in this book.


# VIII
## The Petition

Now, that discourse is called the Petition in which we endeavor
to call for something.

There are indeed nine species of Petition: supplicatory or didactic or menacing or exhortative or hortatory or admonitory or
advisory or reproving or even merely direct.

A petition is supplicatory when we entreat by prayers that something be done or not done. Minors often use this form.

A Petition is didactic when we seek, through precepts, that something be done or not done. It is menacing, when we do it with threats; after all, someone's official office is in a sense a threat, as for instance when a bishop sends a message to admonish one of his subordinates under the force of his office, or when some lord addresses a slave under threat of cutting out his eyes or head or his right hand, and the like.

A Petition is exhortative when we seek through urging that something be done or not done; admonitory, through admonishing; advisory, through advising, reproving, through chiding.

On the other hand, it is said to be direct when we ask that something be done or not done in none of these ways, but only by indicating or writing it directly.

Again, some Petitions are simple, some complex, just as we have set them forth above.

IX

### THE CONCLUSION

The Conclusion, of course, is the passage with which a letter is terminated.

It is customary for it to be used because it is offered to point out the usefulness or disadvantage possessed by the subjects treated in the letter. For example, if these topics have been treated at length and in a roundabout way in the Narration, these same things are here brough together in a small space and are thus impressed on the recipient's memory.

Thus we can use this passage for affirming or denying. For affirming the letter's usefulness, it might be put in this way: "If you do this, you will have the entirety of our fullest affection"; for denying, disadvantage might be phrased thus: "If you fail to do this you will without doubt lose our friendship."

The ending of a letter contains nothing that relates directly to the subject matter of the letter itself. Thus I might say in the first person, "I salute Petrus and Paulus"; in the second person, "Farewell, Petrus and Paulus, my brothers and friends"; or in the third person, "May good fortune be increased for Petrus and Paulus."

## X

### CONCERNING THE SHORTENING OF A LETTER

We have now described the five parts of a letter. But lest it seem by any chance that no letter could be acceptable without all of them, let us see now which parts must remain untouched in the shortening of a letter. Indeed the Conclusion, which is the final part, is many times left out, either because the usefulness or inconvenience of what has been said before is already clear, or because the letter has been lengthy in its other parts and therefore the prolongation of a tedious letter is being avoided.

The Petition is frequently passed over because the sender intends to ask for nothing. Even in this case the letter remains complete with only the three remaining parts.

However, if the Narration is not used, the letter will not be whole with only the remaining two parts. Thus the beginning of a properly shortened letter will be at the Narration, in this way: "It has been indicated," or "It is revealed to us," or "We have learned through the reliable account of many men. . . ."

Again, though, if the Salutation is removed from the beginning, the letter will remain complete with only the remaining four parts. Indeed this is sometimes done, so that when someone wishes to declare the scorn or anger or passion of an indignant mind, he would present no Salutation but would merely use the regular place of the Salutation to list the names involved—for example, "Petrus to Johannes"; or he may wish to indicate something signifying greater disdain of spirit, as follows: "Petrus to Johannes, worthless and deservedly forsaken servant," and the like. On the other hand, the Salutation is sometimes left unsaid out of fear, as in Sallust: "Who I am you will learn from what is being sent to you.[10]

Now if the Salutation is removed in some way, it is necessary for the Securing of Goodwill to be likewise removed, since they are contiguous and mutually connected.[11] Therefore, the letter will

10. The Roman historian Sallust (86–35 B.C.) was widely quoted in the early middle ages, so this citation does not necessarily mean that our author had studied his books directly.
11. This statement apparently contradicts the author's declaration in the preceding paragraph that a letter will still be complete if only the Salutation is removed. This second statement would seem to indicate that the "approved format" would not

remain correct with only the three remaining parts according to the sender.

If the Narration is also removed from these, the letter will remain complete enough with just the Petition and Conclusion. The beginning of this kind of letter will be: "By bearer we entrust writings to you," or "in constancy" or "firmly" "we turn to you, without further delay."

Also we find such a case that many letters remain complete with only the Petition.

Again it should be noted that the Salutation with the Narration alone, or the Petition alone, constitutes a complete letter; but with a Securing of Goodwill alone, or with a Conclusion alone, it does not resemble anything.

## XI
### CONCERNING THE MOVEMENT OF PARTS

Now that the parts of a letter have been enumerated and carefully explained, let us discuss briefly the order in which the parts themselves can be moved about.

Indeed, in order that we may treat the instances useful in the majority of cases, let us state as a rule that they should be arranged in such an order that they are seen by the reader to be clearly used and explained—for example, the Salutation should always come first—so that a letter thus set up would be seen clearly to perform the function of a messenger. By the same token, in a letter using only the other four parts, the beginning should be the Securing of Goodwill, so that when the attention of the recipient is secured in this part, he will be more favorably inclined to understand the rest of the letter. By all means then, the Narration must follow it and after that the Petition; it is especially for the sake of these parts that complete goodwill is sought. Then must follow the Conclusion, which concludes what has been said before and points out what can develop from it.

---

allow the removal of only the first part. Moreover the author again mentions, six paragraphs later, in Chapter XI, the possibility of having a four-part letter without a Salutation.

Nevertheless, even these ways can sometimes be changed without violating correctness.

Now the Securing of Goodwill—which is, of course, written according to the person of the sender or of the recipient or of both at the same time, or according to circumstances—can be placed not improperly in the position of the Narration. This is done in such a way that, after the receptive feelings of the recipient are assured by this part, the place of the Petition will immediately follow, in this way:

*Narration:* "What care and sorrow, what loss and heart-felt grief cruel death has brought upon us with the passing away of our own pastor—surely everyone who knew the life and moral conduct of our devout father can know this only too well! That above all is why, O eminent father, we flee to your paternal love. That is why we seek your kindness in our letters."

*Securing of Good-Will:* "Indeed, who would not freely ask aid of him he knows as one who provides piously for the welfare of his flock? Who would not unhesitatingly seek the comfort of one whom he knows is compassionate and holy? Since therefore, father, we perceive that all these gifts of virtue thrive in you almost bodily,"

*Petition:* "We humbly entreat that you provide for our—nay, rather your—church with the care of a father devout in the lord, and that you arrange to find us a capable father according to the discretion of your stewardship and to assign to us the one you find."

Sometimes the Securing of Goodwill is even placed after the Narration and Petition, and a Conclusion is not even used in the last place. This is usually done to greatest effect in letters of reply, in this fashion:

*Narration:* "Most rarely—or never—does it happen that anyone prefers giving to receiving. Indeed, it is the nature of the human condition that when a man knows he needs a few things, he seeks after and demands a great many. For, each man comes forth naked from his mother's womb, and just as he is deprived of clothing, in other words, so is he in want of all things. Therefore, it is entirely in accordance with man's nature that your parents should send a few things to you, even though less than your filial respect would urge them to send. But I cannot provide in full, my son, what you have asked for."

*Petition:* "I ask on friendly terms that you do not receive this message with annoyance."

*Securing of Goodwill:* "For I know that the wisdom of your good sense is so great that you are worthy of being praised not only by those bound to you by kinship, but also by everyone."

The Petition can even be placed with sufficient correctness before the Narration, if the discretion of the writer takes pains to do it carefully. For when the Narration follows the Petition, it is necessary for it to be so connected that the subject of the discussion is related partly to the Petition and partly to the demonstration of it, just as it is set forth in the format of the following letter:

*Securing of Good-will:* "Since I truly know that you are bound to me both by the tie of kinship and by the unity of warm affection, therefore I do not hesitate at all to ask your kindness with confident boldness, and then to seek from you a favor."

*Petition:* "I therefore ask humbly, I pray most earnestly, I entreat compassionately, that you sustain me generously with your gifts from now until the feast of the Resurrection." [12]

*Narration:* "For indeed you know how scanty are the gifts of parents, how infrequent, how inadequate. If they send a little, they consider it to have been a lot; and they think without cause that the work applied to the study of literature is obviously stupid, and that my worthless labors are in no way productive."

Again it must be carefully considered that often a simple Petition follows a complicated Narration, or that a complicated Petition accompanies a simple Narration, or that both are made simply or complexly.

Now, when a complicated Petition follows a complicated Narration, if particular elements of the Petition correspond to certain elements of the Narration, they can be handled mixed together, in this way:

12. It was, and is, common in the Christian Church to divide the year into periods marked by the great feasts, such as Pentecost, Christmas, or as in this case, Easter. The petition is for enough money to last until Easter time.

*Part of the Narration:* "We have heard it said in public—and we trust some particular parts of this information—that Roger the Tyrant of Apulia has made war against Beneventum,[13] and that he has already seized several most stoutly defended fortifications as bases for his troops."

*Part of the Petition:* "Because of this, we now call upon your loyalty, so that you will attack him with fighting men and throw up against that man all the force you can."

*Another Part of the Narration:* "We have likewise heard that the Anconans, who have changed their loyalty over to him, have resigned the government of their city to his most abominable rule."

*Another Part of the Petition:* "For this reason we also ask that, after the truth of this matter is made known, you either recall them to the constancy of our loyalty, or else chastise and overthrow them as traitors and enemies of Roman rule." [14]

And thus in all similar letters the intermixture can go on quite correctly for as long as desired. Or, after all elements of the Narration have been set forth, all the elements of the Petition can then be placed in unbroken succession, however it pleases the discretion of the letter-writer.


# XII

### Concerning the Grammatical Construction of a Letter

Now that these five parts have been briefly treated, let us turn to the syntax of a letter. But prior to this discussion, it must be noted that in every kind of composition there are three kinds of sentences which both theory and the practice of reading will indicate clearly to us.

13. The use of real proper names in fictitious model letters is a medieval habit that has often confounded historians of the period. It is often difficult to tell whether an actual letter is being copied or whether the author has simply added some recognizable names to an invented example for the sake of versimilitude. Although both Beneventum and Ancona (later in the same letter) are actual Italian places, therefore, this does not necessarily mean that the letter itself is historically genuine. See Jean LeClercq, "Le genre epistolaire au moyen age," *Revue du moyen age Latin* 2 (1946), 63-70.

14. ". . . overthrow them." The Latin text uses the term "those judges" (*eos iudices*) instead of the pronoun "them," but the meaning is obscure.

The first of these is called "suspensive," another "constant," and a third "finite." That one is called "suspensive" by which, when it is heard, the mind of the hearer is virtually kept in doubt and expects to hear something else besides. And this must always be delivered with an acute accent. On the other hand, that one is called "constant" which in fact lacks nothing for the completion of its meaning except whatever the will of the writer wishes to add. We say that that one is "finite" by which the discourse and the intention of the writer is completed.

Indeed, an example of all these is found in the following: "Although it is the property of justice to give itself to every man, nevertheless justice itself loves to be treated with moderation, and solace loves to be employed with compassion for the contrite of heart."

## XIII
### Concerning the Variation of a Letter

For truly every letter must be arranged within the approved format as it is said above, or in accordance with circumstances.

It is especially necessary for this adaptation to circumstances to be made smooth and harmonious and resplendent in the judicious use of words. Since that capacity is acquired by the judgment of the ears and experience in writing—rather than by any very fixed precepts—we are contenting ourselves in this book with providing some basic skills for the untrained.

Now let us postpone no longer the discussion of the syntax of a letter.

[At this point the author adds a brief discussion of the eight parts of speech, the six case endings of words, and other matter concerning the "construction" or grammatical form of a written composition. The discussion of syntax is largely taken from the Roman grammarian Priscian (fl. 550 A.D.), whose *Ars grammatica* concludes with two chapters which circulated separately in the middle ages under the title *On Constructions* (*De constructionibus*).]

Geoffrey of Vinsauf

---

# The New Poetics
## (*Poetria nova*)

Translated by Jane Baltzell Kopp

The *Poetria nova* of Geoffrey of Vinsauf was the best known of all the medieval *artes poeticae* undertaking to teach the principles of poetic composition.[1] This popular work, a metrical composition of more than 2,000 Latin hexameter lines, was a success even in its author's own lifetime (c. 1210). Extremely influential on Latin verse writing of the thirteenth century, it continued to exercise authority, especially in France and England, until as late as the fifteenth century. Chaucer himself, who in one famous instance referred to its author by name, quoted one or two passages nearly verbatim.[2]

Essentially, known facts about the personal history of Geoffrey of Vinsauf are limited to the few simple pieces of information contained in the *Poetria nova* itself: that he was at one time in England, that he went from England to Rome, and that he prepared the *Poetria nova* as a special gift for Pope Innocent III. Yet a traditional and richer account of his life persists. This tradition has

1. Four such treatises—the *Ars versificatoria* of Matthew of Vendôme; the *Poetria nova* of Geoffrey of Vinsauf, and its prose counterpart, the *Documentum de modo et arte dictandi et versificandi*, also attributed to Geoffrey; and the *Laborintus* of Évrard l'Allemand—are contained in their entirety in Edmond Faral, *Les Arts poétiques du XIIᵉ et du XIIIᵉ siècle* (Paris, 1924). In the same volume can be found summaries of the *Ars versificaria* of Gervais de Melkley and the *Poetria de arte prosayca metrica et rithmica* of John of Garland.

2. See, for example, the passages quoted in Caroline Spurgeon, *Five Hundred Years of Chaucer Criticism and Allusion: 1357–1900*, 3 vols. (London, 1925), I, 17, 49. James J. Murphy, "A New Look at Chaucer and the Rhetoricians," *Review of English Studies*, XV (1964), 1–20, calls attention to additional references to the *Poetria nova* in fourteenth- and fifteenth-century manuscripts and offers a bibliography and a skeptical review of scholarship to date on the subject of the indebtedness of Chaucer's style to the *Poetria nova*. Marie P. Hamilton, "Notes on Chaucer and the Rhetoricians," *PMLA*, XLVII (1932), 403–409; and Earl Young, "Chaucer and Geoffrey of Vinsauf," *Modern Philology*, XLI (1943), 172–182, collect and discuss the passages in question.

Geoffrey born in Normandy but initially educated at St. Frides-wide, Oxford. He is supposed to have returned to the Continent for further university study, first in Paris and later in Italy. He incurred the displeasure of Bishop Adam, allegedly after a quarrel in Paris with a certain Robert, once his friend, and was forced to appeal to the mercy of the Archbishop of Canterbury. Later, perhaps through the intercession of that prelate, he journeyed back to England to become tutor at Hampton. At a still later date he is said to have been sent on an embassy to Innocent III, and thus to have developed relations with the Holy See. His designation as "Vinsauf," or "de Vino Salvo," is traceable to a treatise attributed to him on the keeping of the vine and other plants.[3]

Certain topical references within the *Poetria nova*—its dedication to Innocent III (whose papacy extended from 1198 to 1216), its references to the death of Richard Coeur de Lion (1199), and its apparent allusion to Pope Innocent's interdict on England (1208–1213)—point to a date of composition between 1208 and 1213. This is as might be expected, since it associates the *Poetria nova* closely in time with other extant medieval treatises of *ars poetica* and with the culmination of the period of literary emphasis in the Continental cathedral schools.

The title of his work is an implicit claim that he would supplant the Latin poet Horace as arbiter of poetic doctrine. Horace's *Art of Poetry* was known in the Middle Ages under the title *Poetria*, so Vinsauf's use of the title *Poetria nova* was really an assertion that he was presenting "new" doctrines to replace the older ones.

Despite its title, the *Poetria nova*, like other medieval treatises of *ars poetica*, was unconcerned with prosody. Instead, its central concerns are the style and structure considered proper to poetic narrative. On the subject of style, the *Poetria nova* had little to offer that was substantially novel for its age. Geoffrey was content merely to recommend and illustrate the classical catalogue of the *colores*, or figures of speech, already familiar to his age not only from ancient treatises of grammar and rhetoric but from various contemporary manuals of *ars grammatica* as well. (Geoffrey's own

3. A full account, listing sources, may be found in the *Dictionary of National Biography*, XX, 372-373. See also Max Manitius, *Geschichte der Lateinischen Literatur des Mittelalters*, 3 vols. (Munich, 1931), III, 751-756.

highly figured style reflects preeminently the influence of Sidonius Apollinaris, fifth-century Bishop of Auvergne.)

Peculiar to the *Poetria nova*, and perhaps in part responsible for its unusual contemporary vogue, was Geoffrey's recognition of the importance of orderly, planned composition in a narrative poem— for instance, his directions for "ways of beginning" a narrative with a didactic statement of theme, and his presentation of "amplification" and "abbreviation" as alternative techniques for treating portions of narrative raw material to mediate the chosen theme. On these subjects, although influence from classical rhetoric via Cicero's *De inventione* and the pseudo-Ciceronian *Rhetorica ad Herennium* can be detected, the treatment found in the *Poetria nova* is apparently unique.

# The New Poetics

## DEDICATION

O Pope,[1] wonder of the world, if I call you "Pope 'Nocent," I will be rendering your name without a proper beginning; but if I attach the beginning, it will be unfriendly to my meter.[2]

Yet the name "Innocent" has in mind to be like you, not as likes the meter; nor will virtue as great as yours be confined by any measure.[3] There is nothing by which to measure that virtue: it transcends the measures of men.

Yet divide the name—divide it thus: place "In" first and then add "Nocent"—and it is made a sociable participant in my meter.

In like manner, your virtue, subdivided, is equalled by many men, but is found whole in none.[4] In excellent lineage you com-

1. Innocent III (Lothair of Segni), Pope from 1198 to 1216.

2. The vowel quantities of the papal name *Innŏcëns*, constituting a "Cretic" foot, were distressing to Geoffrey's chosen meter, dactylic hexameter, which admitted only dactyls or equivalent spondees.

3. Here Geoffrey plainly plays on the Latin noun and verb for "measure" (*metrum, metiar*) with their nuances of prosodic measurement by syllables and measurement of worth or value.

4. As the name "Innocent" cannot be found whole in Geoffrey's meter, but must be divided into syllables and the syllables separated, so the virtue of the Pope cannot be found intact in any other single man, but its various aspects are distributed among several other men. Geoffrey's ensuing compliments to Innocent are partly inspired by the conventions of medieval panegyric, including the *topoi* ("commonplaces," or conventional themes suitable for development at an individual writer's or speaker's pleasure) of inexpressibility and outdoing: see E. R. Curtius, *European Literature and the Latin Middle Ages,* trans. W. R. Trask (New York, 1963), pp. 70–71, 154–166. However, Innocent himself and his conduct of the papacy provided ideal subject matter for encomium. Innocent could indeed claim excellence of bloodline, being related through his mother, Claricia Scotti, to many noble Roman families; his sermons blended the legal and philosophical-theological thought of the Scholastic age with new expressions of mystical fervor; and he made a particular point of encouraging apostolic poverty and evangelism among

pare with Bartholomew, in gentle heart with Andrew, in precious youth with John, in steadfast faith with Peter, and in perfect learning with Paul: in all these qualities found all together, to no one.

One attribute remains, moreover, which it is given to no other man to approach: that is, grace of speech. Augustine, keep silence! Pope Leo, hold your peace! Desist, John! Gregory, hold your tongue! [5] But why should I mention all these? Granted that, with respect to speech, either this one or that may have a golden tongue, and on the whole be splendid; nevertheless, his tongue is not the equal of yours, and the gold of your speech sets its own precedent.

You transcend humankind altogether: where else such youth of body ingrafted with maturity so great, or heart so seasoned ingrafted with such youth? What a marvelous revolution in the nature of things! Lo, the elder in the boy! [6] At the time when the Faith was new, although our Lord preferred John to Peter in love, he chose to prefer Peter to John in the papacy. Solely in you, O Pope, and in these latter days, has a new thing come to pass: a Pope both Peter the elder and John the youth.

And you have such men as befit a man so great: they reflect the Pope and shine in a circle round him, as constellations do the sun: [7] you alone to the world are as a sun; your men like stars, Rome

---

the clergy and laity, always remaining strictly frugal in his own personal life as well.

5. On this passage, employing the *taceat-* and *cedat-* formulae ("now let so and so keep silence or yield"), see Curtius, *op. cit.*, p. 162. Cf. Chaucer's *Legend of Good Women*, 11. F 249 ff., G 203 ff. and *Merchant's Tale*, 11. IV (E) 1732 ff. Augustine, Bishop of Hippo (354–430), Pope Leo I the Great (c. 461), John Chrysostom (347?–407) and Pope Gregory I the Great (c. 540–604) are invoked as illustrious prototypes of Innocent's eloquence.

6. On the youth-in-age topos, see Curtius, *op. cit.*, pp. 98–101. Originally introduced here in the dedication to Innocent III, the motif appears five more times in the *Poetria nova* (11. 174–176, 674–686 in three variant forms, and 1309–1310). Although Innocent was fifty-four years old in 1213, the supposed approximate date of composition of Geoffrey's treatise, the frequent occurrence of this topos in the *Poetria nova* is probably a deliberate continuance of the compliment here in the dedication. Innocent had been unanimously elected Pope, after only two ballots, at the comparatively youthful age of thirty-seven or thirty-eight.

7. Perhaps a complimentary echo of Innocent's own imagery in a letter written to the Tuscan elders shortly after he was elected pope, in which he affirmed his supremacy over secular rulers, saying that the *sacerdotum* was to the *regnum* as the sun to the moon.

like the sky. England sent me to Rome as from earth to the
heavens, sent me to you as forth from shadows into light.[8]

Do you, O public light of the world, deign to illumine me!
With this your servant, O sweetest of created beings, share of your
sweet nature. You alone are able, obliged, willing, and knowledgeable of how to give munificent gifts: knowledgeable, because of
your good sense; willing, because kind; obliged, because of your
high birth; and able, because Pope. Because you are such a one,
and one so great, this mind of mine, its circuit ended, is at rest;
and you alone it has preferred for all its offerings: its whole capacity it dedicates to you. Accept, great man, this little book;
though slight in compass, it is full of worth.


### INTRODUCTION


If a man has a house to build, his hand does not rush, hasty,
into the very doing: the work is first measured out with his heart's
inward plumb line, and the inner man marks out a series of steps
beforehand, according to a definite plan; his heart's hand shapes
the whole before his body's hand does so, and his building is a
plan before it is an actuality.[9]

Poetry herself may see in this analogy what law must be given to
poets: let not the hand be in a rush toward the pen, nor the tongue
be on fire to utter a word; commit not the management of either
pen or tongue to the hands of chance, but let prudent thought
(preceding action, in order that the work may fare better) suspend the offices of pen and tongue and discuss long with itself
about the theme.

Let the mind's inner compass circumscribe the whole area of the
subject matter in advance. Let a definite plan predetermine the
area in which the pen will make its way or where it will fix its
Gibraltar.[10]

---

8. This is evidently a reference to personal contact between Geoffrey and the
Holy See, for which, however, no evidence outside the *Poetria nova* itself has
ever been found. Further discussion of the matter may be found in Margaret F.
Nims, trans. *Poetria nova*, by Geoffrey of Vinsauf (Toronto, 1967), p. 99, n. 31.
9. With this whole passage, cf. Chaucer's *Troilus and Criseyde*, I, 11. 1065–1069.
10. In the text, *Gades*, i.e. Cadiz or Gibraltar, traditionally metaphorical for a limit
or terminus.

Ever circumspect, assemble the whole work in the stronghold of your mind, and let it be first in the mind before it is in words.

When a plan has sorted out the subject in the secret places of your mind, then let Poetry come to clothe your material with words. Inasmuch as she comes to serve, however, let her prepare herself to be apt for the service of her mistress; let her be on guard, lest either a head of tousled hair, or a body clothed with rags, or any minor details be displeasing. Neither let her spoil anything in one place by overdoing something in another: for if a single part turns out, in whatever manner, to be inept, the whole arrangement can attract blame from that quarter alone. A little gall makes all the honey bitter; a single blemish mars a whole face; therefore consult your material carefully, lest it deserve to dread reproaches.

Let the beginning of your poem, as if it were a courteous servant, welcome in the subject matter. Let the middle, as if it were a conscientious host, graciously provide it hospitality. Let the ending, as if it were a herald announcing the conclusion of a race, dismiss it with due respect. In each section, let everything in its own way do honor to the poem; neither let anything in any section sink or in any way suffer eclipse.

Now in order that your pen may not be uninformed as to what it may look for in the use of a plan, notice that the following discussion provides itself here in advance with a course based upon a plan.[11] And since the ensuing discussion takes its own course from a plan, of primary importance is, from what boundary line the plan ought to run; the next concern, how to balance several weights against one another in the scale, if the *sententia* [12] is to

11. Geoffrey makes the point here that he is following his own advice and exemplifying it even as he writes. That is, he has determined in advance that his treatise will have four parts concerned respectively (as later appears more clearly), with where and how to begin; how to make particular parts of narrative material more or less prominent by augmenting or curtailing the amount of treatment accorded to them; how to enhance style by the use of figures of speech; and how to manage face and voice in oral delivery. This four-fold division is probably derived from classical rhetoric's four divisions (i.e., invention, arrangement, style, memory, and delivery), but obviously it represents a radical transformation of them: classical oratory was concerned with argument, deliberation, and panegyric almost exclusively; Geoffrey, on the other hand, is concerned with literary *narrative*.

12. This term, whose simple meaning is "sense, meaning, signification, idea, notion, proverb," etc. (and probably "theme" in a literary work) is perhaps used in a special sense in medieval literary theory. For extended discussion, see two articles

weigh out correctly; the third task,[13] to insure that the herd of words is not wild but domesticated; the final labor, to see that a voice managed discreetly may enter the ears of the hearer and feed his hearing, being seasoned with matched spices of facial expression and gesture.

Arrangements' road is forked: on the one hand, it may labor up the footpath of art; on the other, it may follow nature's main street. The line of nature's avenue governs when the action and the words follow the same course and the discourse does not deviate from the natural order of events.[14] The work proceeds along the footpath of art, on the other hand, if, as being more suitable, the plan places ensuing things first, or draws to the rear things intrinsically prior. But in the latter arrangement, neither do the things ensuing incur shame from what precedes (their order having been transposed), nor is what precedes shamed by those things that follow; on the contrary, without strife they take up their alternate positions, and freely, and in a spirit of good humor they cede to one another willingly. Skillful art so inverts the material that it does not pervert it; art transposes, in order that it may make the arrangement of the material better. More sophisticated than natural order is artistic order, and far preferable, however much permuted the arrangement be.

The first sort of order is barren, but the second branch is fertile; and from that origin one branch miraculously grows up into many, the single into several, one into eight. Now in the area of this technique the air may seem to be dark, the path rugged, the doors closed, and the problem knotty. The following words, then, are doctors of this malady: ponder them. There will be found the

by D. W. Robertson, Jr.: "Historical Criticism," in *English Institute Essays: 1950*, ed. Alan S. Downer (New York, 1951), pp. 3–31, and "Some Medieval Literary Terminology, with Special Reference to Chrétien de Troyes," *Studies in Philology*, XLVIII (1951), 669–692.

13. In the text, *sudor*, i.e. "sweat." On sweat as a metaphor for literary composition, see Curtius, *op. cit.*, p. 468, n. 1.

14. That is, as Geoffrey goes on to explain, the narrative poet may either keep to the natural temporal sequence of the events in his plot, or, for the order in which he presents them, he may permute the natural temporal sequence.

means by which you may cleanse the shadows from the light, the foot on which you may traverse the rugged ground, the key with which you may open the doors, and the finger with which you may loose the knots. Look, a road lies open! Guide the reins of your mind by the law of this road.

Let the part of the material which is first in natural order wait at the entrance of your work; let the end, an apt forerunner, enter first and preempt a place—as if it were a more distinguished guest, or even the master himself. Nature has placed the end last in order, but art shows deference to it, and, taking up the lowly, raises it on high.

The first peak of the work is not only luminous with light [15] from the very end, but its glory is twofold: coming either from the end of the theme, as has been said, or from the middle of it. Art draws from either an elegant beginning. It plays, as it were, the prestidigitator, and arranges that the last may be made first, the future present, the bias straight, the far near; thus may the rustic be made urbane, the old new, the public private, black white, and vile precious.

If the first part of the work aims at even greater splendor (the natural sequence of the theme being kept intact), let a well-chosen *sententia* [16] incline in no respect to the particular, but rather raise its head higher, to something universal; [17] and in its new splendor, let it not desire to remember the actual form of the material, but refuse to rest in the embrace of that, just as if that were unworthy. Let the *sententia* stand above the given theme, but glance straight at it; let it say nothing outright, but develop its thought therefrom.

This kind of beginning is threefold, rising from three shoots. The shoots are the first, second, and third parts within the material.

15. Metaphors based on light (shining, gleaming, splendor, illumination, etc.) are pervasive in the *Poetria nova*. A possible source is Horace, *Ars poetica*, 11, 15 and 143. The metaphor of food, also frequent in the *Poetria nova*, is discussed by Curtius, *op. cit.*, pp. 134–136.
16. See n. 12 above. In this section of the *Poetria nova*, Geoffrey perhaps means by the word no more than a traditional proverb. But he may also have in mind an original generalized moral, to be drawn by the poet himself after reflection on the implications of his plot.
17. That is, the sententia should not be confined, in the form of its statement, to particulars of the specific plot, but rather should be couched in abstract terms suitable for wider application.

From their common trunk, another shoot sends itself forth, and thus is wont to be born, so to speak, from a triform mother. But it remains in hiding and obeys only when summoned; it is not in the habit of coming forward at the mind's bidding; it has, as it were, a proud nature; neither spontaneously does it offer itself, nor to everyone; it comes only unwillingly, if not, indeed, actually forced to come.

In the aforesaid way, sententiae may lend splendor to the work. And no less appropriately may exempla stand in the foremost position; but the same splendor proceeds from each, and the distinction is equal in each. Indeed sententiae alone compare, for beauty, with exempla. Art has produced other ways of beginning,[18] but it prefers these two; they have more dignity. The other devices are of less worth and considerably more tender age; the greater antiquity is to be found in these two. In them, the footpath winds up more narrowly, the usage is more fitting, the art is greater: a thing we come to see both by art and by experience.

So these are the three principal branches discovered by diligent study: beginning at the end, at the middle, and with sententiae; a fourth way is with an exemplum. But this last also, like the next-to-last, grows up in three branches. And in these eight branches,[19] all told, the pen prides itself.

18. Matthew of Vendôme and Évrard l'Allemand, for example, recommend beginning with constructions featuring the rhetorical figures zeugma and hypozeuxis as alternatives to beginning with a sententia. To these, Matthew as a sole voice adds the possibility of beginning with the rhetorical figure metonomy. John of Garland recognizes the procedure of beginning with proverbs and exempla, but also approves beginning with a simile or metaphor or with an "if," "since," or "while" clause, or (in Latin) with an ablative absolute construction. For Matthew's and Évrard's remarks on ways of beginning, see Edmond Faral, *Les Arts poétiques du xii° and du xiii° siècle* (Paris, 1924), pp. 111–116 and 346–347 respectively; for John of Garland's treatment, see *Romanische Forshungen*, XIII (1902), 905–907.

19. What he means is simply not clear in the Latin at this precise point. From his examples and earlier discussion, it appears that he thinks all the following are artistic or "unnatural" (and therefore, for him, desirable) ways of beginning: 1) at the end of a story; 2) at the middle of a story; 3) at the beginning with a sententia; 4) at the middle with a sententia; 5) at the end with a sententia; 6) at the beginning with an exemplum; 7) at the middle with an exemplum; and 8) at the end with an exemplum. He considers 3 and 6 to be artistic, even though they begin with the chronological beginning, simply because they prefix a sententia or an exemplum. He does not consider beginning at the beginning without adornment as one of the "eight ways discovered by diligent study" because he thinks that to begin so is "natural" and requires no "study."

That your eyes may see as witnesses what we have said to the ear, take that fable in which the first part is about Minos, the middle about the death of his boy, the end about the confounding of Scylla.[20]

Natural order begins it something like this:

> Apart from the gifts of Fortune, whose number streamed to him abundantly, over-flowing as from a torrent, Nature brightens the renown of Minos with another splendor: [21] for she arms his body with special strength; she tints his limbs in a certain novel way; likewise she refines the gold of his mind and the silver of his tongue; she polishes everything fully, infusing a marvelous sweetness into his manners. Charm, as much as becomes a king, answers alike in all his parts.

Or, from the end of the material, art extracts this beginning for the poem:

> The treachery of Scylla led Scylla herself to ruin; she was injured by the same wound with which she gave injury, and she who betrayed her parent lost what most she longed for; and because she wrought destruction, in like destruction she was caught. In suitable requital of her treachery, treachery recoiled upon its authoress in like measure.

From the middle, we are able to imagine a beginning in a form like this:

> Envy, observing the intelligence and the years of Androgeos, perceives him to be in the latter regard a boy, in the former an old man. For, mature in intellect, the boy has no air of boy-

---

20. Scylla was the daughter of Nisus of Megara. For love of Minos, she cut off her father's hair, upon which his life depended; she was transformed as a consequence into the bird Ciris. See Ovid, *Metamorphoses,* VIII. Geoffrey relates the full story he has in mind in the *Documentum de modo et arte dictandi et versificandi,* I. 2–17 (Faral, *op. cit.,* pp. 265–268).

21. Faral prints 1. 161 as "Minois titulos; alios natura nitore," but shows "Minoris" as a variant reading for "Minois" in two manuscripts.

ishness about him. On account of his very triumphs, he begins
to be wretched: because his praises mount on high, he is for
this very reason brought low; in that he is so glorious, he
makes against his own destiny; and his intelligence works
against his own youth.

Or, near the very beginning of the material, this generalization is apposite:

Anything very much wished for is very apt to evanesce.
Everything is certain to pass away, and prosperous times are
all the more prompt of ruin. Cruel Fortune is always laying
her stratagems with an innocent face, and Good Fortune is
always planning her own sudden departure.

In the middle, this common sentiment may be referred to:

Worst of all things is envy, pure mortal venom: to the evil
alone a good, only against the good an evil. It silently conceives in advance of every evil possibility, and gives birth
publicly to whatever bitter thing it conceives.

The ending, in this form of expression, amounts to an adage:

That law is just, which provides that injury strike back with
injury, that hurt redound on the head whence it originated.

This model image may serve at the beginning:

A gloomy wind rages unexpectedly under a clear sky. A
cloudy atmosphere rains beneath a bright sun.

Or, for the middle, choose an exemplum in form like this:

Against the sown seed the weed, foster child of the nursing
earth, gloomily conspires: it contends against the seed when it

is longing to be born, and, blocking all its exits, grudges it the sprouting.

And likewise, with a similar choice, will you be able to prelude the end:

Often the arrow manages to strike back upon the archer, and a blow, reversed, to rebound against the author of that blow.

As aforesaid, art has given a varied purport to the beginning of the poem. Now progress beckons you farther. Direct your step and your course farther along the path, overall structure being now the consideration stressed.[22]

The path is pursued in one of two ways. For either your path will be broad or narrow, either a river or a rivulet; either you will proceed discursively, or you may skip along hastily; either you will note a thing briefly, or draw it out in an extended treatment. Not without toil is either path pursued; if you wish to be well guided, commit yourself to a dependable guide: turn over the following remarks in your mind; they will guide your pen and will teach you those things which are to be taught about either length.

The mass of the subject matter, like a lump of wax, is at first resistant to handling; but if diligent application kindles the intellect, suddenly the material softens under this fire of the intellect and follows your hand wherever it leads, docile to anything. The "hand" of the inner man leads, in order that it may either draw out or compress the material.

If you make your path the broad one, proceed with this first step: though your sententia be one single thing, let it not come content with one costume, but rather let it vary its apparel and

22. Having concluded the first part of his treatise, which was concerned with where and how to begin, Geoffrey proceeds to his second topic, how to make particular parts of the narrative material more or less prominent by augmenting or curtailing the amount of treatment accorded to them, i.e. by "amplification" or "abbreviation." For discussion of amplification and abbreviation as concepts in medieval literary theory see J. W. H. Atkins, *English Literary Criticism: the Medieval Phase* (Cambridge, England, 1943), p. 102; E. R. Curtius, *op. cit.*, p. 492; and Jane Baltzell, "Rhetorical 'Amplification' and 'Abbreviation' and the Structure of Medieval Narrative," *Pacific Coast Philology*, II (1967), 32–39.

assume changes; take up again with other words what has already
been said; repeat one clause in many clauses; let one and the same
thing be disguised in multiple form; be various and yet the same.[23]

Then, it is a step onward when, since a statement merely hops
through the ears if the expression of it be abrupt, a substitute
phrasing is made for it in the form of a long sequence of statements, and a difficult sequence at that. In order that the work may
be longer, do not put down the simple nouns for things: set down
other particulars; neither plainly lay bare, but rather intimate a
thing through little clues; do not let your expression march
squarely through the subject, but, circumscribing it with long
roundabout routes, circle what was on the point of being said
abruptly, and retard your tempo, so giving increase of words.[24]
And a little forethought may spin out the various ways of expressing a thing, when abrupt statements abdicates in order that a long
passage may be its heir. With a threefold lock the plain matter may
be closed up: either in the noun itself, or in the verb, or in both.
Let neither the noun, nor the verb, nor both together specify it,
but let an invented form be offered, either in place of the verb or
in place of the noun, or in place of both.

The third step is a comparison, which may be performed by a
twofold principle, either covertly or openly.[25] Note that certain

23. The procedure that Geoffrey refers to in this paragraph obviously amounts to
a technique of repetition, perhaps to be identified as *expolitio* or *interpretatio*.
This passage from Chaucer (Canterbury Tales, B², ll. 1637–1641) may be an
example:

> My lady Prioresse, *by youre leve,*
> *So that I wiste I sholde yow nat greve,*
> I wolde demen that ye tellen sholde
> A tale next, *if so were that ye wolde.*
> *Now wol ye vouche sauf,* my lady deere?

It should be noted, too, that Geoffrey probably illustrates the procedure with his
own synonymous phrases in this very paragraph of the *Poetra nova.*
24. Periphrasis (*circuitio, circumlocutio*), the substitution of a descriptive word or
phrase for a proper noun or otherwise more straightforward statement, appears
to be the procedure under discussion here in the *Poetria nova.* Cf. Chaucer's
*Franklin's Tale,* ll. V (F) 1016–1018:

> . . . The brighte sonne loste his hewe;
> . . . th'orisonte hath reft the sonne his lyght,—
> This is as muche to seye as it was nyght!

25. The procedure that Geoffrey terms "comparison" (*collatio*) evidently includes
both simile ("that comparison made openly, which signs expressly reveal") and
metaphor ("the comparison that is made covertly").

things are linked with grace enough, but yet certain signs reveal the knot of the joining. That comparison made openly, which signs expressly reveal, behaves in such a manner. There are three of these signs: "more than," "less than," "just as." [26] The comparison that is made covertly, on the other hand, comes with no tell-tale sign; it does not come in its own mien, but disguised, as if there were no comparison there, but rather some new transformation were being marvelously ingrafted; whence the idea may thus cautiously settle in your narrative as if born of your theme. The new concept is, of course, borrowed from elsewhere, but it seems native; it is foreign, but not completely evident as such; and it appears to be integral with your material, but it is not there either. Thus it fluctuates, as it were, between intrinsic and extrinsic, now here and now there, now near and now far; there is a difference and yet there is a similarity. This is that kind of plant,[27] which, if planted in the garden of your subject-matter, so operates that the treatment will be rendered more agreeable; this is that stream in a spring where the spring runs purer; this is the form of subtle joining, the device in which the things joined come together and meet as if they were not contiguous; they are continuous, rather, as if the hand of art had not joined them, but rather the hand of Nature. This mode of comparison has more art in it; there is in it a more distinguished usage by far.

In order that you may run still more at large, let apostrophe be the fourth device of delay, by which you may conserve the material, and within which you may expand by the hour.[28] You may give pleasure with this device; without it your meal may be abundant enough, but with it your mere dishes become excellent courses. A parade of courses coming more numerously, and tarrying at the banquet table that proceeds more deliberately, is a mark of distinction. Long and richly we feed the ears with varied ma-

26. The reference here is apparently to standard introductions for extended similes, as, for example, "*more* savage *than* a lioness when her cubs are threatened . . .," "*less* audible *than* a breeze at dawn . . .," and "*just as* (or *like*) a mountain rising from the plain . . ."
27. Note that at this point, where he begins to introduce several "covert comparisons" of his own, Geoffrey is exemplifying the figure even as he expounds it.
28. Apostrophe, of course, involves direct address of an absent person, an inanimate object, or a personified abstraction.

terial, this food being to the ear flavorful, and fragrant, and precious when it comes. But now let an example of this theory serve me: the eye is a more accurate witness than the ear; neither does one instance suffice: my number of examples will be full; from my copiousness gather fully what kind of instance may justify apostrophizing what kind of thing, and in what kind of form.

If a man's heart leaps up excessively in time of joy, then do you, Dame Apostrophe, rise up and rebuke him thus:

> O why do joys so great unsettle your senses? Bring your hand-clapping to a circumspect end, and do not stretch its limit out beyond what is meet. O mind heedless of disaster about to come, rather emulate Janus: look behind and in front of you, if things are now going well. Regard not beginnings, but rather endings: describe the day by its sunset, not by its dawning. If you would be wholly secure, fear things to come: just when you believe everything to have been won, the snake is lurking in the grass. Take the Sirens for a warning: be taught by them always, when in a better state, to beware a worse. There is no constancy in nature: poison follows after honey, and black night ends the day, and clouds close up a clear sky. Although all human affairs, fortunately, are subject to change, still, adversity has a way of returning with the greater facility.

If a boastful presumptuousness should even more shamelessly puff him up, anoint his swelling with this mild unguent of words:

> Let your eyes run before your stride: search out your own intention, and take measure of your strength. If you are powerful, dare great things; if weak, lay lesser burdens on your shoulders; if of moderate strength, love moderate goals. Take on nothing in which, once it is taken on, you are obviously being presumptuous. In all affairs there is a single virtue: that is, staying within bounds. Recalling this, impress it upon your mind: when you are greater than your fellows, believe yourself lesser and be deceived about yourself; neither

shove others into a bottomless pit nor pitch yourself sky-high. Let your deed outdo your declaration: boasting will diminish your reputation.

If in adverse circumstances a man gives the bit to fear, help the timid fellow with this powerful feat of words:

> Be not afraid; but if by chance you are afraid, have the mind of a man who is experiencing fear, not the mind of a frightened man. Whenever fear manages to penetrate the door of your mind, let it be a mere transient there, not a permanent dweller. Learn how to be afraid: if you are afraid, be afraid by yourself—without any witness. And do not let your face show knowledge of your mind's alarm. For if inner terror consumes and wastes your features, a more jovial state of mind will accordingly nourish and fatten your enemy, and sorrow sucking the marrow from your limbs will afford him delight. More advisedly, then, if fear brings your heart to its knees, simulate an upright bearing, and run to the aid of your fear with a shield for your face, so that if your spirit is afraid, your glance, at least may be such as to be feared. However, may you far rather desire to have hope, and may it shame you, when you are afraid, to turn pale after the fashion of the crowd. If possible, swell your constricted heart; if your body be weak, at least your spirit may be strong. And remember to round out your powers, when they are lacking, with lavish good hope. Lightweight performance should be a heavy disgrace to the man of fighting spirit; and heaviness of spirit should be a light matter to the willing man. In this way, only desire as much and it will be easy to be a man fearful of nothing.

In a time of prosperity, in a time of happy fate, this can you say with your eloquence—this, foretelling of future sorrow: [29]

29. The sorrow in question is, as the ensuing example of apostrophe immediately makes clear, the death of Richard Coeur de Lion. Presumably writing the *Poetria nova* after Richard's actual death, Geoffrey is able in this model to make effective use of dramatic irony.

England, queen of realms so long as your king, Richard,[30] lives, whose glory is the wide fame of so great a name, to whom alone the sway of the world is entrusted, under whose great command the faith is secure: Your king is a mirror in which you, beholding yourself, feel pride; a constellation, in whose radiance you shine; a column, on whose support you flourish; lightning, which you hurl against your enemies; honor, because of which you send up your gables almost to heaven. But why mention details one by one? One better than he could not have been formed, nor did Nature wish him to have an equal. But beware of having absolute faith in his powers: death is that which breaks all strong things. Trust not, England, in your good omens. If for a short while these omens have been bright for you, fateful clouds are about to close out the fair sky, and twilight will lead in the night. Soon now may be shattered the mirror in whose reflex is so much glory for you; the constellation by which you shine may suffer eclipse; the column from which you draw strength may, being broken, sway; the bolt of lightning whereat your enemies tremble will die away; and, from a prince, you will be made a slave. Happy omens are about to bid you adieu: you now take your ease, you will toil; you now laugh, you will weep; you now grow rich, you will be in want; you now flourish, you will wither; you now *are*, soon you will barely be. Still, whence may you know all this? What can you do? Will you examine diligently by ear the murmurings of the birds? Or their motion with your eye? Or destiny with the aid of Apollo? Away with astrologers! The augur is deaf, the soothsayer blind, and the prophet demented. It is permitted to mankind to know the present, and to God alone to know the future. This false hope has no homeland here; that ancient error may take itself home again, and the father of pagan falsehood may feed that which he engendered, since true religion has dragged out of the sight of the Church the tripods of Phoebus and the throne of the Sybil. This one thing you may know in advance; that no power has power to endure, though it be stubborn; that Fortune decrees that

30. Richard Coeur de Lion (1157–1199).

times of prosperity shall be brief. If you want examples, look
back on ancient lives. That flowering prosperity of former
men has withered away: Minos overthrew Athens, the son of
Atreus overthrew Ilium, Scipio overthrew the bulwarks of
great Carthage, and many a one overthrew Rome. The dice-
toss of Fate was reversed in a twinkling. Brief is the extent
both of all happiness and all sorrow; night is the neighbor of
day. These other instances advise, but your own experience,
too, will teach you.

In time of sorrow, express sorrow with these words: [31]

England, once defended under the shield of King Richard,
now defenseless, witness your sorrow with this lament: let tears
ooze from your eyes; let terror distend your lips; let twisting
knot your fingers; let inner sorrow bleed; and let wailing
beat against the sky. All of you dies in his death; the death was
not his but yours. Not private, but public, the source of that
death. O tearful day of Venus.[32] O cruel star! That day was
night for you, and Venus was that poison.[33] She gave the
wound; but worst was that day, the one first after the
eleventh, which, stepfather to life, ended his life.[34] Both days
were homicides shocking in their cruelty. A sheltered man
aggressed against one in the open, a hidden man against one
exposed, a wily man against one unsuspecting; an armed
soldier against one unarmed, and that his own king.[35] Why,
soldier, soldier in treachery, soldier of the troop of treachery, did you dare such a thing—you being the disgrace
of the world, the vilest scum of the military, and sol-

31. The following lament on the death of Richard (cast by Geoffrey in the form
of an apostrophe) is presumably the one alluded to by Chaucer in the *Nun's
Priest's Tale*, 11. B 4537-4544. See Karl Young, "Chaucer and Geoffrey of Vinsauf,"
*Modern Philology*, XLI (1943-1944), 172-182.
32. Richard was wounded in the shoulder by a crossbow bolt on March 26, 1199,
which was a Friday, the day traditionally associated with Venus.
33. Geoffrey exploits the similarity in sound of *Venus*, the Latin name of the
goddess, and *venenum*, the Latin word for poison.
34. His wound mortifying as a result of unskillful treatment or his own neglect
of it, Richard died on April 6, 1199, the twelfth day after he was wounded.
35. This account of Richard's injury makes the slayer a man of the king's own
army.

dier only by the making of his own hands? And did you
dare this heinous crime, this outrage? O woe, O more than
woe, O death, O grim death: would God that death were
dead! What did you think, Death, when you dared such
villainy? Did it please you to take away the sun and to doom
the day with shadows? Do you know whom you took? He
was a radiant star before the eyes, and a sweet thing to the
ears, and a wonder to the intelligence. Do you know, impious
one, whom you have carried off? He was master of arms,
glory of realms, darling of the world. Nature could have invented nothing more to add to him; he was everything she
could produce. But that was why you seized him: precious
things you snatch, and vile things you leave as if unworthy.
About you, too, Nature, I complain, for were you not, while
the universe was still young, while it lay in its cradle newborn,[36] already designing him? Your design is not finished,
then, until his old age. Why so much travail to bring this
wondrous being into the world, if so brief an hour was to see
so much labor carried off? Did it please you to stretch forth
your hand to the world and then withdraw it again? So to
give and then take back your gift? Why do you try the
patience of the world? Either give back the one now buried or
else give us his like again. But you no longer have the where-
withal: all that you had, precious or wonderful, you spent on
him; your treasuries of charms were in him exhausted. In
creating him, you were made most rich; you know yourself
made bankrupt by his loss. If very happy you were, before,
you are now as miserable as previously you were glad. If it be
permitted, I even accuse God. God, best of beings, why in
this case are you so unlike yourself? Why, hostile, do you
strike down a friend? If you recall, Jaffa makes a case for the
king. Jaffa, beleaguered by so many soldiers, which he alone
defended;[37] and likewise Acre, which he restored to you by

36. Faral prints this phrase as *dum nata jaceres / In cunis* (11. 397–399), which
would make Nature herself the newborn; but I have preferred the variant reading
*natusque jaceret* also given by Faral.
37. Ancient Jaffa or Joppa, now part of the metropolis Tel Aviv-Jaffa, was recap-
tured for the crusaders by Richard in 1191.

his valor;[38] and the enemies of the Cross, all of whom he so terrified when alive that he is feared by them even dead. He it was in whose keeping all that is yours was safe. If, God, you are faithful, just, upright, as you must be, and if you are apprised of wickedness, why then did you cut short his day? You could have spared him to the world; the world had need of him. But you preferred him to be with you rather than with the world. You preferred him rather to benefit heaven than earth. Lord, if divine law permit, I will say, and may it please you: you might have acted more ceremonially and less hastily—at least waited until he had put the bit into the mouth of the enemy. (And no real delay would have been involved: victory was at the threshold.) Then he could more honorably have gone to abide with you. But in all this you have given us to know how brief is the laughter, how long the heartbreak of the world.

If you wish to inveigh fully against foolish people, attack in this way:[39] praise, but facetiously; accuse, but bear yourself good humoredly and in all ways becomingly; let your gesture more than your words nip the ones mocked. Lo, what was concealed under shadows will suffer under the light. A quick hit is turned so: "Boys are taken on high and made gods." Or, let this same young lordship move outright laughter:

> Though himself fit still for the ferule, now he sits above others freely endowed with the dignity of a master. To the common people he is authenticated by the freeman's hat on his head, the cut of his clothes, the gold on his fingers, his seat on high, and the numerous commoners in his study.

You may laugh at a ridiculous man—suppose there is such a one: "As much in his own opinion as in the opinion of the vulgar, he is a learned man." But supose you feel exactly as I do: that a

---

38. The long siege of Acre (1189–1191), an epic of medieval warfare, is narrated in detail in the Anglo-Norman poem *Carmen Ambrosii*.
39. The rhetorical effect that Geoffrey begins here to describe, nominally under apostrophe, would seem to be more properly identified as verbal irony.

certain ape is among the learned doctors.[40] I have said as much, but secretly, lest anyone clearly hear. But he nevertheless flaunts himself, and, facing about, he promises wonders indeed. "Now let everyone run up to hear; now the mountain will labor to give birth, but his offspring, in the end, will be a mouse." [41] Anticipating his desire, greet him as "master"; nonetheless, in the meantime, laugh at him obliquely. Peck at him, as it were, with the "beak" of your hands; or writhe your jaws; or hold your nose: to describe such men, not the tongue but the nose should be used.

So, therefore, Apostrophe may change her face: either in the manner of a teacher she may eagerly seize upon a wicked error; or, with a lament, she may plunge into grief about all hard circumstances; or she may swell in wrath on account of a great crime; or she may be carried by ridicule against ridiculous men. When presented in such causes, Apostrophe achieves both beauty and copiousness.

Come, Prosopopoeia, fifth helpmeet in extending the journey. To a thing which has no power of speech, give the power lawfully to speak, and let license endow it with tongue.[42] Thus the earth, having experienced Phaeton's heat, expostulated with Jove; thus Rome with disheveled hair resounded with a tearful voice at the death sleep of Caesar. If novelty of example pleases you, listen to this model: here is a complaint in this form made in the voice of the Holy Cross.[43]

> I, the Cross, having been seized, make wail—seized by force and by bestial hand, and polluted by the touch of dogs. Long ago I was shamefully seized, and not to this day have I been taken back or redeemed by the sword. Tell me, man, did I not grow for you? Did I not bear you fruit? Did I not bear

40. Cf. the *Laborintus* of Évrard l'Allemand, 1. 984 (Faral, *op. cit.*, p. 370).
41. Cf. Horace, *Ars poetica*, 1. 139.
42. Geoffrey's explanation can hardly be improved upon. Prosopopoeia involves investing abstractions or inanimate objects with human qualities, emotions, or abilities, especially the power of speech.
43. The following appeal would have pleased Innocent, one of whose major interests was the organization of Crusades for the relief of the Holy Land. The Cross had been captured by Saladin in 1187.

sweet fruit—salvation—for you? Speak, man, speak to me; tell me, man corrupt whom I redeemed, have I deserved to be so seized without an avenger? And have I deserved so to perish? The power of the enemy could not have brought it to pass that I could be taken from you; rather it was your vice which did so. And since I have seen your crimes to be so numerous, I, being taken, was glad to be taken: it was less shameful to be soiled in foreign camps than in my own. And whether or not you were soiled—even if it escaped the notice of the world—He who sees all things, your God, saw, and knew you to be fully soiled both in heart and in flesh and he took me from you. According to the demanding rigor of the law, a heavy penalty ought to have been inflicted: death without end. But "I have come," the Sympathizer says, "to be wretched with those in misery, not to press for judgment. I have come to spare, not to punish." Beware. Consider. Repent at last, Sunamite, lest you perish. I, if you will turn, will turn toward you, and instantly I will have mercy on your contrite hearts. Rise quickly. Hasten. The hour is speeding and hastening toward you. Why do you sleep? Awake! If the holy Cross redeems you, do you by the sword redeem the Cross, and thereby be made redeemer of that by which you were redeemed. Who that is sound in body can be sluggish in such a cause? The Lord labored on the Cross: and, then, does his servant rest? Take up your cross; He took up his. He tasted vinegar. Do you the same! Will the servant stand upon dignity if the lord does not? If you desire to be his follower, it is necessary to follow in his torments with torments. The road to heaven is not through pleasures: therefore pay that death which you owe to release you from Nature, to God; die in Him. Seeing that death is, of necessity, not to be avoided, translate it into a form of virtue: let me be to you a cause of war and even of death. If you are conquered, as a consequence you triumph. But to be conquered is more than to conquer: a victory enjoys only the hope of a crown; those vanquished by the Cross, the reward of a crown. Therefore, break off delays: impose continence on your flesh; suspend pleasures; and stir a prompt hand quickly toward your weapons, and let a winged will beat back delays.

Another example of prosopopoeia may likewise aid the ornamental object when, now so worn, it says to the table:

> I was accustomed to be an ornament of the banquet table when the springtime of my life was in flower, when I bore a face without a flaw. But since I am old and have a ruined face, I am not willing to come. Table, I am retiring: farewell.

And thus Prosopopoeia performs with two mouths: now she speaks sternly, and now humorously.

Or, if an old example does not suffice, here is a new one. Harsh Pride, natural in a military stronghold commanding the brow of a mountain, was seen to speak as follows:

> Why, France, do you prattle? Whence come such threats? Why such proud language? Lower that eyebrow! Learn something about threatening postures! Whence the shields at your side? Or the spears? Or the swords? Effeminate crew, abandon the mannerisms of men so that your carriage may match your deeds. Strip off your shield and the crest of your helmet. It would behoove you to do the day's spinning and unwind the distaff. Why, therefore, or of what, do you feel proud? Put a lock on your tongue; be wary of puffing up with words; I will give a bit to your jaws and hang chains on your neck, and will render you a slave in no time. I am taken up with a mere nothing when I meet you decked out as if powerful in war; let other enemies arise in numbers as great as you please, they are not equal to me; but I am rather to them good reason for misery—I, fashioned on the model of the heart of Richard the King.

If the lines of the treatise need to be stretched out still farther, step outside the confines of the subject matter and give a little ground and divert your stylus; but do not divert it far off, to a point from which it may be troublesome to recall your step. This device [44] requires a discreet talent lest it be a bypath longer than is meet. Indeed, it is a kind of digression when I pass over things which are near, presenting in inverted order what is at a distance. For now and then, being about to preceed to the middle, I leave off, and by a leap as it were, I vault over a certain matter; then I revert to the point whence I had before digressed. Lest the notion of digression be wrapped in a sooty cloud; I illustrate it in this fashion:

> The knot of a single love bound two spirits into one. An unexpected occasion separated their bodies. But before the departure, mouth fixed kisses on mouth; a mutual embrace circles and strains fast both lovers. The fountain of their eyes pours down tears upon their faces; and an intervening sob cuts parting words asunder. And love is a spur to sorrow and sorrow testifies to the power of love. Winter gives place to spring. A breeze disperses the clouds and heaven woos the earth. Warm and moist he wantons with her, and because the air is masculine the earth feels herself woman. The flower, her son, comes forth in air and laughs upon his mother. The first leaves adorn the treetops; dead seeds wake into life; young corn about to sprout stirs in the blade. This season stimulates the birds. This time of year parted the lovers whom love made not yet separate.

The seventh device, Description, pregnant with words, follows that the work may swell.[45] But though she be large, let her be delightful: let her be handsome as well as big. Let the matter manage to marry with the words in due form. If she seeks to be nourishment and full refreshment for the mind, let not her brevity be too terse nor her conventional nature too trite. Let the follow-

44. Digression, or brief departure from a subject or its main course of treatment, evidently illustrated in Geoffrey's example by the passage on the season of the year.

45. Geoffrey's explanation of description is brief and does little to elucidate the principles that underlie his examples. His exemplar in the matter, however, was evidently Sidonius, whose own technique for the description of persons, like Geoffrey's, involves presentation of details of costume, anatomy, equipment, and the like. Geoffrey mentions Sidonius by name in the *Documentum de modo et arte dictandi et versificandi* II.2.10 (Faral, *op. cit.*, p. 273). For a good example of Sidonius' technique, see his description of Theodoric, *Letters*, Bk. I, ii.

ing stand as illustrations varied by new turns of phrase, so that the
eye and the ear may rove amid variety.

If you wish to shape a full picture of feminine beauty:

> Let Nature's compass describe first a circle for her head. Let
> the color of gold be gilt in her hair; let lilies spring in the
> eminence of her forehead; let the appearance of her eyebrow
> be like dark blueberries; let a milk-white path divide those
> twin arches. Let strict rule govern the shape of the nose, and
> neither stop on this side of, nor transgress, what is fitting. Let
> the lookouts of her brow, her eyes, shine, both of them,
> either with gems' light or with light like that of a star. Let
> her face rival the dawn, neither red nor bright, but at once
> both and neither color. Let her mouth gleam in a form of
> brief extent and, as it were, a semicircle; let her lips, as if
> pregnant, rise in a swell, and let them be moderately red:
> warm, but with a gentle heat. Let order compose her snowy
> teeth, all of one proportion; let the fragrance of her mouth
> and that of incense be of a like scent. And let Nature, more
> potent than art, polish her chin more highly than polished
> marble. Let a milk-white column be with its precious color a
> handmaiden to the head, a column which bears up the mirror
> of the face on high. From her crystal throat let a kind of
> radiance go forth which can strike the eyes of a beholder and
> madden his heart. Let her shoulders adjust together with a
> certain discipline, and neither fall away as if sloping down-
> ward, nor stand, as it were, upraised, but rather rest in place
> correctly; and let her arms be pleasing, as slender in their
> form as delightful in their length. Let substance soft and lean
> join together in her slender fingers, and appearance smooth
> and milk white, lines long and straight: the beauty of the
> hands lies in these qualities. Let her breast, a picture of snow,
> bring forth either bosom as if they were, in effect, uncut jewels
> side by side. Let the circumference of her waist be narrowly
> confined, circumscribable by the small reach of a hand. I am
> silent about the parts just below: more fittingly does the
> imagination speak of these than the tongue. But let her leg
> for its part realize its length in slenderness; let a foot of excel-
> lent smallness sport in its own daintiness.

And thus let beauty descend from the top of the head to the very
roots, and everything together be highly polished down to the
very fingernail.[46]

If to beauty so portrayed you wish to add clothing:

> Let her hair, dressed down her back in braids, be entwined
> with gold. Let a band of gold give radiance to the brightness
> of her brow; let her face be bare, clothed only in its own
> color; let a starry necklace circle her milk-white neck; let
> her hem be white with linen, her mantle burn with gold; let
> a girdle everywhere bright with jewels cover her waist; let
> her arms be rich in bracelets; let gold circle her fine fingers,
> and a jewel prouder than gold pour forth its beams; let art
> contend with fabric in her bright attire. Let neither hand nor
> imagination be able to add anything to such array. But her
> face will be more than all the rich apparel. Who is there who
> is ignorant of the fire in this torch? Who is there who has not
> discovered this flame? If Jove in his time had seen her, he
> would not have sported with Alcmena in the shape of
> Amphytrion; nor assumed Diana's speech in order, Callisto,
> to deflower you; nor deceived Io by the cloud; nor Antiope
> by the satyr; nor Agenor's daughter by the bull; nor you,
> Mnemosyne, by the shepherd, nor Asopo's daughter by the
> fire, nor you, Deo's daughter, by the serpent, nor Leda by the
> swan, nor Danae by the gold.[47] He would have courted her
> alone and seen all others in a single woman.

But since the description of physical appearance is, as it were, a
thing trite and outworn, let an example be found in these lines, in
which the usage is more unusual: [48]

> With kings and potentates of the realm reclining on the wel-
> coming couch, Ceres adorned—the very image of milk

46. Cf. Horace, *Ars poetica*, 1. 294. H. Rushton Fairclough, ed. *Horace: Satires,
Epistles, and Ars Poetica* (Cambridge, Mass., 1961), p. 66, explains that the Latin
expression (*ad unguem*) "involves a metaphor from sculpture, for the artist would
pass his finger-nail over the marble, to test the smoothness of its joints."
47. With this whole sentence compare Ovid, *Metamorphoses*, VI, 11. 110–120.
48. The following example is of another kind of description, representation of
what might be called an "action scene." The procedure in this case seems to be
presentation in rapid-fire order of many individual visual, aural, and kinaesthetic
images.

whiteness—introduces the delights of the feast. An old wine [49]
grows young again in a gold goblet: there alone, or imbued
with nectared fragrance if you will, he allows his bouquet to
escape and wanton round. Royal pomps of courses, coming
on armed in gold, by turns are vain of themselves and of the
gold. The guests note, above all, the paragon of the board: His
countenance vies with Paris, with Parthenopaeus his age, with
Cresus his wealth, with Caesar his breeding. If you would
consider the rest—what is on his body—his linen vies with
the snow, with flames the purple dye of it contends, his
jewel with a star. You would see that particular details savor
the more, seasoned, as they are, to the taste of the guests.
Other delights, which the eye may covet and the ear, an enter-
tainer affords. Taste is not the same for everyone, and to each
his own! A varied pleasure has more honeyed sweetness.
Tinkling tambourines fly, feasting the eyes of kings, and the
hands alternate, and against one lively tambourine another
rises in the clash. They hasten out and they return; and
they rise again and fall again; and they feign threats,
and put on the likeness of friendly combatants; and they
flee from each other and pursue each other. Here in
another sporting hand, twin cymbals play in the face of the
sound. Nor does the foot go idle; rather, it frequently moves
out, returns, and flits back with a light step to the same place.
Charming voice and charming step. At the same time, in the
air there sounds a song and the noise of a cymbal sounds in air.
A third man spins himself with agile motion in a circle, or
flies full length, or lifts up his supine limbs in a graceful leap,
or bends his flexible joints in the form of a bow, neck to
ankles, or sends up the point of a sword, and, resolute, leaps
in amid its juggled edges. These individual things you may
admire. But, even though up to this point you have proceeded pleasantly, now the clapping grows rapturous, now
the fingers snap in playful art, now the arms, undivided,
curve in a graceful arch, the motion of the shoulders is made
frenzied by the swift and sidewise movement of the hands.
And you may see the instruments follow the action, there

49. In the text, "Bacchus senex," literally old Bacchus.

being from them for every man his own kind of pleasure:
the feminine hautboy, the masculine tuba, the raucous tym-
pany, the clear-voiced cymbals, the harmonious symphonia,
the sweet pipe, the soporific cithers, and the jolly fiddles. All
applaud vigorously; such pleasures both lengthen out the
hour and are becoming to the banquets of kings.

Thus you may celebrate feasts of kings and the joys of the banquet
table; thus we protract a brief theme with long speech.

There remains even yet something which yields copious language: any statement you please may be dressed in twofold form.
One sets out the thing proposed and the other denies the reverse of
it.[50] A twofold mode thus harmonizes into one statement, and the
stream of words flows in two branches. The two streams flow
together; the words issue from a double stream. Let this be an
example:

That youth is wise; his form is youthful and not aged. Give
youth of countenance and take away age; give maturity of
mind and take away juvenility. His mind is mature and not
juvenile.

As is possible, too, if, for instance, your tongue discourses within
limit such as this:

His cheek is not that of an old man, but that of a youth; his
mind, however, is not that of a youth, but that of an experienced man.

Or, taking up something associated with the idea, you will go
even farther—like this:

That face is not wrinkled, nor is the skin dry; the heart is not
weakened with age, nor are the lungs spent, nor the limbs

50. The procedure in question here is close to both oxymoron and paradox. That
is, a suggestion is first made positively and then seemingly denied. Thus, "a *twofold* mode harmonizes into *one* statement," "the streams *flow together,* [but] the
words issue from a *double stream.*"

stiff, nor the spine bent: his body's age is youth, his mind's, long-lived maturity.

Thus may a great deal of corn spring from a paucity of seed: great rivers have their source in an insignificant spring; from a slender sapling a great tree evolves.

If you wish to be brief, first cut out all the aforementioned devices, which make for conspicuousness; and let there be compressed into a modest circumference a little summary of the material, which you may effect by this sort of process: Let Dame Emphasis,[51] acting as speaker, bind many things straitly; let Articulus,[52] chopped off in short phrases, compress broad roundabout things in a brief expression; the Ablative has certain abridged constructions in which it may stand alone without a "rower" [i.e., a preposition];[53] let the same thing disdain to be heard twice; let the skill of your expression signify what is not said in what is said; let no conjunction be at the joining of clauses, but leave them to go alone; or the hand of the artificer may so combine many matters in one, that by the insight of the mind many things may be apparent in a single statement.

By means of this brevity you can cinch in an extensive theme; in this small boat you can cross an ocean. Narration of action elects this form of expression, which, performed discreetly, does not spread a cloud, but, every such cloud being far away, ushers in the sun.

These abbreviating devices may operate together, therefore, but always only as is fitting: emphasis, articulus, the free ablative case without a rower, skillful indication of one thing among the rest,

51. The rhetorical figure that leaves more to be suspected than has been actually asserted. See [*Cicero*] *ad C. Herennium*, trans. Harry Caplan (Cambridge, Mass., 1954), IV.liv.67, pp. 401–403. Subsequent page references to this work, which will hereafter be designated the *ad Herennium*, are to Caplan's translation.

52. The classical figure indicated by this name involved single words set apart by pauses in staccato speech, as, for example: "By your vigor, voice, looks you have terrified your adversaries." Cf. the *ad Herennium*, IV. xix. 26, p. 295. However, as Geoffrey explains it here, and as he appears to illustrate it in the "Snowchild" anecdote, articulus seems to involve the deliberate use of sentence fragments.

53. That is, the Latin ablative absolute construction.

chains removed from between clauses, the sense of many clauses in one, no repetition of the same word. Use either all these things, or at least whatever the particular instance itself allows. Here is a model of abbreviation that reflects the whole technique: [54]

> Her husband being away at some distance engaged in increasing his wealth, the wife, adulterous, gives birth to a child. To him, returned after much time, she pretends that the boy was conceived of the snow. A reciprocal fraud: wily, he goes along with it. He carries off the child and sells him, bringing back to the mother a mocking likeness which he represents as the boy melted by the sun.

If your brevity needs to come to a stop at a still shorter boundary mark, let the whole of your *sententia* [55] at first be dormant. Consent not to be mindful of the verb, but with the heart's pen write only the nouns that belong to your notions: in the nouns all the strength of the theme dwells. In doing this, work as if by the process of a blacksmith: [56] the iron of the subject matter, seethed with the fire of the mind, transfer to the anvil of study. Let the hammer of the intellect, whose close coming to grips may form from the unformed mass words more fit, work it all through. Later, the bellows of reason may fuse verbs (the elements being also added which follow verbs)—the nouns to verbs and verbs to the nouns—which express nothing either more or less than what is fitting.

The practice of the new brevity is more penetrating. This subscript serves as a brief example of it.

> Whom the adulterous mother represents as having been conceived by the snow, the husband, selling, represents as having

---

54. P. S. Allen quotes medieval analogues for Geoffrey's tale of the Snowchild in *The Romanesque Lyric* (Chapel Hill, N.C., 1928), pp. 215–276 and 357–358.

55. See notes 12 and 16 above. Here, Geoffrey probably means simply "thought" or "idea."

56. The blacksmith metaphor for the writer appears in several places in the *Poetria nova.*

been melted by the sun. The husband, because his wife pretends that he whom she has brought forth was engendered by
the snow, sells him and pretends by analogy that he has
melted from the sun.

Be it brief or long, let your discourse always "color" itself
[i.e., with figures of speech] within and without, the color being
chosen by a careful plan.[57] First, muse upon the spirit of an expression, and only lastly upon its countenance; and be not credulous
about the color of the latter: unless the inward color conforms
to the outer, it is insulting to the intelligence. To paint the surface
of an expression is like a picture made of mud,[58] a thing fabricated,
a false beauty, a whitewashed wall, and a mime feigning some
speech for himself although he has none. Its form conceals its
deformity; it flaunts itself outwardly, but has nothing within; it
is a picture that pleases when distant, that does not please when
near. Therefore remember: be not hasty; but in those things that
you intend to say, be an Argus and spy out words for your proposed subject with sharp eyes. If your meaning be dignified, let its
dignity be preserved to it: let no ignoble word dishonor it. But in
order that all things may be governed by rule, let rich content be
dignified by rich expression; do not let a wealthy matron blush
in a pauper's gown.

In order, then, that your theme may assume a rich costume, if
the expression is old, be a physician and make the old veteran a
new man. Do not always be willing to allow a word to rest in its
usual place; such monotonous lodging is a shame to the word it-

---

57. Cf. the *ad Herennium*, IV. xi. 16, p. 269: *quae si rarae disponentur, distinctam
sicuti coloribus* ("distributed sparingly, these figures set the style in relief as with
colors"). In his discussion of the "metaphorics" of medieval poetics, E. R. Curtius
(*op. cit.*, pp. 128–144) does not mention the very common one of color. But
cf. Chaucer, *Franklin's Prologue*, which also uses the images, dear to Geoffrey as
well, of "dyeing" and "painting" and of a "flowery meadow." In this section of
his treatise, Geoffrey expounds the so-called figures of diction, or tropes. Cf. the
*ad Herennium*, IV. xxxi–xxxiv, pp. 333–347. Geoffrey first considers the four tropes
*transferatio*, or metaphor, *permutatio*, or allegory, *pronominatio*, or antonomasia,
and *nominatio*, or onomatopoeia, under the general heading of "transsumption."
58. Cf. Horace, *Ars poetica*, ll. 361–362.

self; let it avoid its usual haunts, and wander elsewhere and build a pleasing abode on another's site; let it be there a novel guest and give pleasure by reason of its novelty. If you mix this antidote, you will make the face of a word grow young.

This method teaches how to "transsume" words properly.[59] If it be a person about whom the discourse is made, let your speech transfer to its subject something *like* the thing being portrayed: when I see what its proper apparel is in a similar situation, I change it and transform for myself, out of old clothes, something new. See, here, what I mean: In strictly correct speech one says "yellow gold," "white milk," "scarlet rose," "sweet-flowing honey," "fiery flames," "white mass of snow." Say therefore: "snowy teeth," "flaming lips," "honied taste," "rosy face," "milky forehead," "golden hair." Well suited to each other are: "teeth" and "snow"; "lips" and "flames"; "taste" and "honey"; "face" and "rose"; "forehead" and "milk"; and "hair" and "gold."

And, because an association of very similar things is obvious in that case, too, if the object of which you speak is not a person, twist the reins of the mind around to what it would be in the case of a person. Tastefully substitute a verb that a similar statement fittingly places in the same position. So that, if you wish to say vividly that "Springtime adorns the earth, the first flowers thrust up, the weather becomes pleasant, storms cease; the sea is smooth, its motion without turbulence; the valleys are deep, the mountains lofty," then consider a like theme in the life of us men, which has verbs of its own to express it. If you are producing ornament, "you paint"; finding your beginning, "you are born"; if mild in speech, "you soothe"; ceasing from all action, "you sleep"; motionless, "you stand with fixed foot"; borne down, "you plunge"; raised in air, "you loom up." Then the verb has good savor if you say:

59. Under discussion first is the trope metaphor (*transferatio,* in Geoffrey's terminology). Geoffrey first illustrates the two main possibilities: metaphorical transfer of the attributes of inanimate objects to man; and metaphorical transfer of human attributes to inanimate objects. Next he discusses certain refinements: metaphorical use of adjectives to clarify the significance of metaphorical verbs; apparent opposition of meaning between noun and verb (i.e., paradox); and union of literal and figurative meaning in the same verb. Finally he shows how the metaphorical effect of a verb can apply either to its subject, to its object, or to both; and how an adjective, similarly, can have metaphorical force variously, according as it modifies different units of the syntax of a sentence.

Springtime "paints" the earth with flowers; flower buds are "born"; pleasant weather "soothes" us; the storms, now ceasing, "sleep"; the ocean "stands" as if immobile; the deep valleys "plunge"; the lofty mountains "loom up."

When you transsume your own material, it has more pungency because it derives from what is your own. Such transsumption of language is like a mirror for you, since you see yourself in it and recognize your own sheep in a strange field. Now look at several such transsumptions—as, perchance, if we should wish to present in such transsumed form winter's shameless behavior:

Winter, hardened in despotic cruelties, is always "opening wide his jaws"; clouds during his reign "grieve" the sky; fog "blinds" the day; the wind "gives birth to" storms; snow "closes" the roads; winter's season "pierces" the bone marrow; hail "lashes" the earth; ice "locks" the waves.

Or, if we speak of weather fit for ships:

The north wind does not "chide" the waters, nor does the south wind "inebriate" the air; but the ray of the sun, like a broom "sweeps" the sky clean of murky air, and with bright face the season "flatters" the sea; the wind with secret whisper makes the ocean "stand still" and the sailing vessels "race."

Or if we speak of a blacksmith's procedures in this language:

The flames "wake" to the bellows; the unformed mass is "buried" in the fire; a pair of tongs "transmits" the fired mass from the freshened fire to the anvil. The hammer, as teacher, administers frequent "blows," and vigorously "corrects" it with hard strokes, so that it performs as he wishes. Either he "entices" from it the circle of a helmet, useful "counsel" for the head, or he "fathers" a sword, lawful "companion" for a man's side, or work proceeds on a coat of mail, "host" for the body. The more lowly greaves are "born" together with these, a "shield" which the shins "elect," and the spur, the horse's "instigator," which the ankle "adopts"; and likewise the other kinds of armor which cunning prepares. Such a "dissonant" array of things, such varied kinds of arms, "exhaust" the iron. The hammer then "restrains" its blow; the bellows, their journey ended, "pant"; the work "crosses the finish line," and "completes its meal."

In this fashion, place your verbs with distinction; so placed, they will be transparent to the mind's eye. But to place the verbs is indeed a weighty matter, as regards the application required. This mode of expression is both burdensome and easy: the discovery of the verb is a heavy task; the heart is easy after it is hit upon. So opposites mingle; but they pledge peace, and enemies stay on as friends.

In this, there is a certain blending process. Let not the verb be light, cheap, or rude: a verb draws charm and worth from a degree of seriousness. But let not its gravity be swollen or obscure; a light touch [60] will promote clarity and check bombast; let the one correct the other. Therefore so speak, so join the sober with the light, that the one thing may not detract from the other, but that they may meet and enjoy the same abode, and a harmonious discord reconcile their quarrel.

In order that the transsumption of a verb may be more urbane, let it not come in the sole company of a noun. Give it an adjective, and let that be such as may be fully helpful and clear away the cloud, if there be any such present in the verb; if not, let it elucidate the verb more fully and shed full light upon it.

See now, if I portray something in the following form—the laws are "soft" or the laws are "stiff"—it does not yet adequately shed light, but the transsumption of the verb lurks, as it were, under a cloud. And whereas, so placed, the verb remains in obscurity, an adjective may lend light and assist it. Better say, therefore: "Merciful, the laws are 'soft'; strict, they are 'stiff.'" Now the adjective conveys the verb, for certainly strictness conveys rigor and rigid

---

60. Pervasive in the section of the *Poetria nova* devoted to style, the concepts of "lightness" or "ease" and of "heaviness," "seriousness" or "soberness" require clarification. Words are considered to be used with a "light touch" when they are employed in their literal senses. They are regarded as "heavy," "dignified," or "sober" in effect when they are used not literally but metaphorically.

measures, whereas devout mercy tempers and softens the laws. But
what if the transsumed verb is quite clear, in and of itself? Nonetheless, an adjective may help it; the light therefrom redoubles that
of the verb. Suppose that I speak felicitously enough if I say: "The
earth drank the dew of the sky more than was meet, and the rain-
storm doled it out irresponsibly." Nevertheless, you will express
that better and more sweetly if you say: "A sottish earth drank the
waters more than was meet, and the spendthrift rain distributed
them irresponsibly"—because these images accompany each other
and intertwine in the manner of ivy, as if they would not suffer to
be separated from each other. Rather they swear a merger into one
entity, and are companions of a single mind. Discrimination of this
kind has "rubbed the file," since the rust has been removed from
the words.

But your picture masters this color better still when the substantive has strife with the verb, and they have the appearance of hating
each other, and yet within all is love and concord in meaning.
A technique which this illustrates:

> He pours out lavishly, but in pouring out his riches, he renews
> them; his hand is never tired except when it rests.

And also this: "Before the face of God, devout silence cries aloud."
Consider other instances and you will be surprised to find the same
possibility in them: [61]

> When lovers make war with mutual wrangling, peace of mind
> grows from the strife of tongues. By this hate, love is estab-
> lished.

So it is, too, with these examples: their inner statements love one
another, although their exteriors are at enmity. The quarrel is all
in their sounds, and the sense of what they say settles all the dispute.

Yet another light by which a transsumed word may shine is
when, once chosen, it is at the same time a transferred and a proper
usage—as, for example, in this passage:

61. Faral prints the following paradoxes about lovers (illustrating opposition of
meaning between a noun and its verb complement) as a part of Geoffrey's remarks
rather than as an italicized example.

That ancient skill of Rome armed tongues with laws and bodies with steel, in order to prepare tongues and bodies for war at the same time.

Or let this be an example, since this brief speech has more savor: "Faith arms them in heart, steel in body."

So verb, adjective, and noun seek to be transsumed. But the transsumption of a verb may be varied, by reason either of the words preceding or of those following, or of both cases at once. By reason of the words preceding, as in this example:

In springtime the clouds "stand still," the air "grows tame," the breeze "hushes," the birds "joke," conversing among themselves; the sea "sleeps," the streams "frolic," the branches "sprout beards," the fields are "painted," and the land "frisks."

By reason of what comes after, as in this example:

If the Pope, mighty in word, loose his tongue, he "sows grain" from his mouth, whence he "feeds" the eyes and "makes drunk" the ears, and "sates" the whole soul.

By reason of both, as in these examples:

When the mouth of the Pope "pledges a toast" in sweet words, alert ears, while he speaks, "drink" the words from his mouth as he speaks, and the things heard "sleek down" their spirits with peace.

The adjective may similarly be transsumed in three different respects. Either by reason of its noun, to which it joins itself in an unusual way, as in this example:

Do away with speech that is either "raw" or "boiled to pieces," "watery" or "desiccated," "shaggy" or "combed to death," "uncouth" or "effete," "penniless" or "vulgarly wealthy."

Or by reason of the complement of the noun, as in the passage below:

> What may our king do, "unarmed" with counsellors, "girt round" with ill will, and "naked" of friends?

Or by reason of both, as when "eloquent in speech" is expressed as "flowery in eloquence," or "an old man weak with age" as "a pauper in the thing you possess."

Next follows transsumptions of the noun.[62] If the noun transsumed is a common noun, it gives to the verbs some such color as this: "the 'thunder' of the people struck the city"; or of this sort:

> A "trumpet" of lightning, a "shock" of air, "quarrels" of the winds, "din" of the sea, the "wrath" of tempests.

If it should be a proper noun, it is transsumed either on the one hand, to the end that you may praise or blame with it, as if it were a nickname—you may praise with such words as "that Paris," similarly you may blame by saying "that Thersites"—or, on the other hand, to the end that there may be a kind of analogy, as, obviously, in this example: "that master, our Tiphys, rules the boat—or, as I may give it again, "that rustic fellow, our leader and our Automedon." [63] Or I transfer a noun for other reasons, that it may not be a true resemblance, but rather through antiphrasis, derision as it were, as when someone deformed in body is called "Paris," or someone savage at heart "Aeneas," or when someone of feeble strength is called by the nickname of "Pyrrhus," or someone of rude speech "Cicero," or someone wanton "Hippolytus." [64] Such change rejuvenates a word.

62. The first means of transsumption of a noun treated by Geoffrey is onomatopoeia (*nominatio* in Geoffrey's terminology), i.e. a figure of speech whereby a thing that has no name, or an inadequate one, receives an appropriate name. Cf. the *ad Herennium* IV. xxxi. 42, pp. 333–335.

63. Here the second means of transsumption of a noun is indicated, namely antonomasia (*pronominatio* in Geoffrey's terminology), the figure of speech whereby another epithet is substituted for a common or proper noun. Cf. the *ad Herennium* IV. xxxi. 42, p. 335.

64. Finally Geoffrey discusses transsumption of a noun by allegory (*permutatio* in his terminology), i.e. the figure of speech whereby one thing is denoted by the letter of the words but another by their meaning. Cf. the *ad Herennium*, IV. xxxiv. 46, pp. 345–347.

Thus a simple change transsumes a single word. When there are several, it is as in this pattern of speech: "the shepherds are stealing the sheep." Here you transfer the two nouns "shepherds" and "sheep": you transsume the noun "shepherd" to prelates and the noun "sheep" to their subjects. Moreover, the whole location is transsumed, and not part of it, a technique which a speech like the following illustrates: "He plows the seashore, he washes a brick, he flogs the air." These are the ways in which *transsumptio* colors words.

Transsume by well-tried methods. Yet be moderate, neither inflated nor swollen. Honor and the onerous, these two, are intermingled: it is onerous to transsume a word as is fitting, but it is an honor when it is transsumed fittingly. Whenever your meaning comes clothed in apparel of this sort, the sound of the words is sweet to the happy ear, and it soothes the inner mind with an unexpected delight.

*Transfero, permuto, pronomino, nomino*—these verbs produce from themselves further words,[65] and they are the names of rhetorical colors, all of which transsumption alone includes in itself. Get for yourself these viands and these liquors: this feast gives content; this drink makes drunk the ears.

Skilled art has woven other garments of lighter value, but still there is in these, too, weight and a becoming usage. There are ten such bouquets of words, counted on this side and that: six on one side and four on the other.[66] This ten-count of colors dyes words with a gravity that is foreign, not intrinsic; their sound colors by an artificial technique. One thing is common to all: clearly, the position [67] of the words is uncommon and the choice of words is exotic. Lest perchance your mind, doubtful, should hesitate about this, the following examples will give it confidence.

65. That is, the Latin verbs just mentioned yield the Latin nouns *transferatio, permutatio, pronominatio, nominatio*; "they" (the nouns) are the names of rhetorical figures.
66. Geoffrey has previously dealt with four tropes (*transferatio, permutatio, pronominatio, nominatio*). He states that he will now proceed to consider six others. Again, cf. the *ad Herennium*, IV. xxxi-xxxiv, pp. 333-347.
67. Here in question is not word order, i.e., a word's "position" in the syntax of a sentence, but rather figurative as distinguished from literal usage. A word is in normal "position" when used with its literal meaning; used figuratively, it is in uncommon or exotic "position."

Let such a thought as this come forth for general consideration:

> The sick man seeks a doctor; the mourner, consolation; the needy man, relief.

The words flower better in this arrangement:

> Sickness needs a doctor; mourning, consolation; neediness, relief.

Intrinsic to these words is the charm of placing the abstract for the concrete: [68] thus, changing "the sick man" into "sickness"; "the mourner," into "mourning"; "the needy man" into "neediness."

What does dread produce? Turning pale. What does anger produce? Turning red. Or what does the plague of pride produce? Swelling. So, we rephrase: "Fear pales; wrath reddens; pride swells." And it delights greatly and savors more sweetly in the ear when I apply to the cause what the effect claims for itself.

> Let service of a comb part in order the hairs of that head that has first been washed. Let scissors cut away from the hair every superabundance, and a razor renew the face.

Thus art teaches us to attribute to an instrument (in a facetious manner) that which in fact it is the user's to do with it. So arises, from art, the power to avoid trite paths and to proceed with greater distinction.

Likewise splendid is speech chosen like this:

> We stripped bodies of their steel, purses of their silver, fingers of their gold.

---

68. In the preceding example Geoffrey has illustrated the trope metonomy, i.e. the rhetorical figure whereby the name of one thing is substituted for the name of another that it suggests or is closely related to. Traditionally, metonomy has (and Geoffrey explicitly distinguishes) several subdivisions: the abstract for the concrete, the cause for the effect, the instrument for the user, the constituent material for the object, the container for the contained. Cf. the *ad Herennium*, IV. xxxii. 43, pp. 335-337.

—not because zeugma paints the words with its colors,[69] but because, about to convey the whole of something, I suppress the abstract word for it and instead make a point of the constituent material. A more unsophisticated technique states both, but art is silent about one, and so serves two in one. This method, once introduced, brings with it three advantages: for it cuts down on expenditure of words, it "colors" the topic, and it is good for the work with respect to meter. The mode of expression cuts down on verbiage: i.e., a word is more succinct than a statement; and the more skilled word usage in this artistic arrangement gives aesthetic "color" to your material; and it is good for the work with respect to meter where the oblique case [70] requires a word whose company the verse must avoid. All of which is evident in the following: "My finger sports in gold." "Gold" is a shorter word; "a ring of gold" is more drawn out. The latter expression specifies the object itself, the former puts it more subtly. In the one instance, the metrical feet go along with the case requirements; in the other, they are rebellious.

Use the thing which contains, rather than the thing contained, putting down verb, noun, or adjective as you please, so long as it is done suitably. Insert the noun thus: "drunkard England," "weaver Flanders," "braggart Normandy." Or place the adjective thus:

The "loud" forums; "close-lipped" silence; the "mournful" prison; the "cheerful" house; the "quiet" night; the "busy" day.

Likewise, use select verbs:

Salerno by its medical virtue heals the sick from diseases. Bologna with its laws arms those bared to litigations. Paris dis-

69. The foregoing example happens, incidentally, to be an instance of zeugma (the stylistic figure whereby a word is used to modify or govern two or more words, with only one of which it makes strict sense: here the verb "stripped," which Geoffrey considers to be only appropriate, strictly speaking, to "bodies" in the quotation); but Geoffrey's interest in the example is, as he explains, something else, namely its illustration of metonomy.
70. The oblique case is any case except the nominative and vocative. Latin nouns in their oblique cases may of course be considerably changed from their forms in the nominative, and their forms in the oblique cases may be inconvenient or impossible for a given meter.

penses through its arts those loaves wherewith it gives the hardy to eat. Orleans educates infants in their cradles with the milk of the great authors.

Give hyperbole [71] its head, but do not allow the speech to gallop away out of hand: let reason rein it in and let it give pleasure by a sensible termination, so that neither the mind nor the ear may abhor the excess. As, for example, in this passage:

A heavy rain, as it were, of javelins is falling on the foe. The shattered heap of spears resembles a forest. A wave of blood is flowing, after the fashion of the sea, and corpses burden the valleys.

This technique wonderfully diminishes or augments praise. Even excess pleases, when both ear and usage approve it.

When you are about to say, "I have studied three years," you may, if you will, color your words more attractively than that. The "color" above is a color crude and outworn. Rework that raw material as follows. Let your file redo the old phrase with these words:

A third summer found me in study; a third autumn enveloped me; a third winter involved me in its cares; three springs I completed.

I express a statement more subtly when the whole is so subordinated, when, by the methods aforesaid, I imply a whole by its parts.[72] Suppose part of the year is wet: say "it is a wet year." If part is dry, "it is a dry year"; if part is hot, "it is a hot year"; if part is mild, "it is a mild year." I appropriate for a whole year what belongs to part of it. With that same figure of speech, you, Gion,[73]

71. Overstatement. Cf. the *ad Herennium* IV. xxxiii. 44, pp. 339–341.
72. This trope is usually known as synecdoche. Cf. the *ad Herennium* IV. xxxiii. 44–45, p. 341.
73. This reference is obscure. A likely explanation is Gihon, the river mentioned in Genesis ii. 13. It may, however, refer to one of the two French towns of Guillon. Guillon in the department of Yonne is traditionally famous for its wines; Guillon in the department of Doubs, for its mineral waters. There is also the Spanish port Gijon, famous in Roman times for its mineral baths. The Gion

will be assessed for your various attributes: muddy and clear, narrow and broad, bitter and savory. Again, the day should be described by a like process as "dry" or "wet" still according to one of its parts. Since either color may be pleasing, you will please with either color.

And it is polite *abusio*,[74] when neither the proper nor the conventional word is chosen, but rather one that is a neighbor to the proper one. Consider if this be proposed: "The strength of the Ithacan is 'little' but his wit is 'great.'" *Abusio* may change the word like this: "Ulysses was 'short' on strength, but 'long' on wit"; for there are some boundaries belonging in common to the words "long, great" and "short, small."

In the figures mentioned above there is a certain effect of color and a certain gravity which arises from the fact that the statement does not show itself in public with a bare face or avail itself of its own voice, but rather uses a strange voice. And thus it covers itself, as it were, with a cloud (still clear, however, under its cloud).

In addition, a certain gravity arises out of mere word order when what the grammatical construction associates, the order separates [75] —as is the case in this permuted construction: *rege sub ipso; tempus ad illud; ea de causa; rebus in illis;* or an inversion of this kind: *Dura creavit pestiferam fortuna famem; letalis egenam gente fames spoliavit humum.* Thus stand separated in order things which properly constructed would instead stand close. Correct close structure manifests the meaning more readily; but a judicious distance be-

---

referred to by Geoffrey appears to be a liquid of some kind: depending on what liquid, the various adjectives employed would lend themselves to slightly different translation.

74. Catachresis, or inexact use of a merely like and kindred word in place of an exact one. Cf. the *ad Herennium* IV. xxxii. 45, p. 343.

75. The trope hyperbaton. Cf. the *ad Herennium* IV. xxxii. 44, pp. 337-339. Under consideration here is the violation of normal word order, common in Latin but comparatively uncommon in English. The orderly translations of these Latin phrases would run "under the king himself," "up to that time," "for that reason," and "cruel Fortune created a pestilential famine; fatal famine despoiled the impoverished land of its yield." A complex instance of hyperbaton in English is Chaucer's *Troilus and Crisyelde*, I, 11. 1-5:

> The double sorwe of Troilus to tellen,
> That was the kyng Priamus sone of Troye,
> In lovynge, how his aventures fellen
> Fro wo to wele, and after out of joie,
> My purpos is, er that I parte fro ye.

tween grammatically related words hangs more upon the ear and
has move savor.

If you would trust in gravity, use these sails; keep to this harbor;
here let the anchor of your mind be fixed. Yet be weighty in such
wise that the topic is not covered with a cloud; let your words
make for the meaning to which they are bound by rule.

The words that unlock a closed mind are words carefully hit
upon, like so many keys to the mind: anyone who wishes to open
a closed matter refuses to introduce a cloud of words; however, if
he has introduced it, an injury has been done to his words, for he
has made a lock out of a key. Be the bearer of a key, therefore;
open up your subject the more speedily by means of your words.
For if a speech enters through the ears into the mind's sight without
light, it builds on river water, it plants in dryness, it flogs air, it
draws a furrow in sterile sand. If, therefore, you use exotic or
abstruse words, you are only making a show of your powers and
you are not observing the law of discourse. Let your tongue re-
cover itself from such a blot, and see that you fasten a padlock
on obscure vocabulary. Use good judgment: it is permitted to you
to innovate in all things, being one greater in this than other men;
yet still be, in your words, one man among others; be not exclusive
but rather social in your eloquence. The advice of the ancients
runs: "Speak as the many; think as the few." But at the same time,
do not make yourself vulgar: you can be at the same time pleasant
and skillful in speech. Therefore, do not have regard to your own
powers, but rather his with whom you speak. Give a weight to
your words that is suited to his shoulders, and speak words proper
to your matter. When you teach a craft, let your speech be that
native to the craft; every craft delights in its own vocabulary. But
let the craft's words be content with the craft's boundaries. When
you come outside into the common forum, let the craft be satisfied
to use common terms. In its own house a speech may be its own
man; in public, let it suit the public. Thus for each business its own
custom should be satisfied. In speech, this is the better practice.

If your language is intended to be light and yet beautifully colored also, do away with all devices of dignity and use instead the

plain—the plainness of which, however, should not alarm the ears by ugliness. Here are the colors with which may be colored whatever you choose.[76]

Evil matter! Matter more evil than all others! Worst of all matters! Oh apple! Oh wretched apple! Miserable apple! Why did Adam's tasting touch you? Why do we all lament the

76. The apparent source of Geoffrey's thirty-five plain colors is the *ad Herennium* IV. xiii. 19–xxx. 41, pp. 275–333. The effect of a few of the so-called "plain colors" (or figures of diction) illustrated in the long example that Geoffrey here appends is dependent upon sounds in the Latin of the original. To obtain a sense of these, Faral's text should be consulted. In the order of their appearance in the *ad Herennium* and also in Geoffrey's example, the figures in question and their definitions are as follows: *repetitio or epanaphora*, repeating a word at the beginning of successive clauses or sentences; *conversio or antistrophe*, repeating a word at the close of successive clauses or sentences; *complexio*, a combination of repetitio and conversio; *traductio*, repeating a word (in any position) for emphasis; *contentio or antithesis*, antithesis of words or thoughts; *exclamatio*, an exclamation expressing vehement anger, grief or the like; *interrogatio*, a rhetorical question or summary challenge; *ratiocinatio*, a question addressed to and answered by the speaker himself; *sententia*, a traditional saying, e.g., a proverb, or a generalization; *contrarium*, denying the contrary of an idea instead of or before affirming the idea; *membrum or colon (or clause)*, a brief sentence member which, though complete in itself, does not express the entire thought but is in turn supplemented by another membrum or by several; *articulus or comma (or phrase)*, single words or sentence fragments set apart by pauses in staccato speech; *continuatio or period*, a close-packed, grammatically continuous group of words embracing a complete, usually complex thought; *conpar or isocolon*, a figure composed of membra (q. v. above) that consist of an approximately equal number of syllables; *similiter cadens or homoeoptoton*, two successive clauses ending in words with the same inflexional endings; *similiter desinens or homoeoteleuton*, two successive clauses ending in indeclinable words with similar sounds; *adnominatio or paronomasia*, punning word play; *subjectio or hypophora*, asking and suggesting the answer to a rhetorical question put to an adversary; *gradatio or climax*, repeating the opening word of one clause as the closing word of the next (a linking effect); *definitio*, a brief explanation, a definition; *transitio*, a brief summary of what has been said, with a brief forecast of what is to follow; *correctio*, substituting a more suitable word or suggestion for one previously advanced; *occupatio (occultatio) or paralepsis*, refusing to describe or narrate something (a means of referring briefly to a subject under cover of passing it over); *disjunctio*, using different verbs to express similar ideas in successive clauses; *conjunctio*, using one verb (interposed) to serve two phrases; *adjunctio*, using one verb either at the beginning or the end to serve two phrases; *conduplicatio*, repeating a word as a means of expressing emotion; *interpretatio*, repeating the same idea in different words; *commutatio*, in balanced clauses, reversing the order of the first in the second; *permissio*, an admission or concession, or an appeal to the mercy of the court; *dubitatio*, expressing doubt as to which of two or more words had best be used to express something; *expeditio*, eliminating all but one of various alternatives; *dissolutio or asyndeton*, omitting connective words; *praecisio or aposiopesis*, leaving a sentence unfinished (a device of insinuation or emotion); *conclusio*, a brief summing up.

guilt of one Adam? That tasting of an apple was a general cause of evil. Adam our father, and yet to us a remorseless enemy, shows himself to be not a father—he, from a condition of wealth a pauper, from a situation of bliss one wretched, from light so extreme thurst into darkness.

Where now is paradise and that pleasure of which you were lord? I say to you, most powerful of created beings, how did you become guilty of such a crime? You err by condoning in your mind the deed of your wife, by making trial of what was forbidden, by defending your deeds with speech. Therefore, you, condoning, making such trial, and defending yourself, do you not fall deservedly? Answer therefore: Why then did you touch the baleful apple? "My wife brought it to me." But why did you eat? "She persuaded me that the thing was not harmful." And why were you her accomplice? "I was afraid to annoy her." After the deed, why were you slow to lament the crime by petitioning God for pardon? Speak: What was the reason for this deed of death? "Sin alone was the reason."

That man is free who is not a slave to vices. Yet when he, Adam, was a slave, shall we enjoy liberty? If he, so able in virtue, did not resist the Foe, with what shall we weak ones resist? The Fall began with the Foe, and by that one's art are we fallen; and we, being corrupt, are not able to live without falling. Useful to us in our fallen state is this kind of help: tears, fasting, and psalms.

To him for whom God is more precious than the world, the unclean Spirit is not harmful. From whence, in him who does not place his hope in the Foe, can fear of the Foe arise? If he is wont to be oppressively injurious only to his own, the law, which is just, prohibits our being of his mob. Lest perchance tempests overwhelm us with their might, let us defend what is honest and avoid what is evil, since virtue is the best of all things, and vice (nothing else is equally destructive) the worst of all things.

This had He put to the test, this pitied, who, deigning to be born, came from death to be reborn, one who was able to be something of good profit to us all. This one, in the flesh, yet without corruption nor caught on the hook of sin, a man simple and humble, wagered with the iniquitous Snake who defeated us in the game; and having been made a sacrifice, he slaughtered his enemy; and, dying, he bit the snake in return.

Serpent of ill will and enemy of our race, why did you damn Christ to the cross? Did he deserve it? But he was void of all sin. Did you think his body an illusion? But he took flesh from the Virgin. Did you think him to be all man? But he proved himself to be God in virtue, by which merit he earned the right to damn you. Remember: The servant who damns his lord will be damned by him. Thus, justly, in him through whom it had begun, damnation perished. For first the Foe damned Eve, second Eve damned the man, third the man damned all that were of his posterity, fourth his posterity damned God, lastly God damned the Foe, to whom he was death itself. He was that, and therefore he was of good profit to the world; he became manifest and he was of good profit to the world; he was manifest, inasmuch as he redeemed the world.

If He had been contending in his own power, he would have saved us all without effort, for certainly his power is omnipotent virtue, and to him is given all power, at his nod or at his word, or at his mere wish. You see what He could do: it follows why he was not willing. Lo, the trend of his thought: If violence had been done to the Enemy, He could—rather he would—have appeared to be doing something unjust in the matter. Whence—but I pass over it as being well known —the rule of the law said that, just as the Foe deceitfully slew man, so should man slay the Foe, ingeniously capturing him by the lure of his Godhead. For this reason, God came to dwell among us in true flesh; he could not be disgraced by the stain of our flesh, and ultimately he washed us with his blood; he, potent over both life and death, shattered both the first and the last. For, dying, he shattered life, and, rising, death; and it is not by his first life but by the life that he resumed, that he redeems his own.

Betrayer of our human nature—betrayer, I say—where now is your power? Where is your power? Death has broken your chains. His death, by its miraculous virtue, has broken your chains. How happy is death! Death, how happy! It is our redemption. This, his death, has healed the spirit's wounds, has washed away its uncleanness, taken away its sins.

O how holy the grace of Christ, how gracious the holiness! Wellstream of righteousness, from this time forth I dedicate myself wholly to you. Give, take away, scourge, forbear, command, forbid, do what you will: lo, I am your servant. Lord, use your servant as you see fit; whatever you do, I will give thanks. Jesu so good, what shall I call you? If I call you righteous, or righteousness itself, or wellstream of righteousness, or whether I augment all these expressions greatly, you are greater still.

The One so great desired to be least of all. Coming in the guise of a slave, he came to win back those sheep he had lost, who were seized by force by the enemy: not through a judgment, unless perchance he might conquer the enemy as man before had been conquered.

But such a one had to be either pure man, or an angel, or God. He could not be pure man, because the Foe overcame one purely man. And, were he impure, his infection would incur the Fall. And [yet, God,] you could not be angel, for since your own nature had fallen, you would not stand fast in ours.

But suppose it had been so. Suppose that, in one nature or the other, He had stood fast in resolute virtue and redeemed us. It is established that to be created is a lesser thing than to be redeemed. Man, redeemed, would have been possessed less by his Creator and more by his Redeemer; and thus the creature would have been greater than his creator. Therefore it was necessary that the man be God, whose full wisdom ruled the human senses by the rein of his Godhead, to whom alone the world owed both being created and being redeemed, and to whom the world paid adoration as One God.

And even as the need was, so the plan proceeded to the act itself. One unifold nature remained among all the Persons: the Son united himself to our nature, and was enclosed in the royal chamber of a virgin; her womb contained him whom the uni-

verse was not able to contain; within time there began that
which was before time.

True man, true God, he bore patiently all that belongs to
our nature except sin. Undergoing scorn, he kept silence;
beaten, and bearing stripes, he slipped through the chains of
death; his tender body hung on the hard cross. As a rare kind
of guest, breathing forth his spirit, he came to Hell. After three
days a victor, he returned to life by his own virtue.

So the Shepherd led his stolen sheep back to the sheepfold.
How great a deed it was! And how . . . but I omit the word,
since a word cannot be found adequate to so great a miracle.
Therefore, since we could not have been redeemed unless he
were God, God was made man (and was not made man except
that he purposed to conquer death). Death overcome, He redeemed his own from death.

This theme brings together in one example all the verbal flowers
in which there is both lightness [77] and literal use of words. Not one
was left out of their number, nor is their order neglected. If I sometimes used expressions unorthodoxly, on the other hand, it was suitable to use serious words intermingled with the light to the end that,
although it might savor sweetly enough by itself, lightness might
have the more savor by reason of seriousness in its hidden taste.[78]
In this way, then, the finger of the heart may cull flowers in the
field of rhetoric. But let your speech flower sparingly with them,
and with a variety, and not be thick with them. That fragrance is
better that arises from an assortment of flowers; the vice of repetition can render insipid what has of itself a fine flavor.

Moreover, there are flowers in which the very thought that the
words convey is the flower, all of which I include in what briefly

77. Most of the so-called figures of diction illustrated in the foregoing example
are considered to have "lightness," or to be "easy," in that their ornamental effect
derives from the polished selection and positioning of words in their literal senses.
Again, these particular figures of diction are thus distinguished from ten other
figures of diction, the so-called tropes, in which words are not used in their ordinary meanings and which accordingly are considered to have not *levitas* ("lightness") but rather *gravitas* ("heaviness" or "seriousness.")

78. That is, in the foregoing example Geoffrey has occasionally used a trope, so
varying the prevailing "lightness" of effect with moments of "seriousness," when
words were not used in a literal sense.

follows.[79] When the thought is colored, it works like this: it distrib-
utes distinct functions among various things or among various persons; [80] at times it accuses either lords or friends honestly and lawfully, without giving real offense with its words; [81] at times it
intimates more about a thing than is actually said in speech, and
understates something with a word, but in discreet fashion; [82] and,
too, it describes things that will follow and things that can come to
pass as a result of something under discussion [83] (nevertheless, it
explains everything plainly and with a certain seriousness); or, dis-
tinguishing one topic from another, each with the idea that it entails,
it frees both; [84] or again, single things come together in one, and it
gathers up elements that have been scattered everywhere.[85]

Sometimes, by repeating something and ever changing the color,
again and again, I seem to say several things, but I always abide in
one, so that I may polish it fully and, as it were, refine it with a
brisk file.[86] This may be done by a twofold method: either by stating the same thing in various ways, or by saying various things
about the same subject. We may say the same thing in three different ways, and some one subject may be discussed in seven different
ways. All of which, read about fully in Cicero.[87]

79. The nineteen so-called figures of thought now to be described and illustrated
derive their distinction from the form of the concepts behind them, not from the
words in which the concepts are expressed. Cf. the *ad Herennium* IV. xxxv. 47–lvi.
69, pp. 347–409.
80. The figure *distributio*. Cf. the *ad Herennium* IV. xxxv. 47, pp. 347–349.
81. The figure *licentia*. Cf. the *ad Herennium* IV. xxxvi. 48–xxxvii. 50, pp. 349–
355.
82. The figure *deminutio*. Cf. the *ad Herennium* IV. xxxviii. 50, pp. 355–357.
83. The figure *descriptio*. Cf. the *ad Herennium* IV. xxxix. 51, pp. 357–359; "Vivid
description is the name for the figure which contains a clear, lucid, and impressive
exposition of the consequences of an act."
84. The figure *divisio*. Cf. the *ad Herennium* IV. xl. 52, p. 361: "Division separates
the alternatives of a question and resolves each by means of a reason subjoined, as
follows: 'Why should I reproach you in any way? If you are an upright man, you
have not deserved reproach, if a wicked man, you will be unmoved.'"
85. The figure *frequentatio*. Cf. the *ad Herennium* IV. xl. 52–xli. 53, pp. 361–365:
"Accumulation [frequentatio] occurs when the points scattered throughout the
whole cause are collected in one place so as to make the speech more impressive
or sharp or accusatory."
86. The figure *expolitio*. Cf. the *ad Herennium* IV. xlii. 54, pp. 365–367: "Refining
[expolitio] consists in dwelling on the same topic and yet seeming to say something ever new. . . . We shall not repeat the same thing precisely—for that, to be
sure, would weary the hearer and not refine the idea—but with changes."
87. That is, in the *ad Herennium*, which was attributed in the Middle Ages to
Cicero. The treatments of "saying the same thing in three different ways" and

Either I come down on one same point, and dwell there over and over,[88] or else, when I compare two things, the propositions clash head-on;[89] frequently, I derive an analogy from something quite dissimilar;[90] or I supply an exemplum, using the name of a particular author and something he once said or did;[91] or I omit the aforesaid colors and another color enters in: a comparison made of one kind of thing to something similar, under a ruling principle of likeness;[92] or there is a color closely related to this one, when I either portray or suggest the very appearance of someone's body to the extent that suffices.[93] Next, I provide certain little clues, very definite signs, by which I quite clearly describe what a man's character is:[94] this color gives more and better color; and see, yet another flower, when the style of the dialogue is adapted to the person who is speaking, and the language smacks of the speaker;[95] finally, coloring even inanimate objects with yet another freshness, I sometimes, by giving speech to something to which nature denies the power of speech, form a new "person,"[96] or, by a method of suggestion, I give away more than my words are proof of.[97] Sometimes I compress a whole topic into a few brief words:[98] those which the topic absolutely requires and no others; or sometimes an action manifests itself so openly that it seems to be present before the eyes (this may be done to perfection by these five means: I show what happened before, during, and after the event, and what circumstances surrounded it, and what resulted from it).[99]

---

discussing some one subject in "the seven ways" may be found in the *ad Herennium* IV. xlii. 54–xliv. 58, pp. 365–375.

88. The figure *commoratio*. Cf. the *ad Herennium* IV. xlv. 58, p. 375.

89. The figure *contentio* (antithesis). Cf. the *ad Herennium* IV. xlv. 58, p. 377.

90. The figure *similitudo*. Cf. the *ad Herennium* IV. xlv. 59–xlviii. 61, pp. 377–383.

91. Cf. the *ad Herennium* IV. xlix. 62, pp. 383–385.

92. The figure simile. Cf. the *ad Herennium* IV. xlix. 62, pp. 385–387.

93. The figure *effictio*. Cf. the *ad Herennium* IV. xlix. 63, p. 387: "Portrayal [effictio] consists in representing and depicting in words clearly enough for recognition the bodily form of some person."

94. The figure *notatio*. Cf. the *ad Herennium* IV. l. 63–li. 65, pp. 387–395: "Character delineation [notatio] consists in describing a person's character by the definite signs which, like distinctive marks, are attributes of that character."

95. The figure *sermocinatio*. Cf. the *ad Herennium* IV. lii. 65, pp. 395–399: "Dialogue [sermocinatio] consists in assigning to some person language which as set forth conforms with his character."

96. The figure *conformatio*. Cf. the *ad Herennium* LV. liii. 66, pp. 399–401.

97. The figure *significatio*. Cf. the *ad Herennium* IV. liii. 67–liv. 67, pp. 401–403.

98. The figure *brevitas*. Cf. the *ad Herennium* IV. liv. 68, pp. 403–405.

99. The figure *demonstratio*. Cf. the *ad Herennium* IV. lv. 68–69, pp. 405–409.

In the aforesaid list, note what the figures of speech are, how many they are in number (for there are twice ten if you subtract one), and how they stand in order. For the order that I have followed above will not be changed, when, below, I provide examples to clarify the matter:

It is for the Pope to pronounce the sacred laws, and for lesser beings to observe the form of the law prescribed. But very many do now err, whose erring, O Pope, contradicts you. You pardon, and do not punish, those who are pursuing irregular profits. They sell and buy illegally, without an avenger of their guilt.

Powerful Pope, you whose power is not short, be mindful of vengeance. Gentle father, draw someday your sword. If vengeance sleep, the Erring One will circle about like the impudent wolf or like the little fox treacherous to the deer. Here he will practice his wrongdoing, there he will purpose it; hidden here, manifest there: either way, full of evil. There are two evils: the fraud of simony, the sangfroid of avarice. Both the one and the other are embraced, not despised. But I labor with an empty voice; whatever I say in this matter, I merely wash a brick. If I condone the one, he does not get his desert, if I approve the other, his crime does not move him. Read what venom is his. It will read off as follows: present a flatterer, absent a detractor, visible a friend, hidden an enemy; a stingy owner, a hard creditor, a grievous robber, an ambitious trader, an illegal buyer, swift to the evil of simony that is so widespread. Best holy father, avenger of crimes, send your hand against this crime. The wisdom of a pope desires to and ought to destroy iniquity. Neither this work nor this intent is foreign to a wise pope.

Good Pope, muse often with yourself as follows: "Oh how wonderful is the power of God! How great his might! How great I now am! How insignificant I was. Suddenly, from a little sapling, I have grown into a great cedar. That God of gods has made great his own creation; he desired me, though in the flower of youth, to be captain of his elders. Marvelous gift! He gives to a youth the keys of the celestial kingdom and the empire of the world. Not much time has elapsed since I bore about me a head smatteringly informed; my speech was unpolished, my power little. But now my heart and lips and power he has so exalted and preferred before all others, that I am the unique wonder of the world. That doing is not mine; the grace of the Most High has made me supreme; the glory for that is not mine, but to him be the thanks, from whose gift we all benefit. Whence I am more closely bound and strictly obligated to Him to put down what he wishes to be put down, to raise what he wishes to be raised, to desire what he desires, to hate what he hates. And I desire it to be so, since I am so constrained; and I shall put down all things that he orders to be put down; I shall raise what he orders to be raised—on only one thing intent: to desire what he desires, to hate what he hates."

Who is there, so empty of mind, so crafty of heart, so beside himself, that he would not praise this chosen work— that he would not pronounce it drawn from a vein of wisdom? Thus endowed with wisdom, all his work the Pope builds on the fact and on account of the fact that so much power falls to him. And since God so raised him on high for this work, it is his concern that he perform it, to the end that he may take away the stains of the world to make the world pure, in order that he may lead it by the right-hand path to paradise. And therefore when he is remiss in this work, he is the font and origin of a double wrong: for he is at once his own and the public enemy.

Is it better to do mischief to the world by torpid sleep than to do it good with watchful care? Do not fail to note this: The Pope in the likeness of a good shepherd saves his sheep- fold from the mouth of the wolf; or, after the fashion in which a physician heals bodies, he thus heals their souls and wounds as a physician and a shepherd. Our God, healing all, laid down his life for the sake of his sheep; the carrying away of the sins of the world is thus proved right, both by the strength of reason and by Christ's example. Therefore, holy father, end these crimes, walk in the footsteps of Peter, and let simony along with Simon Magus be given over to ruin. Everyone takes delight in his own particular crime; upon you alone does the general evil weigh heavily. This one sin is undermining all men. If only no mortal sin gnawed at them! Since, nevertheless, it does stand in their way, the death of the soul may occur from one cause as well as from many: a ship no less by one than by various cracks may be flooded with rising waters. But either bane has the same result.

Nevertheless, hardly may it be that a man live without crime, whence moral Cato: "No one lives without sin." That Spirit of malignant nature, our public Foe, circles anxiously about man on hidden wings, that he may regain what he has lost. Christ, our gladiator, carried that one off by his wonderful lion's strength, with his serpent's wisdom and his simplicity of a dove. Who is He? Indeed, he is that one of twofold nature: wholly unacquainted with sin, fiery in aspect, sweet of countenance and angelic in visage, lovely in form surpassing the loveliness of man, likeness of our extraordinary Father —He, that second Adam, who with the key of his death threw open to us the gate of life.

When summoned to those joys, what do we do? We are torpid in the manner of a sluggard. Do you know about the temporizing of the sluggish man? If called in the morning, he ignores it. If aroused still further by a repeated loud summons, he snorts through his nose, even though awake. Finally, urged by a bellow, but still sluggish in speech, he moves his tongue, and "What do you want with me?" he says. "Rise! Come!" "It is night, let me sleep." "No, it is day: arise!" "My God, look I am getting up. Go and I shall follow." And he does not follow him, whom he deceives; and then: "You are not coming?" "Just now I would have come, but I am looking for clothes for myself and not finding them." "It doesn't matter. I know you, Birria. Rise quickly." "Lord, I am ready." However, he is not; instead, he turns his head this way or that, or rubs his arms, or stretches his limbs. So he seeks for delays for himself, wherever he can find them. To judge from his words, he is always on the way; to judge from his feet, not so. Although he is always on the way, he never arrives in person.

If perchance compelled, he drags his heels, moving with the speed of a turtle.

We are of this man's likeness when we are called to the true joys. Captivated by various delights, either we stop up the ears of our heart, or if the ear be open, we always delay to come to those joys. If finally we come, perchance dragged by force, we move with the slow motion of the tortoise. Forgetful of ourselves, we rank God after the Foe.

Alas, we wretched ones! Why are we unwilling to remember the day of counsel, on which, with his hand, he redeemed us from the talon of the Foe? Why do we not remember the things he bore, the kinds and the numbers of things, in torments and derisive words? The servant of the chief priest maliciously found fault with the responses given by our Lord, and, striking him, said: "You answer in such a manner to the high priest?" Christ submitted patiently to this. "Friend, if I have said anything ill, tell me in what respect. If well, why do you strike me? Likewise, Pilate, you may war against me in proportion to the power given to you." Then Judea cried out, trembling, "Crucify!" repeating it and crying out again, "Crucify!" Another threw out this taunt, with hammering blows: "Prophesy, Christ, who is it that struck you?" And another impertinent one added these words: "He will save others, and he fails himself! He hoped in the Lord; let Him free him, if he choose." He desired to be handled thus scornfully, who, beaten with rods, hung on wood, given vinegar to drink, transfixed with iron, beaten with a rod, his head hedged in with the points of thorns, having passed through every torment, so many kinds of death, finished all in one death. Insults, whips, threats, ignominy, nails, lance, thorns—these are, in this happy end, the turning point in our downfall. By these delights, man, by this art of the cross, he redeemed you; bravely weak, then, he redeemed death through death.

While he suffered death, Nature said: "It is necessary to suffer: the Lord is suffering. Lament with me, every kind of thing; heaven, close up your lights; air, be dark; sea, cry out; earth, tremble; weep together, all you elements." She thereupon shook terribly with grief and broke down altogether. Every kind of thing gave indications: the sky closing up its light, the air growing dark, the sea crying out, the earth trembling, every element in tears. Nor did that happen after the customary order of events, but it happened because the Lord of Nature had suffered the power of death. At the same time, Nature suffered that power, compelled by her bitter grief. Only the depraved breed whose posterity are in infamy laughed at the dying God: Treacherous stock! People of stiff neck! Teach that heart so hard to soften. Remember the terrible ruin of the obdurate Pharaoh. Learn righteousness.

Examine the characteristics of the Christ; you will see clearly. Ought not Christ to have suffered in this way? As it was written on the inscription there, the Lord ruled from the cross, and thereon won his victory, and expelled the Enemy, and redeemed the world. Thus, as man he fought for man, but the man fighting then was God himself, who now is holding the sceptres of royalty and shortly is to be our judge! That God and no other, that the Son Himself, not the Person of the Father nor that of the Holy Spirit, had to be the salvation of man, now deduce from a few reflections.

Having been born in heaven with the other created angelic citizens, Lucifer of surpassing light (he took on more of the light of the Creator than the others) became presumptuous on that account; and then, swollen, he began to presume against the Highest Light. For he saw Light brought forth from Light, the Word from the Father; likewise he saw the Holy Spirit come forth from both; he saw the same Triune Nature; he saw those three various persons. And he grudged the sole Word, and, created being as he was, he desired to be equal to the Father's Son. "I intend to dwell in the regions of the north," he said, "and appear like to the Most High." He desired sin thus to become a citizen of heaven.

But it was a brief sojourner there, since heaven could not tolerate crime. But from there, soon, Lucifer fell as he had risen, and suddenly morning was turned to dusk for him, his good into a worse condition, his eminence into abasement, his holiness into diabolism; and he had two shapes within a single hour; bright and dark, good and evil, high and low, angel and demon. And having suffered his own ruin, he dragged down to the depths with him a tenth from all the orders of angels, each alike to its own ruin.

After the passage of five days, on the sixth, God made Adam, and he made Eve: your two citizens, Paradise. Their Author said to them: "Taste every kind of tree, both good and evil; but the Tree of Knowledge, do not touch." He added a reason, moreover, that it was lest from the taste of it they might die the death. What did Lucifer do? He saw them and saw them formed so that they might fill out the number of angels with whom he had fallen and so that they might enjoy those delights which he as angel had lost. Then, considering what he might do, having taken on the likeness of a serpent, coming privily, straight, and upright, he came to Eve, not daring to accost Adam. "Why," he said, "are you kept back from eating from the aforesaid Tree?" She replied, "For this reason: lest perchance through it we die." Indeed, in that "perchance" he saw that she was the less convinced. And then, more boldly, he overcame her with these words: "Not so, he said, "rather, eat; and so you can be knowledgeable of both good and evil, as are the gods." Hope, aroused by such diplomacy, inflated her; she tasted what was forbidden; and her master did likewise—although conscious of what he did—lest he annoy her. That was the first sin. But the second sin, which was more degenerate, was not to wish to bewail his crime or besiege God with entreaties. Instead, Adam turned the crime into the doing of his wife. And what did the wife do? She turned it into the deceit of the serpent. And their defense of their crime was the major source of their offense. Thus, Paradise, they fell from your throne, both damned; and thus the race of humans perished. Neither natural law, nor legal right, nor any virtue could have availed it that Tartarus should not swallow up all souls.

Such enormous wrath bellowed for many thousands of years; nor for that long did so fearful a tempest subside. Therefore the Son of God said to himself, "Because Lucifer presumed against me, he fell and perished. That fall was the root of this one. Thus I am, as it were, the remote cause of this plague; I will be the near cause of its salvation. If I choose to fight in my own strength, the Foe will easily fall. But if I win that way, I shall be resorting to my power and not to justice. Wherefore, since the shrewdness of the Foe conquered man, it is essential by the law of reason that it be a man who conquers him; and that he who slipped and fell may rise from the fall; and that, strong, he tear himself from its clutches and walk free and upright—he who surrendered to the servile yoke; and that he live a joyful life who perished in misery. But it is also necessary that he be God. Not otherwise may the virtue of man overthrow the Foe, except God clothe himself in flesh. Since human virtue was, thus, one with God's virtue, therefore it is necessary that, just as the enemy overthrew man, he be overthrown by man himself; that just as the enemy won by means of a Tree, he be conquered by the same; that whom he captured through a trick, he should be captured by." Thus spoke the Son.

The Holy Paraclete, then, was the author of His conception; and with his own hand he wove for him the garment of a human—for him who secretly descended into the royal chamber of a virgin; and, entrances thereto still closed, he emerged from the virgin chamber, its door still closed. Whence, every way a miracle: miraculous entrance, miraculous exit, and all His life a miraculous progress.

The Foe perceived nothing in Him to make his own. But still he attackd a being not his own: damning Him, damned by Him, to the death of the cross he damned Him. On the cross He bore our sins, not his own. There He expiated our crimes; and that debt He had incurred not, he then discharged. But death itself did not escape when it thus attacked him: what then swallowed the man was, by the hook of his Godhead, intercepted. And having so swallowed Him, death expected to conquer, but was aghast to be conquered: for His spirit robbed the infernal regions of their right, transformed the grief of His friends into raptures of light. Whom the country of death held, grace alone so redeemed. Through Him by whom it began, so wrath was ended.

If you will fully examine these figures of speech, the sense in all of them demonstrates the topic clearly. Two instances only can you raise where it does not put its point openly.[100] That is so in this proposition: "My power is not small, nor my rank insignificant," for I intimate more than I say and the concept is larger than the statement itself. If by chance I speak on behalf of my own affairs or of what pertains to me, this way of speaking is tasteful; and with such a form of speech I am more modest. In this way, the thought appears covered over; the meaning is not plainly opened up; rather, the thought is larger in itself than the speech which pertains to it.

"Out of all the riches, so many and so extensive, left him by his father, the spendthrift not only has no means with which to conceal his poverty, but he even has no pot in which he may beg a fire." Thus, about a trifling fact,[101] I say too much;[102] I speak immoderately what is not moderate: no temperance in the subject, no temperance in the speech. And even if the subject is more moderate than the speceh, still, excessive speech about it intimates that it is the less so.

"That man is remarkable"—this word "remarkable" sounds as if it means "excellent." However, its other sense of a "very bad" man gives us a sidelong glance; this it also means. This word doublecrosses the vision, or else the vision errs in its ambiguities. The statement is covert, but the jest is open.[103]

"When the boy saw the switch, ruddiness instantly left him and his face was bloodless." This appearance signifies that he himself

100. The "two instances" are contained in the two members of the quotation that follows, "My power is not small nor my rank insignificant." Both are examples, as Geoffrey intends them, of *significatio* (mentioned earlier in the *Poetria nova*, ll. 1269–1270), the figure that implies more than is explicitly asserted. Cf. the *ad Herennium* IV. liv. 67, pp. 401–403. *Significatio* may take six different forms (understatement, hyperbole, ambiguity, mention of effect instead of cause, aposiopesis, and pointing of an analogy). Having already illustrated understatement in "the two instances," Geoffrey takes up each of the remaining five in turn in what now follows.

101. In the text, *de re minima*. The Latin perhaps means instead, a condition of abject poverty. Faral shows *nimia* as a variant reading for *minima*, however, in which case it would be the improvidence ("excess") of the spendthrift that was in question.

102. Hyperbole, the second category of *significatio*.

103. Ambiguity, the third category of *significatio*.

was afraid. "Redness overspread the girl's face." This sort of face indicates that she was ashamed. "In her strolling, she went about with her hair adorned." This mode of expression reports her to have been a wanton. Attribute the signs associated with it to any given concept: make known the signs themselves, but do not make them known for their own sakes, but rather as the mere indications of the things they signify: [104] fear by pallor, lust by excessive adornment, shame by sudden blushing. And show the concept by definite signs, the cause by the effect: such and such a color, sex, age, or appearance.

"Lately in another man's bedchamber . . . but I will not tell." In such manner I break off my words,[105] nor do I say what man, and by no means what his age or appearance.

"You are great, and the world kneels on bended knee to you. But although you have the power, do not be cruel: remember Nero." Having made such an analogy,[106] I add nothing further. Or here I elaborate a subtle exemplum with this speech:

> When Alexander the Great was at war with Athens, none of the terms for reestablishing peace were pleasing to him, unless perchance if the elders of the city were given as hostage. One wise man replied to that proposal with these words. "Suppose the wolf made war on the shepherd. And each side negotiated for peace; but no formula for peace pleased the wolf except that the keeper of the flock be given over to him as a mortgage and pledge of love. This was done, therefore, but whereas before the enemy felt some fear, he was afterward the more confident.

When he had said this, he stopped. The speaker wished his point to be compared to the exemplum. And since he cleverly gave only part of his meaning to the ear, he saved part for the mind. This is the method of a man of skill—to compass in half a speech all the force of a whole speech.

104. Mention of effect instead of cause, the fourth category of *significatio*.
105. Aposiopesis, beginning a statement and then stopping short, so that what has already been said is enough to arouse suspicion: the fifth category of *significatio*.
106. The citing of an analogue without explicitly showing or expounding its relevance, so that by means of it an opinion is intimated: the sixth category of *significatio*.

The thought that has arrived at elegant "color" by such means does not come so as to be clearly detected, but instead reveals itself through signs. It sheds its light from off to one side; it does not care to proceed directly into the light. There are five varieties, but it is all one and the same color.

Unite the flowers of diction and of thought in one, so that the meadow of your speech may bloom with both varieties of flowers. For there arises a certain harmony of fragrances, and it will have a rich odor mixed of both kinds of colors.

You know what is fitting and you utter things fit to be said, but perhaps led by chance, not art. Nor do you have a feel in composition for the kind of thing that you should observe at first sight, and on which you should expend effort—in other words, what the point is from which you may anticipate the direction of the effort to be made, what the source is which may beget ornament of words. Instead, your mind wanders this way and that; and the footprints of your dubious mind are aimless, like those of a blind man, groping for where or which the proper way may be, whose eye is a staff and whose guide is chance. What, then, to do? By art you may train the mind, which like an idler is drifting.

Select a definite "place." There are only three places: [107] first, an expression that can be varied through tenses; next to that, an expression varied by grammatical cases alone; lastly, an expression that resists inflection. And this is the way it may be done.

Here is the first place: think of a verb. Let that convert into a noun, either one that derives from the same stem, or one that derives from the same stem as a verb that has the same meaning;

---

107. "Place" is a technical term here. At this point in the *Poetria nova* Geoffrey begins to expound the theory of "conversions," which involves, as is soon apparent, the "conversion" of Latin nouns and adjectives into their declined forms (and into their synonyms and the declined forms of those); the "conversion" of Latin verbs and their synonyms into their various tenses and declining forms (e.g., participles); the "conversion" of nouns and their synonyms into cognate verbs and vice versa; and finally, the "conversion" of indeclinable Latin forms into periphrastic forms that do decline. All of these maneuvers are designed to promote variety of vocabulary and of forms of expression and to help solve metrical difficulties.

or let it be approximated by a satisfactorily expressed synonym.[108] The noun comes forth from the verb like a branch from a trunk, and it keeps the flavor of its root. But whereas the noun only means the same thing as the verb and is not sufficient to the matter, the whole fire will be revived out of this spark—with the help of other closely related words and by the craft of the mind. With this, therefore, as the basis of your effort, go about the matter as follows. You may vary the case of a particular noun, and, to it, adapt whatever sequence of construction will properly serve the subject proposed.[109] But to this end you will travail with your whole heart: hammer diligently upon the anvil of your mind, hammer again, and finally strike out something that is fitting. But let this be the order you follow. Collect beforehand in your mind all the various grammatical modes. After this, select the best one, the case form in which the thought will infuse into the ears most felicitously. Let shrewd judgment be operative in this, and scan critically the possibilities. This decision, if it is to be discerning, must bring to bear both art and experience. The point should be clear in an example. Take this brief theme: "As a result of this 'I grieve.' " Use the rule that has just been established as follows:

> "Grief" flows to me out of this fountain. From here rises to me the root (or the seed, or the fount, or the source) "of my grief."
> This matter provides the substance and the cause "for my grief."
> This sows (or brings forth, or issues in) my "grief."
> You, "O woeful grief," come hard against me with cruel wounds.
> My mind, as if hardly sound, and sick "with grief," collapses.

108. The first "place," as Geoffrey explains, is the conversion of a verb into a noun.
109. Once a Latin verb has been converted into a Latin noun, the noun itself is, of course, susceptible of declension into various cases; and, for the various cases of the noun, various appropriate sentence structures may be devised. Thus, in the example that Geoffrey presently appends, the Latin noun *dolor* ("grief") is used in all its grammatical cases (nominative, genitive, dative, accusative, vocative, ablative—in that order), a different statement that exploits the nature of the grammatical case being constructed for each such case in turn.

Thus, from the verb "I grieve," you take the noun "grief," and you so change its case however you like: to any case you like, you may add a corresponding sequence of construction that suits the topic itself.

Or again, you may take as noun, not the stem noun of the verb, but rather one from a similar verb signifying grief, such as "sigh, lament, moan, weep"—whence the nouns are "sighs, lamentations, moans, weeping." Then in this way the nouns express the sense of the verbs:

> From my soul come sighs; from my mouth lamentations; tears pour down upon my face; and my moans I renew continually.

But say that still more felicitously:

> From the depth of my breast my sighs break forth; my breath bursts out in lamentations; the fountain of my eyes wells tears; and moaning breaks my spirit.

So thought should bind nouns to verbs with a certain knot of artifice. There is a pleasant enough charm in words used literally, but in things well transsumed [110] we know a pleasure more complete.

The expression that is inflected by case alone may enjoy a two-fold consideration.[111] The adjective, for its part, needs one approach, but it is otherwise with the noun. You consider the one apart from the other; but in this treatment have regard for the former first.

The above rules gave instruction in how to convert the verb; the adjective changes according to a similar pattern: [112] you should proceed with the same steps in both the one affair and the other,

110. Expressed metaphorically.
111. Turning now from verbs to declining forms, Geoffrey divides the latter into the two categories adjectives and nouns.
112. Like a verb, an adjective may be converted into a noun; and the noun is again susceptible of declension into various cases. Again, too, for the various grammatical cases of the noun, various appropriate sentence structures may be devised that exploit the nature of the particular grammatical case. Thus, from the adjective "white," comes the noun "whiteness." For the noun "whiteness," different sentences are constructed that utilize its various cases (nominative, genitive, dative, accusative, ablative—in that order, the vocative being omitted).

for both courses keep the same road. This is apparent in the theme: "Her face is white." Alter the adjective thus and observe the rule stated:

> "Whiteness" lights up her face.
> With a ray (or a light) "of whiteness" it shines.
> "To whiteness" her face is wedded.
> Her cheek wears "a whiteness" like the sun.
> Dawn breaks on the world "out of the whiteness"
>     of her cheek alone.

This is a satisfying device. In a miraculous way, such hyperbolic style either augments or diminishes praise or else blame for a crime. And praise or blame is the suitable application of it. Thus, derive "whiteness" from "white" so that a better mode of expression may result from case variations. Or if you like, choose nothing from the "white" stem, but rather from "snowy," because it is similar to it; and then, choosing the noun from thence, think "snow," and take this course:

> "Snow" and her cheek are not far apart in appearance.
> Whiteness shines in her face with as much light as if it were
>     emulous "of snow."
> Her face is near "to snow" in brightness.
> Her face in its own brightness has imitated "snow."
> Sure of victory, her face competes "with snow."

I pass by the fifth case, which is to be used only when apostrophe requires it.

Thus you may change the adjective into a noun derived either from it or from a similar adjective; and the prudent innovator will add other words, and so make pleasant their sequence that the succession of words, all related through the noun used in the original version of the material, may keep the meaning and vary the color. And it will mean the same thing, although not sounding the same.

Apply this rule to the noun. If the noun is well off, as regards case, it does not need the care of artifice. But if it does not possess distinction in the case in which it is written, a declension of one case into another should be performed; [113] and strive to weave a fabric of words such that the unadorned theme may take to itself a garment of new beauty. The face of this theme is without ornament: "I did the foul deed by premeditation." I freshen the cheek of the expression as follows:

> A plan "was my goad to acting" or "was the agent of the foul deed."

Or like this:

> A suggestion of wicked premeditation "offered itself as a cause for the crime" or "came forth as a cause."

Or write it in this kind of statement:

> The act was "in accord with a plan" or "A wicked hand was evident in it."

Or derive the expression like this:

> A wicked hand put plan into action.

Or again, if someone puts this to you, a bald statement, as it were, "All men are talking up this deed," concoct a statement like this:

> This "deed" is the talk of the people.
> Public rumor is witness "of the deed."
> No one tongue clamors with respect "to the deed," but the voice of the people publishes it, one and all.

---

113. No less than a verb or an adjective, a noun, too, may be converted: either by manipulation of its own grammatical cases, or by conversion into a synonym or paraphrase, which in turn may be given supporting sentences that use various declined forms. Thus, starting with *consilio*, the ablative of the Latin noun *consilium* (the ablative being translated as "*by* premeditation,") Geoffrey first uses the nominative *consilium* ("plan"), then the genitive *consilii* ("of premeditation"), then the dative *consilio* ("in accord with a plan"); then he resorts to the paraphrase *paruit illi flagitiosa manus* ("a wicked hand was evident in it").

Should I go on with more examples? To what purpose? Meaning does not reject a single case; indeed, though itself one and the same, the thought may be adapted to all the cases. Apply yourself, so as to be able to find the way: it suffers itself to be found if you are able to find it. If the way is not open to anyone, it is not the fault of the way, but of the man to whom the counsel of art is wanting; he does not have as an ally one whom he can consult—experience. Three things perfect the poem: art, by whose rule you should be governed; practice, which you should cultivate; your betters, whom you should imitate. Art makes artists sure, practice makes them quick, imitation makes them tasteful: all three combined produce those artists that are preeminent.

That stiff-necked mob of words that refuses to be inflected is, though allowed to be passable in speech, best done away with: the oftener the better, let the plebeian word retire from court, a matter to be attended to according to a certain model. Let this be the model: consider what such a word signifies, then express the thing it signifies in a noun or in a verb so that a new form emerges and one better than the first.[114] Take this brief theme: "He will come then." "Then" is a sign of time. Express that time through a noun, maintaining the same sort of purport: "That day will produce him." If the theme be this, "He will come here," the following way of putting it will add ornament to the words: "This place will admit the one who is coming"; or "It will be host of him who is coming, whether for a long time or for a day." Again, if you choose to speak rather more ornately, take this as a model. If you intend to say " 'Once' or 'twice' or 'frequently' I fail in duty," say:

It is the 'sole' or 'second' or 'the repeated' infection of my soul.

Or:

Sin just now begins.
Sin returns to me.
Sin grows by use.

114. Certain Latin words, especially adverbs such as *tunc, huc, semel, bis,* and *frequenter* ("then," "here," "once," "twice," "frequently") do not decline. For these, periphrastic constructions are recommended.

By the same rule, where "this" or "that" is written, substitute "the one" and "the other." [115] If a subdisjunctive statement is being made, write "the one or the other"; but if you would oppose two things, say "the one . . . the other." But you will not bring it forward as "If this man should come, that one would depart," but rather as "This man when he comes will effect the retreat of that one." The former statement was the style of inexperience; the latter, the style of art. This is the same kind of thing again: "The people run all around the city" [*versus*] "The people compass the circle of the city with swift foot." [116] Or: "He is justly punished for the crime" [*versus*] "His crime was a cause commensurate with his punishment." [117]

Lest these examples weary anyone, I am covering many typical instances under a few illustrations, and all the rest under them. If you wish to understand the effect of the majority of instances, take this minority: the majority behave like the minority. Look over these few instances: what the rule is for the few, it is also for the many. Another author adds examples in the *Topics*, where the theory is greatly curtailed but the overall treatment is more lengthy.

Lest, therefore, I wander off into long discussions, my illustration should not go on with individual instances; but rather, by way of more striking counsel, let many instances be comprised in a brief illustration.[118] You take the role of malcontent and you have as

115. The Latin words *iste* and *ille* ("this" and "that"), although themselves susceptible of declension, may also at times be replaced by the Latin words "alter" and "alteruter," which decline, too.

116. The Latin phrase *undique circa* ("everywhere around") is considered to be inept; it is replaced by the more fluent *urbis . . . circinat orbem* ("compass the circle of the city").

117. The indeclinable Latin adverb *juste* ("justly") is replaced by a paraphrase.

118. The point of the subjoined illustration is somewhat obscure. But probably the idea is that the apprentice writer whom Geoffrey imagines as reading the *Poetria nova* is impatient by now with Geoffrey's involved counsels, which the novice sees as "obstructing his progress" when he is eager to hasten on with his composition. Geoffrey portrays the young writer, then, admonishing himself to be patient, to allow time to "think" and to "produce" (say) better, "converted" forms for his first impulsively chosen words. If this understanding of the lines in question is correct, then they are a dramatic representation of those struggles of the mind against itself so movingly described by Geoffrey in the concluding paragraph of this section of the *Poetria nova*.

theme: "You are trying to obstruct my progress." [But admonish yourself:]

> You want results immediately; I ask for delay. I request time
> to think. You are too headlong, my exacting friend. I am not
> able at the moment; have patience: delay will be able to pro-
> duce what the present moment cannot.

This skill does not come easily or without labor. But the mind when it labors, struggles like a wrestler, anxiously. For it contends against itself. It seeks that it may consult with itself and yet it does not give itself counsel. And it seeks again, and again it suffers repulse. It fervently insists, and still it stands fast against itself; anxious with cares it writhes itself, at length wrings out from itself, what it wishes, by violence. And thus, both victor and vanquished, it triumphs over itself. But if you wish to rejoice in happy success, supply what is lacking, shave down what is excessive, comb what is shaggy, make light what is dark, emend what is vile. By these pains all things will be made well.

Add these principles to those proceding: since a word that is heard by itself is, as it were, raw material, stuff crude and formless, give it a helpmate: [119] the addition will give it beauty.

In order that your diction may have real sheen, let transsumption paint the clause, as when two words associate in such a joining as "the meadow laughs," or "his study is flourishing." Or collect many interrelated words in this sort of aggregation:

> Dirty silverware, coarse bread, rough food, bitter drink, and a
> servant dressed in rags appeared, to the disgrace of the
> banquet.

119. At this point in his treatise, Geoffrey begins to expound the theory of "determination," which, as is immediately obvious, involves elaborating a theme by means of syntactically parallel phrases. Thus a noun may be "determined" by verbs, by single adjectives, by several adjectives all in the same case as one another, or by other nouns all in the same case as one another. An adjective may be determined by nouns all in the same case as one another; and a verb may be determined by nouns in the same case, by parallel adverbs, or by other "determinations."

Or the adjectives may be doubled, like this:

> The banquet was poor and skimpy: the napkin was worn and
> not fresh, the food raw and horrid, the very drink vinegary
> and clouded, the waiter foul and rude. The whole affair was
> without grace.

Or the noun may determine, as follows:

> You are Cato in temperament, Tully in eloquence, Paris in
> countenance, and Pyrrhus in vigor.

Or you may transsume it as follows:

> The rose of your face, the lilies of your brow, the ivory of
> your teeth, the flame of your lips, the balsam of your breath.

Or thus (figuratively, but with distinction): for "Tiphis," say
"Love's own"; for "Delilah," say "Samson's"; for Martia, "Cato's."
 Let adjective determine adjective in a like case, and I "determine" the noun with a noun in a different case. Or the genitive of
the noun may also determine the adjective—as, for example, if an
avaricious man is described:

> Full "of riches," empty "of virtues," very greedy "of prop-
> erty": prodigal "of another's possessions," stingy "of his own."

Or the dative may determine the adjective, as here, if in speech I
describe Nero:

> His mind with its vices so numerous is made evil "to strang-
> ers"; worse "to his intimates," worst "to himself," helpful "to
> no one" and destructive "to all."

Or here are the ensuing cases:

> This man at table is filthy in his every remark, and always,
> throat burning, he is ready for excess: not approving the wine
> unless the things he has swallowed return in vomit, he is in the

habit of defiling feasts, breathing out filth, throwing up wine, and belching poison.

The supreme model of this style is from the mouth of Sidonius.[120] But it is better if the adjective associates itself with two nouns in a case, which this example clearly illustrates:

> The table silver pleases by the novelty of its pattern and by its brightness; the food is seasoned with cost and art; the drink tastes not so much like wine as like nectar; the servant is distinguished both in behavior and in livery. The charm of the presentation of the banquet and the face of the giver of it are the twin glory of the board.

Indeed, by a similar law, I bring nominative cases together with verbs:

> Now my skin cringes, my heart quakes, my lungs labor, my loins stiffen, my back curls, my body trembles, and death is at my door.

Or I apply the nominative to the verb in a manner like this:

> He is wise as Cato is; he speaks as Cicero does; he is energetic as Pyrrhus is; he is handsome as Paris is; he is bold as Campaneus is; he makes love as Theseus does; he plays the harp as Orpheus does.

Or you may subjoin the oblique cases of the noun as follows:

> He boils with wrath, is terrible in aspect, roars with his tongue, ramps with his sword, rages in his gestures.

Or collect clauses like this:

> Divine Love, pitying the contrite heart, dismisses its debts, remits its sins, infuses love of Himself, and promises the joy of true life; but the heart foregoes that joy unless it stands firm in love of Him.

120. Apposite passages, including two that Geoffrey presently quotes verbatim, or almost so, are to be found in Sidonius, *Letters*, Bk. I, ii and Bk. II, i.

Or you may fit adverbs to verbs as follows:

> The actor gorges in the morning, drinks greedily, dissipates himself immoderately, lives foully.

Or say it with mixed endings, as follows:

> He picks up the dice rapidly, scrutinizes them acutely, shakes them craftily, suddenly throws them, chides them amiably, and, patient, waits to see. When the dice are well thrown, he sits back, silent with the pleasure of his mind. At his bad luck he laughs. In neither case is he upset in mind. About both the former and the latter he is philosophical.

This is the method and the manner of Sidonius, and such heaping up of clauses is an excellent technique. In two ways is inculcation [121] becoming to your verse, and these two cases are the praise or blame of deeds. In praising, inculcation builds up approval; and in blaming, inculcation is a brisk hammer for battering.

The pen of Sidonius in particular appropriated this practice for itself: to lengthen verse by introducing numerous clauses. The contrary practice of Seneca is quite different from Sidonius' style: "Free is he who is not a slave to vices; rich is the man for whom what he has enough; poor is the man who wishes any more." This is the manner of Seneca: to round off the verses with a quick conclusion. Each is worthy of respect, but which of the two should I follow? The former or the latter? Since novelty delights more and sameness of mode surfeits us, I will be neither like the one, nor yet like the other: I will be neither as long, nor as short, rather both long and short, being made both out of neither.

If you mark well these remarks and accurately fit words to concepts, in so doing you will speak suitably. If perchance mention of something is raised, whether of sex, of age, of station, of circumstance, or perhaps of place or of time, that propriety is due which the thing, the sex, the age, the station, the circumstance, the time or the place demands.[122] Elegance in this regard is especially to be

121. Heaping up of syntactically parallel clauses.
122. Cf. Horace, *Ars poetica*, ll. 156–157.

desired; for when I expertly handle specific detail, I round off the whole [123] with similar beauty. When the particular is well done, the whole work has relish.[124]

Control the detail and conserve the meaning. This principle is of as much service to prose as to poetry. And one art pertains to both, however much they differ in form.

Meter is straitened by laws, but prose wanders in a freer road: the public thoroughfare of prose admits both wagons and carts at random; but the narrow footpath of a line of verse does not want things so gross, rather desires the same words in graceful form, lest the rustic chassis of a word shake with its weight and defile it. And Poetry desires the meter to come like a handmaiden, with hair adorned, cheek shining, body slender, and beauty exceptional. The delightful comeliness of meter knows no equal for sequence of such sweetness to the ear. The prosaic line is a grosser thing: it loves all words indiscriminately, except for those which it reserves to the very last place in the line (such are those with accented penults); it is not becoming to reserve others for final position. In such form Aulus Gellius [125] treats the subject, and he adds a reason: lest the number of syllables be deficient and not enough to conclude the line. If the final word of a clause be, as it usually is, of another cursus, yet nevertheless this rule is more decorous, for a better reason supports it, as well as the witness of the author Aulus Gellius.

Reason does not vary the other [rules of art], but, whether a poem is straitened by the laws of meter or unbound from its law, art is always the same—although what is decided by art is not always the same.

In either case words should be ruled thus: Let them not be dry, but let the thought press juice into them, and let them be full of juice and blood. Neither let them sound of anything puerile: let them be of great weight, but not bulky: that way they are onerous rather than honorable. Let them not come with an ugly exterior

---

123. *Bene cum determino / totum termino.* The foregoing theory of "determination" is recalled here.

124. *Res condĭta / Tota est condīta.* Note the play on the two forms of *condita*, which, differently accented, have different nuances.

125. Aulus Gellius (born c. A.D. 130), author of a miscellany entitled *Noctes atticae.* The passage Geoffrey alludes to is at I. 7. 20.

either, but let there be color both within and without, and let the hand of art paint the color in both places.

But for all that, it is sometimes a color to avoid colors, except those that common speech knows and that common usage affords. For certainly a comic subject rejects speeches labored at with art: all it requires is the plain style—which fact this joke demonstrates in a few words:

> We are three friends sharing expenses and we do without a valet. This we established for a rule, that we would prepare our meals, each of us in his turn. The other two having served as cooks, then, lo, the third day, and the kitchen hour calls me. About to make a fire, I use my own breath for bellows. A lack of water also requires my attention. My hand takes up the jug: the fountain is sought out. A stone obtrudes, my foot slips, the urn is broken. A happening of double injury: both lack of water and lack of jug. What should I do? While I am thinking it over, I enter the forum. A man sits there, surrounded by jugs. While I turn the choice ones in my hand, while I eye them, he, seeing me penniless, fears theft and insults me with foul words. Befuddled, I return home. I find my friend. I tell the tale. "Let me go back to him," I say, "and you follow, crying out the death of my father." I disguise myself and seek out the place again. This hand seizes one jug, this hand another. My friend, crying out, says, "What are you doing? What are you doing here? Poor chap, your father who was ailing, lo, he is dead, and still, witless, you tarry?" At that "he is dead," my grip, as I clasp my hands together, dashes the jugs to bits. I flee. He who confounded me, I confound him, the villain, and in such sort I get back at him for his earlier libel.

By this reasoning is a humorous speech designated "light": humor proceeds from lightness of heart. And a joke is a youthful thing and is agreeable to those who are in their green years. And a joke is a "light" thing to which the more sprightly age applies itself easily. And third, the action is light. Therefore let everything to do with it be light. The whole is in harmony with itself throughout if the heart is light, the action light, and the words light.

If you treat serious things, your speech and your attitude should be serious: the spirit responsible and the words responsible, too; and color both the topic and the words after the methods previously described.

In the beginning, therefore, you should clean the poem itself of filth and root out its vices. What, of what kind, and how many the things are which vitiate the flow of speech, gather now from a few examples: *Ecce deae aethereae advenere.* Hiatus of the vowels [126] shudders through this passage. Art gave this law to the vowels: namely, that their juxtapositions should not be frequent. Juxtaposition it endures, but it forbids frequency; and here, since they are frequent, the sound of the vowels is disfiguring and heightens the hiatus.

*Tu, Tite, tuta te virtute tuente tueris.* So, the same letter is a disgrace when it is shamelessly repeated.[127] But a less insistent repetition is a becoming ornament.

*Cum non sit ratio rationis de ratione, hinc non est ratio praebere fidem rationi.* So the same word defiles when so often repeated and so pointlessly.[128] A moderate repetition of words is a color, but too much of anything is without true color.

Sometimes similar ending of words serves as ornament; but the frequency of the same sound in these words so joined is unseemly: *Infantes, stantes, lacrimantes, vociferantes.*[129]

These four effects constitute a vice.

A fifth infection it is when something comes suspended in too long a construction.[130]

126. Frequent juxtaposition of vowels. Cf. the *ad Herennium* IV. xii. 18, p. 271. The Latin example quoted by Geoffrey would translate, "Behold, the heavenly goddesses have come."
127. That is, an inordinate amount of alliteration. Geoffrey's example would be translated, "You, Titus, protect yourself, keeping safe your security."
128. The "same word" here is the Latin noun *ratio*, appearing in four different grammatical cases. The translation of Geoffrey's example: "Since there is no reason to the reasoning of the reason, there is no reason to trust reason."
129. The Latin words in series here all have the same ending, i.e., *-antes.* The translation: "Children—standing, weeping, crying out."
130. That is, a periodic sentence that is too long, forcing upon the hearer too many subordinate clauses or too long a subordinate clause before delivering the main statement.

A sixth is added when the violation of normal word order is awkward, as in *Luci misimus Eli.*[131]

Lo, I have given you a comb, with which, if they be combed, your poems may gleam—as well those in prose as the metrical. And if you will ply the comb well, you will be able with this mirror to discern beauty plainly: when you consider the appearance of a word, to see if perchance some lurking worm befouls it, let not the ear nor the mind alone be judge. Let the triple judgment of mind, ear, and usage decide it. My own way to polish words is by sweating: I chastise my mind, lest it stagnate by resting in one technique. For stagnation spoils standing water, but I, ardent, am transported hither and thither, and now I paint the action with this color, now with another. Nor do I revolve it in my mind a single time, but rather often. At length the agile mind, when it has made a complete circuit, chooses one out of many possibilities. It comes to rest there as being, it thinks, a place without shame. But the augur is deceived in many instances. As long as they are buried away in the mind, many things satisfy the mind which the ear nonetheless will not approve. But supposing that it allays the mind, it likewise appeases the ear, and both approve at once. Still, that is not enough; I do not yet trust it, unless I try it again. The first consideration neither well, nor fully, decides a matter: the more I revolve a thing, the more I evolve it. If malodorous, the thing emits, when much thought about, an even worse smell; if full of savor, it savors even more upon reflection. Therefore let the judge of a proposed expression be threefold: first the mind, second the ear, and third and last, that which should conclude the matter—usage.

If you wish to remember all that reason demands, or order arranges, or ornament refines, bear in mind this advice, which,

131. Cf. the *ad Herennium* IV. xii. 18, pp. 273–275. Translation: "We dedicated to you, Lucius Aelius." The full quotation (from L. Coelus Antipater's *Punic War*) read: *In priore libro has res ad te scriptas, Luci, misimus, Aeli*—"In the preceding book we dedicated an account of these things to you, Lucius Aelius." The word order is awkward in that the two members of a proper name are separated from each other.

although brief, is useful.[132] The little organ that remembers is an organ of pleasure. It thirsts after delight, not tedium. Will you please it? Then do not burden it: it wants to be kindly treated, not hard pressed. Since it is a chancy thing, it is not much good for hoards of facts. Feed it thus, when you appease its hunger: be not so generous of food that you have nothing more, let it be fed more than half-full, less than full. Put into its stomach not as much as it can hold, but just as much as contends it: its nature must be nourished, not burdened; and to stop between the two extremes and on this side of satiety is the healthier practice. For you drink in the same way: you moderate your drinking by reference to reason. "Master yourself," [you say,] "and do not drink. Let drink be taken for pleasure and not for a burden. Drink sparingly, not like a sot. The thirsty man finds fault with wine more gracefully than the drunkard refutes him." Knowledge, the food and drink of the mind, is to be enjoyed by a similar law; it should so feed the mind as to prove itself a pleasure, not a burden.

You thirst now to understand this whole art. But instead, slice off small portions, and do not take up several together, but instead lift one at a time—a very small one—and less by a good bit than your shoulders are willing and able to bear. So it will be a pleasure and nothing heavy to lift. Let usage be your companion: when the subject itself is recent and new, turn it over frequently and reflect; after this, wait and delay awhile, and take a breath. And after a short delay has intervened, let another part be summoned up. When it in turn has been retained by a similar process, two of the afore-mentioned memory cells will at last be associated, and well cemented, and use then will glue them together. A third may then be joined to the first two by a similar association; and a fourth to the three. But in all this you err unless you always insist that it be done in the manner described—so that you stop on this side of tedium. The law of the faculty of memory extends to all men: it sharpens dull minds, softens hard heads, and raises both keen and soft wits to something better. What is too much for some men is too little for others; an equitable law should fit to each man the load for him, and its pattern should be one and the same for all.

132. With Geoffrey's remarks on mnemonics, compare the *ad Herennium* III. xvi. 28 – xxiv. 40, pp. 205–225.

Add other techniques which I use and which it is expedient to use. Whenever I want to remember things seen, heard, remembered from the past, or done previously, I talk them over with myself like this: "Such and such have I seen, such and such heard, such and such thought, such and such done in this place or that." Places, times, shapes, or other similar cues are reliable roads for me which lead me back to the details I want. And I know through these cues; this or that was the case, and I call up an image of this or that.

Tully [133] relies on a theory of exotic images, which it is well to remember; but he is teaching himself and is, as it were, the sole devotee of his subtle system, which is of a subtlety unique to himself. But my own subtle scheme may please me and not please him. To every man what pleases him and helps him!—for pleasure alone makes the recollective faculty strong. Wherefore, believe not his methods, but neither believe in these of mine, if they seem to you hard or the less acceptable. But it you wish to proceed the more safely, fashion little cues for yourself, whatever your mind's free will suggests. If they delight you, then you will learn by using them. There are some people who wish to learn, but not to work or to suffer study and pain. That is the way of a cat: it wants a fish but does not want to go fishing. I do not speak to them, but only to any there may be whom the labor of getting knowledge rejoices as much as the knowledge itself does.

These languages should be heard in reciting: [134] first, that of the mouth; next, that of the speaker's countenance, and, third, that of gesture. The voice has its own laws, and observe these as follows.

Let the period keep its pauses when spoken, and let pronunciation preserve accent. Those words which the sense separates, separate; those which the sense joins, join. So tame your voice that it is not at odds with the subject, nor let it be inclined down a path other than that which the subject matter intends; let both go to-

---

133. Cicero, who, as has been noted, was believed in the Middle Ages to be the author of the *ad Herennium*.
134. On delivery, cf. the *ad Herennium* III. xi. 19 – xv. 27, pp. 189–205.

gether: some particular tone of voice will be the perfect reflection of the subject matter.

As the subject behaves, so let the speaker behave. Let us see this by one example:

> Wrath, offspring of flame and mother of madness, deriving its origin from its own bellows, poisons the heart and the innermost parts. It blasts with its bellows, burns with its flame, and confounds with its madness.

In this very same order, a bellowing voice goes forth, the countenance is inflamed, and the demeanor disturbed: the external behavior follows the internal, and the inner and outer man are identically moved.[135] If you represent the person of this angry man, what, as a speaker, will you do? Imitate true rages. Yet be not yourself enraged; behave partially like the character, but not inwardly. Let your behavior be the same in every detail but not to such an extent; and suggest wrath becomingly. You can also present the gestures of a rustic character and be humorous. Your voice may suggest the character's voice, your face his face, and your gestures his gestures—through little clues. This is a disciplined charm; this technique of oral recitation is appealing and this food is flavorful to the ear.

A voice decently moderated, and one seasoned with twin flavors of face and manner, should therefore be so conveyed to the ears that it may feed the hearing. Power comes from speech, since life and death rest in its hands; however, language may perchance be aided, in moderation, by both expression and gesture. So, therefore, all combine: apt invention, fluent speech, sophisticated construction, steadfast memory. Read poorly, compositions have no more glory than has, read charmingly, a composition composed without reference to the principles that herein have gone before.

## Epilogue

Now I have crossed the ocean; I have anchored on the shore at Gibraltar. And you [136] I establish as harbor before me, who, most

135. That is, a speaker delivering the preceding passage would do well to *dramatize* the effects of wrath as he enumerates them.
136. Here again, as in the dedication, Pope Innocent III.

great of created beings, are neither God nor man: you are, as it
were, "neuter" between the two, whom God has chosen for his
companion. With you He walks sociably, having shared the world
with you. He did not wish all things to be his alone, but willed the
earth to you and heaven to himself. What could he have done
better? What greater? To whom better or greater? I will put it
even more conservatively—rather, to whom equally great or comparable? Therefore, father, vicar of Christ, I commit myself wholly
into your keeping, whose wisdom flows forth as a fountain, whose
sharpness of reason is as fire spitting out sparks, whose ready eloquence is like a precipitate rushing torrent, and whose grace is
marvellous. I could wish to express fully how you excel in every
human quality, but the truth is very much more eloquent than my
tongue. Crown of Empire; you whom Rome, capitol of the world,
serves on bended knee; you, full of sweet nectar, who are fragrant of learning seasoned by the spice of good character: by your
leave—and briefly—let me speak. Although you have power to do
most things, may you desire only the power to observe the mean.
Remember, and impress this on your mind: Although able to do
harm, be unwilling to do it; sufficient injury it is to be able to
injure. Do nothing that you might afterwards wish not to have
done, but let thought be cautious preamble to any deed. Do you
not see, if you observe the true facts about our ruler, that he has
proved himself a soldier both of the cross end of Christ, and the
sword of the whole Church? Such devotion deserves love, not
hate; praise, not blame; reward, not punishment. Therefore, you
who overcome others, submit to be yourself overcome; and desire
to turn and be reconciled with the king.[137] O flower of the clergy
and its crown, let pour forth from the honeycomb of your heart
the choicest of its honey in accustomed sweetness. For our prince I
pray. I am least of beings, you are most great. But for all that, be
merciful, and may it be better for him by reason of this, my plea.

Accept, O flower of the realm, the special gift I have composed
for the Pope in the form of this little book. May you possess the
first honor of this private work. But take not it alone, for with it

137. Geoffrey apparently appeals to Innocent on behalf of King John. The exact
circumstances that might have necessitated such an appeal (and thus, what date
for the Epilogue might be indicated) are a matter of controversy. See Nims, *op.
cit.* (n. 8 above), pp. 109–110, note on lines 2081–2098.

I give to you all of myself, William,[138] man of gold. I am entirely at your disposal. Your heart full of all things is not taken up with insignificant matters but ever aspires on high. Nobility of giving—which moderns know not—is innate in you, who alone, jewel of donors, give in such manner that no hand may be more open in giving, or mind gladder, or hesitation briefer. You alone are a man upon whom God has poured out whatever is fitting: namely, a heart full of great wisdom, upon which heart the hearts of other kings are wont to lean in carrying out the negotiations of the realm. You are singular in giving, prudent in judgment, faithful in alliances. God as helper always multiples your victories, and you rise continually in eminence. But granted that every eminence of fame should be added to your rank in honor, you could never gain in reward as much as by right you merit.

138. Probably either William of Wrotham, archdeacon of Taunton, or William de Sancta Maria Ecclesia, Bishop of London. See Faral, pp. 32–33, and Nims, p. 110, note on l. 2100.

Robert of Basevorn

---

# The Form of Preaching
## (*Forma praedicandi*)

Translated by Leopold Krul O.S.B.

Robert of Basevorn is a fourteenth-century writer about whom very little is known. His preaching manual is the only work attributed to him, and indeed it is only from chance remarks in the *Forma Praedicandi* that we have learned anything at all about him.

His name has been learned from an acrostic combination of the initial letters of the fifty chapters in the book, as he points out in the introductory section:

> Should any one wish to know who and of what status is that friend to whom this work is dedicated, and who I am and what is my status—I write all this from beginning to end— let him look at the capital letters and he will learn.

The letters spell out "To Lord William, Abbot of Basingwerk, (from) Robert of Basevorn" (*Domino Willelmo abbati de Basingweek Robertus de Basevorn*). Unfortunately the acrostic does not actually reveal the status of the author as he promises.

The date of 1322 appears in one manuscript of the work, and there seems little reason to doubt it.

Basevorn was familiar with what he calls the "Method of Paris" and the "Method of Oxford," although his impartiality suggests that he was connected with neither of these universities. Indeed he castigates both of them for their tendency to "appertain more to curiosity and vanity than to edification." It might be noted that he is somewhat more critical of the English than of the French, though this in itself does not necessarily indicate his nationality. He does not seem to belong to a religious order, though he dedicates the treatise to a Cistercian Abbot.

The *Forma praedicandi* itself is a fine example of the medieval

preaching manual dealing with the so-called "thematic" sermon.[1]
This type of sermon takes its name from the Scriptural citation or
theme used as the base for division and amplification by the
preacher. The elaborate discussion of theme choice in Basevorn's
work demonstrates the importance of this one feature.

The origins of the thematic sermon are obscure. Despite the continuing influence of Ciceronian rhetoric throughout the eleventh
and twelfth centuries, no one had constructed a new theory of
preaching. During the academic year 1230–1231 at the University
of Paris, however, a number of Latin sermons were preached to
the university community in a manner which revealed the presence
of a new homiletic practice.[2] (The thematic sermon is sometimes
also called the "University-style sermon" because of its frequent
association with academic centers like Paris or Oxford.) It was not
until later in the century that theoretical treatises or manuals began
to appear; or, at least, we do not now possess records of earlier
works of this kind. Since the thematic sermon appeared at a period
of high interest in the newly-popular Aristotelian logical works,
some modern scholars have seen the thematic sermon as an out-
growth of the "scholastic method." [3] Others, however, point to the
evident influence of Ciceronian rhetoric in the manuals.[4]

In any case Basevorn's treatise represents an extremely popular
type of theorizing about oral discourse—the medieval analogue to
the oratory of ancient pagan Rome. It was itself extremely influential, finding imitators well into the fifteenth century; one of the
most famous, the historian Ranulph Higden (died 1349), followed

1. The translation is of the text in Th.-M. Charland. *Artes praedicandi: Contribution à l'histoire de la rhétorique au moyen age* (Paris, 1936), 233–323.
2. Texts in M. M. Davy. *Les sermon universitaires parisiens de 1230–1231: contribution à l'historie de la predication medievale* (Paris, 1931).
3. The so-called "scholastic method" of inquiry and expression is actually an out-
growth of medieval dialectic which used the logical works of Aristotle as a base.
See Martin Grabmann, *Die Geschichte der scholastischen Methods.* Two vols.
(Basel, 1909–1911; reprinted Stuttgart, 1961).
4. For the scholastic influence, see Charland, *op. cit.,* pp. 9–10. For the Ciceronian
influence, see Harry Caplan, "Classical Rhetoric and the Medieval Theory of
Preaching," *Classical Philology* 28 (1933), 73–96. A good survey of preaching
theory from Augustine to the fifteenth century may be found in Dorothea Roth,
*Die mittelalterliche Predigttheorie und das Manuale Curatorum des Johann Ulrich
Surgant.* Basel and Stuttgart, 1956 [Rev. in *Journal of Ecclesiastical History* 8
(1957), 242–243.]

Basevorn's lead and buried his own name in the acrostic pattern of initial letters when he wrote a preaching manual. And Basevorn's obvious knowledge of his field enables him to range over the work of his contemporaries to give the modern reader a revealing insight into other preaching theories prevalent in the early fourteenth century.

# The Form of Preaching<sup>*</sup>

*The Lord stood with me, and strengthened me, that by me the preaching might be fully known* (2 Tim. 4:17). As the Philosopher says, they who seemed experienced reasoned falsely through bad logic. Not knowing the syllogistic form, they called themselves philosophers, in vain professing Philosophy, of whose beginning and in a way foundation, namely logic, they were ignorant. Grasping some parts of Philosophy's cloak, they vainly thought that the whole of it fell to them, as says Boethius.[1] Thus also many presume to preach on Theology and to call themselves preachers, when they do not even know the form of preaching, which is the system and method of preaching on every subject, as logic is the system of syllogizing in every field of knowledge.

Since preaching and teaching are necessary for the Church of God, that science which presents the form of preaching artistically is equally necessary, or even more so. For this reason I have tried to present this small offering of mine especially for the honor of God and His holy Church, although other concurrent motives strongly suggesting it are also involved. Therefore, since I was in many ways bored, and since I was importuned with many insistent requests by different Religious of various Orders and at the same time by Seculars, and also since I was not pressed by other occupations as once I was, I undertook to write this book. I have done so in the hope that it would please you to whom above all things I am humbly grateful; in the hope that applying my mind to other

---

* Scriptural citations are to the Douay-Rheims version.
1. Boethius, *Consolatio philosophiae*, Book 3. For a translation see Boethius, *The Consolation of Philosophy*. Trans. Richard Green. Library of Liberal Arts No. 86. New York, 1962.

things I might lighten my boredom; in the hope that in my own little way I might satisfy my companions, whose ardent and constant insistence spurs me on; in the hope that the memory of you, my friend, might be the more precisely fixed in me and in our posterity; and, finally, in the hope that I, too, might not grow stale through leisure. It is in these hopes that I undertook to write the present work, which may be called the Form of Preaching.

When after such a beginning some things which ought to be included seemed difficult for me to invent, I began to be moved by doubts about my ability to bring to perfection what I had begun. And when I was anxiously pondering thus, suddenly and wonderfully there rose before my mind and vision the authority touched upon in the introduction above, and fixing itself with vividness it filled me with unwonted joy, so much that it dispelled a great part of my former sadness. Thus when I clearly saw that the first part of the authority was fulfilled in me, namely, that *the Lord stood by me*, strengthening me, I had no doubts about its remaining part, and made bold to continue what I had begun, rightly judging that I must begin from the place in which could be assigned the four causes of this work such as are usually noted in Introductions.

The final cause is designated when is said: *The Lord stood by me and strengthened me.* For this end the Apostle invites his followers (Eph. 6), saying: *be strengthened in the Lord and in the might of His power.* For he who rightly considers ought to establish Him as an end Who is a soothing consolation in dejection, complete satisfaction of desires, a charming alliance in friendship, and a profitable delight in studies. This end can be rightly expressed in the saying (Ezek. 3:14). *The hand of the Lord was with me, strengthening me.*

Secondly, the efficient cause is designated when is said: *by me.* May God, who is also the end, be primarily the efficient cause influencing the whole, as it were. You, my friend, are like a special attracting force, and the insistence of my colleagues is like a certain continual driving force; whereas I am more immediately the instrument putting the task into execution. However, because the primary cause has more influenc, I do not dare to attribute anything to myself as proceeding from me; but I say with the Apostle (Rom. 15): *I dare not speak of any of those things which Christ worketh by me*, and (Gal. 2): *And I live, now not I, but Christ liveth in me.*

Should any one wish to know who and of what status is that friend to whom this work is dedicated, and who I am and what is my status—I write all this from the beginning to the end—let him look at the capital letters and he will learn.

Thirdly, the material cause is designated when is said: *preaching*, because the form of preaching is here considered as the matter. On this subject, because I know well enough that I am less fit to speak, I must say with Psalmist: *It is good for me to adhere to my God, to put my hope in the Lord God that I may declare all thy praises* (Ps. 72:28), that is, compose a form which should be a guide for all methods of preaching.

Fourthly, the formal cause is designated implicitly when is said: *may be accomplished*, as some books have it. A thing is formally transmitted and taught when a continuation carries through in an orderly way what the beginning of the work promises or proffers for investigation, and what the end brings to a conclusion, as the Apostle enjoins upon Timothy (2 Tim. 4): *do the work of an evangelist, fulfill thy ministry.* As St. Gregory says in the prologue to *Moralium super Job:* [2] *He who treats sacred eloquence ought to imitate the way of a stream. A flowing stream, if it touches hollows along the side, immediately turns into them, and when it has sufficiently filled them, immediately flows back into its bed.* So says Gregory. In a similar way a stream moves gradually, in an orderly manner, from its source to its mouth. Thus one who deals with the divine word—yes, with any orderly treatise—should make sure that in discussing a subject he has an organized method of procedure. He should not dwell too long on the same point nor should he repeat more often than is right. He should hastily progress from one thing to another as the matter allows. An exception may be made when—without deviating too far from the matter—he finds along the way a source of edification into which, as I might say, he turns his stream of language as into a neighboring valley. When he has sufficiently filled the place of added instruction he turns back into the channel of the intended sermon. Whence the saying, in Ecclus. 24, about God, who brings about this formal

2. For text see *Patrologia Latina.* Ed. J. P. Migne. Vol. 75, column 513.

filling, and from whom primarily comes that which seems to come from us. It is said that *He filleth up wisdom as the Phison,* and again, that *He filleth up wisdom as the Phison,* and again, that *He maketh understanding to abound as the Euphrates.* In other words, just as those two rivers, Phison and Tigris, fill their beds in an orderly way, so does God do in the case of those who deal with his wisdom, pouring into them the grace and wisdom, or the knowledge of proceeding in an orderly and formal way, that thus by the opening of His hand all things may be filled with an agreeable goodness.

This filling, the formal cause, or method of procedure (if we may now turn to our proposal, having completed the foregoing Prologue) is treated and taught in fifty chapters. For, as is clearly evident, the Prologue shows to whom this treatise is dedicated, why its title, and its four causes. Here ends the Prologue.

The index for the following work, which is called The Form of Preaching, was composed in the year of our Lord 1322.

First chapter: What in the proper sense preaching is, and how much time one sermon should take.

2nd. Who should rightly be called a preacher, and when he deserves the aureole.

3rd. The difference between preachers by office and preachers by privilege.

4th. That three things are necessary for one preaching rightly, namely a good life, sufficient knowledge, and legal authority—that is conscience, knowledge, and power.

5th. That above all a proper limit must be established and fixed beforehand in sermons, from which follows that those eager for gain must not be listened to.

6th. What was the first sermon and who the first preacher if we extend the name "preaching" to "persuasion"; and that Christ did not deign in his preaching to refuse to accept the theme of his precursor; and that Christ's method and that of the great teachers differ among themselves.

7th.  That the modern method varies from all the methods mentioned above.

8th.  In what ways Christ and His precursor preached.

9th.  In what ways St. Paul preached.

10th.  The method of St. Augustine's preaching.

11th.  The method of St. Gregory.

12th.  The method of St. Bernard.

13th.  Disproof of the prevailing notion that preaching should not be embellished.

14th.  That twenty-two ways of ornamenting a sermon are observed in the English method.

15th.  What things are required for a good Invention of the Theme; first, that it fit the feast and create a full understanding.

16th.  Secondly, that the theme must come from a common text of the Bible.

17th.  Which parts in a theme may be skipped and which not.

18th.  That a text may not be perverted, and that it is not always perverted when given another sense.

19th.  How a theme of three statements or one which is convertible into three should be selected.

20th.  How, according to some, there can be a division into many statements, and yet it is incorrect to put into the theme more than the appropriate number of statements.

21st.  That a sermon can be built upon one statement, and how it is built up in respect to the antetheme.

22nd.  That one must foresee that vowel concordances can be found for the statements of the theme, and the number of these.

23rd.  That the theme and antetheme should be the same, and in what way.

24th.  Concerning the second ornament, namely Winning the Audience over and the five methods of its use.

25th.  Concerning the third ornament, namely Prayer, and how it is exercised.

26th.  From which Books and passages of the Bible the theme can be taken.

27th.  What themes can be taken according to the aforementioned method *De tempore*, whether in general or in particular.

28th. What theme, according to the same method, can be taken from the saints in particular.

29th. What themes can be taken from the saints in general and from concurrent feasts.

30th. What themes can be taken from emerging material.

31st. Concerning the fourth ornament, namely the Introduction, where note the way in which different preachers use different methods of quoting, and four usual methods of Introduction.

32nd. How the Introduction should be formed when the theme consists of one statement.

33rd. Concerning Division, the fifth ornament.

34th. Concerning the sixth ornament, the Statement of the parts.

35th. Concerning the seventh ornament which is the Proof of the parts, and especially about the very unusual method of the Parisians.

36th. The usual method followed by the Parisians with respect to the antetheme.

37th. Their usual method with respect to the treatment, which does not extend beyond the seventh ornament, namely the Proof of the parts, except in the case of Conclusion.

38th. How the Oxonians use this ornament.

39th. Concerning the eighth ornament, namely Amplification, and its eight methods in general.

40th. The method of Amplification in particular, which the Oxonians especially use, and which is called the Subdivision.

41st. Concerning the ninth ornament, by some called the Digression, and incorrectly so, because it is properly the Transition.

42nd. Concerning Correspondence, which is the tenth ornament.

43rd. Concerning Agreement of Correspondence, which is the eleventh ornament.

44th. Concerning Circuitous Development, which is the twelfth ornament.

45th. Concerning the thirteenth ornament, which by some is called Convolution—to wit, all for all and each for each.

46th. Concerning the fourteenth ornament, which is called Unification.

47th. Concerning the fifteenth ornament, which is called Conclusion or Ending.

48th. Concerning sixteen other and diverse ways of preaching, whose subtleties can be understood from what has been said above.

49th. Specially devoted to one method which is in part similar to that of the Parisians, a method which is very effective in every language.

50th. Specially devoted to one peculiar method used in Latin which in part is like the Oxford method, and also briefly to the seven remaining ornaments, namely Coloration, Modulation of Voice, Appropriate Gesture, Timely Humor, Allusion, Firm Impression, Weighing of Subject Matter.

## Chapter I

First we must show what preaching is. Preaching is the persuasion of many, within a moderate length of time, to meritorious conduct. For, when some determine questions, even theological questions, such determination is not preaching, because it is not persuasion by intent, but rather an investigation of truth. When one exhorts one person or two to goodness, that is not properly preaching, but admonition or exhortation or the like. Therefore, it is improper to say that Christ preached to the woman.

Similarly, an orator or narrator who is a good man, experienced in talking, or a speaker who publicly persuades many to fight bravely, commending the brave and disparaging the cowardly, or doing the like, is not properly a preacher, because that serves the end of preserving the State, not of acting meritoriously, as we now speak of the merit which pertains to eternal life. And if he does achieve this end, he does so accidentally, because it is not his special business. The same must also be said about a lawyer or a narrator or others to whose function this purpose is accidental.

In like maner, if someone with one small reason persuades many of something which pertains to the merits of eternal life, that is not properly preaching, for I could then write on this page forty sermons, a thing that is hardly possible. Therefore, preaching requires time that is not too short, nor too much beyond the customary. Just as to know how many particulars make a universal, which is the beginning of art, or to know precisely how many beautiful days make a beautiful summer (for example, if there were relatively few beautiful days, they would not make a beautiful summer), so it is difficult to know how many acts of preaching properly entitle one to be called a preacher, or precisely how much time is needed in order that it should properly be called preaching. It is definite that Christ was a good preacher, of whom is said in Matt. 4, that *He began to preach* and said: *Do penance, for the kingdom of heaven is at hand.* No more is said about His sermon at that time. Paul extended his sermon to midnight, and St. Andrew preached alive on a cross for two days. But I believe that Christ took those words: *Do penance,* etc., for a theme, and added much persuasion that is not mentioned. For not all His miracles are recorded, and even fewer of His words. In like manner it can be said that Paul taught, then, more than he preached.

At the present time, however, it is commonly held in many places that preaching should last no more than the space of a Solemn Mass with music, nor less than a Low Mass without music. Although some saints' sermons are found to be well drawn out or shortened, this does not happen commonly. And they should not properly be called sermons but persuasions or exhortations or the like, although they are called sermons by extending the name.

## Chapter II

We must now see who is rightly to be called a preacher. The Pope, Cardinals, Bishops, and those having the care of souls by ordinary jurisdiction are preachers by office. Religious, constituted by privileges given them, are preachers by commission, even though they never preach; but then they do not merit the aureole of teachers, although they may have the will to preach unless prevented from doing so. The *aurea*, or palm, corresponds to the will, the aureole to the deed.

A preacher by practice is one who preaches frequently. For just as one beautiful day does not make summer, nor one battle a fighter, so also, it is clear, one sermon does not make a preacher. Therefore it does not seem that one sermon merits an aureole. If this is true, it is difficult to know how many acts render a preacher worthy of an aureole. It seems to me that if a person preaches once legally, and as far as he can is prepared to fulfill this office fittingly, and if he is not legally kept from doing so, that such a one merits the aureole. And this is what is said in Dan. 12: *they that instruct many to justice, are the splendor of heaven.* Nor does he specify by saying: *they that instruct many to justice* twice, thrice, or frequently. I have said *legally*, because the aureole is not only a reward for an act of preaching, but for the act done legally. Hence the Apostle: [3] *no one will be crowned unless he strive lawfully.* Therefore, impostors and such as have not been ordained by the Church, nor sent to Israel, do not merit the aureole.

This also makes clear the falsity of the opinion which holds that the aureole is due only to them who have the duty by office as long as they perform it; because, as is evident from the words of the Apostle, nothing more is required than that one strive legitimately. But he preaches legally who does so by commission.

## CHAPTER III

The difference between preachers by ordinary institution and preachers by commission must be noted. The first are held to preach by necessity of salvation, through themselves or through others if that is fitting. If they do not do this, they are guilty of a mortal sin, as is made clear by Boethius, by John, and by other wise men; the subject is discussed almost everywhere. If they preach through others—the Friars or substitutes—it is not altogether safe, because they who preach through others are either able enough to preach or they are not. If they are, they must be ex-

3. 2 Tim. 2:5.

cluded from the joy of the Lord, since they hide the talent entrusted to them, like wicked servants putting it into a handkerchief; if they are not able enough, it is dangerous to preach through others because they thus obligate themselves by accepting a benefice for that which they do not know how to execute. Since they consider such substitutes capable enough, they ought also at the same time to consider these substitutes more worthy of the benefices which they themselves occupy incapably, and to yield the goods of the Lord which they hold unworthily, according to the saying: *He is judged unworthy of the milk and wool who does not shepherd the sheep.*

Preachers by commission can preach if they wish. If they preach, they merit the aureole. If they do not wish to preach, they are not obligated to do unless through perfection. And then, if they do not preach, they do not merit an aureole. And this is the reason why the Church has ordained that stipends be given to ordinary preachers, through tithes and the like, and this of necessity, because of necessity they are burdened with sowing spiritual thoughts in their subjects. Therefore, by just necessity, from pure debt, temporal rewards are due them. To such, however, as preach through perfection, the listeners are not bound to give a stipend except by reason of perfection. He whose place they take is also held by necessity, as it seems to me, because he has the goods of the Church for that purpose. As Gregory explains it in Job 31: *If I have eaten the fruits thereof without money, and have afflicted the soul of the tillers thereof.*

## Chapter IV

It must also be noticed here that the members of the preceding distinction are not so different that they ought not to overlap, because the second member presupposes the first. I mean that a preacher in practice is first of all a preacher by office. Three things are necessary for the one exercising an act of preaching. The first is purity of life, without remorse of conscience with respect to anything grievous; otherwise, according to the scholars, the preacher sins grievously. *For God said to the sinner: Why dost thou announce my justice?* (Ps. 49:16) And there follows: *I will accuse you and stand against your face* (Ps. 49:21). The reason is that he enjoins upon himself a duty whose end in itself is to make others good. In this there is a great, even a very great, presumption that he is initiated into hierarchical acts, yes divine acts, and publicly shows himself to be, as it were, divine and godlike, although actually deformed. Although one may say that he is good when he is not, yet it could be that he does not sin mortally because this is not an hierarchical act. Thus a lecturer in a school may be in mortal sin and teach in it, and because his act of itself is not immediately directed to making others good as such, I do not believe that he sins mortally. But as it seems to me, we must on this subject say what we would say about one administering some Sacrament in mortal sin, that if he can refuse ministering it without confusion, scandal, or ultimate danger to him to whom the Sacrament ought to be administered, by all means he ought so to do; otherwise he commits a new mortal sin. If he cannot refuse, he ought to be sincerely contrite, and in that case the saying applies: *I said: I will confess, and you forgave* (Ps. 31:5). Thus refraining for the most part from that sin, he can administer the Sacrament. That is what I believe should be said here.

The second need for one actually preaching is competent knowledge. He must at least have explicit knowledge of the articles of Faith, the Ten Commandments, and the distinction between sin and non-sin; otherwise, *the blind leads the blind, and both fall into the ditch* (Matt. 15:14, Luke 6:39).

The third need is authority, and with this the preacher is sent out by the Church. *How*, says the Apostle, *will they preach, unless they be sent* (Rom. 10:15)? Wherefore we learn: No lay person or Religious, unless permitted by a Bishop or the Pope, and no woman, no matter how learned or saintly, ought to preach.[4] Nor is it enough for one to say that he was commissioned by God, unless he clearly proves this, for the heretics are wont to make this claim. From this it appears that parish priests cannot preach unless permitted by the Bishop or the Pope, nor is it enough that they be allowed by the rectors. This I think is true if consideration is given

---

4. Here and in the following section Basevorn cites Canon Law, the official church law, in support of his definitions. For passages cited, see *Corpus Juris Canonici*. Ed. Friedberg. I:86, I:592: II:786.

to the intention of the legislator in the aforementioned laws. The intention is to avoid teaching error, and if such people preach indifferently, there is no doubt that they teach many errors.

Still it must be held that connected with their duty are both public preaching and private teaching, especially of the articles of Faith and the Commandments, and they have the power of teaching other things, even subtleties, if they know how to do so. The aforementioned laws consider a rector, vicar, and canon the same. Therefore from the very fact that their rector or vicar is appointed to an office with which preaching is connected, a canon—who by ordinary power takes care of it in his stead—is constituted in the same office in his stead. I nevertheless think it good for them that they do not go too far, but keep themselves within the articles of Faith and the Commandments and their opposites.

## CHAPTER V

Let the preacher see to it above all that he have a good purpose for his sermon—such as the praise of God, or His saints, or the edification of his neighbor, or some such object deserving eternal life. If, secondarily, he also includes another purpose—that he be famous, or that he gain something temporal, or the like—he is an adulterer of the Word of God, and this is considered a mortal sin. But if such a subject occur to him that he cannot profit by his teaching unless he say something by which he shows himself learned and capable, he may have that intention not as an end and direct it to the purpose of edifying.

Likewise, if anyone intends to acquire some temporal goal for the maintenance of the holy, then the end he has in view ought to be called the sustenance of the holy and not the acquisition of temporal goods. And so with the rest. (This is evident from VIII, q. 1 Olim, and the Chapter *In Scripturis.*) [4]

It is, therefore, clear that seekers after gain should in no way be accepted as preachers; (1) because it is frequently found that they have wives or concubines, and do related things, which are opposed to the purity required of a preacher; (2) because they are generally uneducated, which is opposed to the knowledge required of a preacher; (3) because they are not accepted but universally rejected; and finally (4) because as far as is evident they do not have in view the proper end, since they accept such things conditionally. Those, then, who permit them to preach, sin mortally, and just as they are bound to prevent anyone from sinning grievously, so ought they to prevent them from preaching.

I think that the same should be said about those preachers (if there be such) who are known to accept some limitation, an agreement, as it were; for example, if they should receive something by preaching, they would return three parts to the community and retain the fourth for their own use.

## Chapter VI

The prefatory remarks having been made, we must now come closer to our task, which is to show the required form of preaching. Here we must realize that different preachers have from the beginning used different methods—which is still true—so that there are almost as many different ways of preaching as there are capable preachers. Therefore it would be impossible to explain the art of all these, nor is it our purpose to do so here, but only to present some rather well-known methods which accord with modern practice.

After creating man, God preached (if we extend the word 'preaching'), saying to Adam (Gen. 2:17) *For in what day soever thou shalt eat of it, thou shalt die the death.* This was the first persuasion of which we read in Scripture. The preceding words, however, pertain more to a precept when is said: *of every tree of Paradise thou shalt eat;* or to prophecy when is said: *increase and multiply,* etc.; or, according to some, to establishment in power and possession. Afterward He preached frequently through angels who assumed bodies or, as some would have it, some other corporeal likeness which He Himself assumed not in union of substance, but only as moving as perhaps He spoke to Adam and many others. Then He preached frequently through Moses and some Prophets, and finally, with the approach of the end of the Old Testament, through John the Baptist, of whom is said (Matt. 3:1): *In those days came John the Baptist preaching in the desert of Judea, and saying, Do penance for the kingdom of heaven is at hand.* And at last He Himself, taking on a human soul and body in the unity of substance came preaching the same theme which His precursor had preached before, as is seen in Matt. 4:17.

In this it is clear how proud and deserving of confusion are those who reject themes undertaken by others, and in order to speak novel things strive to avoid repeating well what has been well said by others. If this must be done, everyone's books should be burnt at his death lest things said well in them should be said again. The absurdity of this is clear first of all from Christ. Again, after Christ the Apostles and disciples arose, among whom St. Paul is first, and later different Confessors and Doctors, among whom Saints Augustine, Gregory, and Bernard seem preeminent to me, and whose more solemn sermons and homilies are listened to up to the present day. Hence, as it seems to me, it would be quite praiseworthy to try to imitate the methods which any of the five preachers, Christ, Paul, Augustine, Gregory, and Bernard followed.

## CHAPTER VII

Among the modern methods those more commonly used are the French and English, emanating from two quite famous Universities. They have their origin in the aforementioned Doctors and others, and yet follow no particular one. They use in part the method of one or the other and in part their own and also add many devices which, as it seems to me, appertain more to curiosity and vanity than to edification: that concordances be vowels—e.g. if the theme is Veni, Domine Jesu (Come, Lord Jesus), the gerundive, *veniendi,* or the noun *adventus,* or the verb *dominari* or the noun *salvator* (which is equivalent to Jesus) could not function at all. And there are many like things. But this practice is characteristic more of the English method.

What excuse they have before God I cannot well see. They say that a preacher should preach in such a way that he makes the doctrine as well known and honored as he can, because his audience will all the more for this reason adhere to it. Indeed, so great is men's vanity, especially that of the English, that they only consider the curious and do not commend anything else. That makes it necessary to lean on such methods. Then immediately they say: "Our brother is already beyond his theme." This I have myself heard. Likewise, many uneducated men would usurp the act of preaching, except that they see this great finesse to which they cannot attain. And for the same reason, when they preach to lay people, they give their theme with its division in Latin, because it is difficult for the ignorant to do this.

These reasons notwithstanding, it seems safer to propose another goal. The blessed Bernard did not wish to be bothered with things that were vain and hardly necessary for salvation by also giving natural reasons; though had they been given, his teaching would have been more honored. Because I can be deceived in my judgment, and in order to satisfy the requests of others, I will explain each method as far as I can. In order to make them understandable, I will first run through the five approved and honored methods.

## Chapter VIII

It is not easy to understand all the methods which Christ used in preaching. He, as I believe, included all praiseworthy methods in His own, as the fount and origin of good. He preached now by means of promises, now by threats, now by examples, now by reason. He preached now to be understood easily, now clearly, and now profoundly and obscurely.

(1) By means of promises, as is evident from His first theme: *Do penance; for the kingdom of God is at hand,* where he first invites to virtue, and then promises subsequent salvation. That method according to Aristotle, is good and agreeable to good men—or at least to those who are not stubborn. Good and generous minds are more easily drawn by sweet and beautiful promises than by any other means. And in this manner He turned the Apostles to Himself, *Follow me, I will make you fishers [of men],* giving them an inner light, so that they would follow immediately at one word. This is not in our power, but we can be quite like Him through manifest sanctity and through good reputation, which draws men as it were in a similar manner.

In that style also He preached the wonderful Sermon on the Mount, where He showed that that blessedness which is the highest good desired by all can be obtained in eight ways and that it consists in those eight ways.

(2) Christ also preached by threats, as seen in the quote: *unless your justice abound more than that of the Scribes and Pharisees, you shall not enter into the kingdom of heaven* (Matt. 5:20); and again: *it shall be more tolerable for the land of Sodom*, etc. (Matt. 10:15). This method is suitable for the stubborn who, according to Aristotle in the *Ethics*, are not moved except by terrible punishments.

(3) By example: e.g. *Neither do men light a candle*, etc. (Matt. 5:15). It is clear that He used this method quite extensively. Hence in one place it is said that He did not speak to them except in parables: *and without parables he did not speak to them.* (Matt. 13:34). This method is now extensively used in Paris and in many other places.

(4) By reason: e.g. *what therefore God has joined together, let no man put asunder.* (Matt. 19:6); this method is commonly used;

(5) Obscurely: because it is frequently said about His hearers that they did not understand the Word; and

(6) Clearly: e.g., *Behold, now thou speakest plainly, and speakest no proverb* (John 16:29).

These methods He used so wonderfully that the human mind cannot, I believe, fully understand them, for in them, it seems to me, no necessary subtlety or appeal to the emotions is lacking. To show this would require an extensive work. His precursor, the Baptist, used a similar method, as is evident to anyone who looks at the Gospel.

## CHAPTER IX

Paul used reason with great success, especially together with authority—now taking a reason from authority, now conforming reason with authority, now commending the hearers, now saddening them, now flattering them, now disparaging them, now totally committing himself to God, now helping himself with human industry. In all things and all ways he showed that his writings and words flowed from the great charity which he had towards his listeners. These methods are particularly recommended, especially when he confirms example or reason by authority. I boldly state that if one diligently studies Paul, he will find moving themes more quickly and easily because Paul includes the entire Gospel, the Law and the Prophets, as it were, in his Epistles and sayings.

## CHAPTER X

From what I have said it seems to follow that among the Doctors and Confessors, the blessed Augustine holds the most important place. He, more than the others, read Paul the Apostle, and it is his custom sometimes to explain one whole Gospel, or some great passage of Scripture and to do so diffusely, as is clear from *De Verbis Domini et Apostoli*. Sometimes it is his habit to take one theme and follow it up extensively, as in the sermon on St. Paul: *Benjamin a ravenous wolf*, etc.,[5] but always, as far as he can, he rests his case on reasons. This is why he says that where authority is lacking, we must rest on reason, without which even authority is not authority.

The first method should be good for those who have poor or weak memories, because the thread of some great Gospel can be mastered more easily than that of a subtle argument, or a small division of one member. The second method is more common, because it is more novel.

## CHAPTER XI

Gregory has a praiseworthy method, one that operates mostly through figures of the Old Testament, tangible examples, and entreaties. Devoutly and movingly, in almost every homily, he tries to use his persuasion in matters which have more to do with morality than with faith, and especially to the end that we may condemn things temporal. He carries out a whole discourse either about the Gospel or something pertaining to Faith, now with concordances of word and matter, and again only with those of matter. Frequently he multiplies authorities for the same matter and frequently divides one noun into many significations. The latter two devices

5. Gen. 49:27.

are allowed only with reason in common sermons to lay people, nor are they used much, as will be made clear later. All the first are rightly held because they are moving and novel. He also adds to his discourse edifying stories.

## CHAPTER XII

Now about St. Bernard. It must be realized that his method is "without method," exceeding the style and capability of almost all men of genius. He more than all the rest stresses Scripture in all his sayings, so that scarcely one statement is his own which does not depend on an authority in the Bible or on a multitude of authorities. His procedure is always devout, always artful. He takes a certain theme or something in place of it—i.e., some matter which he intends to handle—and begins it artfully, divides it into two, three, or many members, confirms it, and ends it, using every rhetorical color so that the whole work shines with a double glow, earthly and heavenly; and this, as it seems to me, invites to devotion those who understand more feelingly and helps more in the novel methods which we are now discussing. No one, in my opinion, has so effectively joined the two at the same time, except perhaps St. Anselm in the *Meditations*, as St. Thomas the Martyr thinks, or Ambrose, as others think, because they move us more quickly to tears.

There are also other learned men—Chrysostom, Fulgentius, Leo, and others—whose methods I do not specify because to me they do not seem to be different from the methods of the aforementioned.

## CHAPTER XIII

What some say therefore seems to me altogether reprehensible: that preaching ought not to shine with false verbal embellishments—for in very many sermons of St. Bernard the whole is almost always rich in colors. The same is true in the sermons of other saints, as is clear to one who knows rhetoric and examines those sermons. Further, Pope Leo says: *this is the virtue of eloquence, that there is nothing foreign to it that cannot be extolled, nothing so incredible that it would not become plausible by previous adornment of it, nothing so abhorrent or unrefined that it would not shine in its style.*

Who will hesitate to say that wisdom and eloquence together move us more than either does by itself? Thus we must insist upon eloquence and yet must not depart from wisdom, which is the better of the two. If both cannot be achieved, neither can wisdom be achieved. It remains then that it is better to have eloquence than to lack every good. For of what use would an opinion be in which there is neither eloquence nor wisdom? Therefore let those who are not productive through wisdom strive to be eloquent. *In vain does eloquence for a cause bear the burden,* as the poet says, *with the result that in one in whom reason has availed very little, oratory seems to avail very much,* as Gerald of Cambridge says in the prologue to *The Wonders of Ireland.* It does not follow from this that they present their hearers a right reason for judging them by the desire for human respect. But, as I have said, they can for a just and meritorious reason strive after eloquence. It is without doubt very blameworthy that one should prefer to strive after eloquence when he can have wisdom by the striving, as St. Augustine teaches in IV *De Doctrina Christiana,* where he wants a preacher to strive to teach, please, and move. About those who try only to please so that they neither teach nor move, he says that their eloquence is the more damnable the more eloquent it is. Therefore they are better when joined, as is a sweet mixture of good things.

## Chapter XIV

We must come now to our proposal to discuss the ornamentation which is used in sermons by certain of the careful craftsmen. It must be realized that in the most carefully contrived sermons twenty-two ornaments are especially employed. These are: Invention of the Theme, Winning-over of the Audience, Prayer, Introduction, Division, Statement of the Parts, Proof of the Parts, Amplification, Digression, which is properly called 'Transition,' Correspondence, Agreement of Correspondence, Circuitous Development, Convolution, Unification, Conclusion, Coloration, Modulation of Voice, Appropriate Gesture, Timely Humor, Allusion, Firm Impression, Weighing of Subject Matter. The first fifteen of these are inserted into their proper places once, or at any rate into a few places; the remaining three, and generally Allusion and Firm Impression, can be placed almost anywhere. The element that follows after these, Humor, ought to be used in a few places and very sparingly. The last must be observed in all places. All these, when concurring, embellish a sermon elegantly, and so can be called the ornaments of a sermon. And if perhaps there are more elements than have been enumerated, they can be reduced to these.

CHAPTER XV

For a good Invention of the Theme the following are required: that it concur with the feast, that it beget full understanding, that it be on a Bible text which is not changed or corrupted, that it contain not more than three statements or convertible to three, that sufficient concordances can be found on these three ideas, even vowel concordances, and that the theme itself can serve in place of the antetheme or protheme. For example, concerning the first, suppose that someone has to preach about Advent and he takes as his theme: *Come, Lord Jesus,* from the Nativity: *the Grace of God has appeared,* from the Epiphany: *A great sign has appeared;* thus he will find the above-mentioned conditions concurrent.

Likewise concerning the saints. He should consider what or which things about the saints or saint about whom he preaches he especially wishes to commend. For example, as I consider St. Andrew, I see much that is especially commendable in him: that he hung on the cross for so long and did not waiver, that in spirit he seemed rather affixed to Christ than corporally to the cross. And thus the saying of his fellow Apostle is seen in his own person: *with Christ I am nailed to the cross* (Gal. 2:19).

Likewise I consider St. Nicholas who was much given over to works of piety and devotion, because of which he was made a bishop. Then one could say about him: his throne is prepared in mercy. And so concerning the rest. All of those fit their feasts well.

The second condition is that the theme create full understanding, that the statement be not uncertain or doubtful, lacking a verb; for example, if the theme on St. Catherine should be: *the virgin daughter of Sion,* such a theme would be judged faulty. This fullness of understanding must be looked at according to the situation, for it should not always be the greatest possible fullness. For example, suppose that the theme about St. Nicholas should be: *and all the Church of the saints shall declare his alms*. This is a full construction. But it is not so full as it would be if the following should be said: *it will declare the alms of the Bishop*, etc. It would be even fuller if the sentence were: *the alms of Nicholas*, etc. But the fullness in the first example is sufficient, and is frequently found to be better.

<h2 style="text-align:center">CHAPTER XVI</h2>

Some, on the other hand, use a good and commendable method in addition. They choose such a theme that immediately excites the audience to devotion, no matter what idiom is used, as in Advent: *Come, Lord Jesus;* or on the feast of St. John before the Latin Gate: *The just one is delivered out of distress;* and so concerning the rest. For this reason also such themes as invoke mercy, and consequently indicate misery, are often used by very many preachers, as *Have mercy on me (Lord)*, and *Jesus, son of David, have mercy on me* and the like.

Others also, for the same reason, choose themes in which there is this word which arouses emotion, as from Advent: *Let us put away the works of darkness;* and from Nativity: *Let us see this word;* from Passiontide: *His blood be upon us;* and on the feast of any martyr: *My life is wasted with grief.*

Let a preacher see to it that his theme is from a text of the Bible and not from any antiphonary. Hence that theme is wrong which some take on the feast of the Trinity: *He saw three and adored one*, because it is not a text from the Bible.

Likewise when Holy Writ contains a relative pronoun, in the theme it should not be changed to its antecedent: for example, if the following theme should be used on some saint: *my foot has followed God's step*, this would be faulty because it is not the letter of the Bible. Literally it reads: *His steps*, etc., and it ought be used in that form.

Indeed it is considered incorrect if one puts in his theme a quotation from another translation than the one commonly used. Hence, if for Passiontide the theme would be chosen which has the translation from Ps. 95, *Sing,* i.e. *Say among the nations, the Lord reigneth from the wood (cross),* it would be incorrect, because literally from the accepted translation it is: *Say among nations, the Lord reigneth,* without anything more. I wonder about this, and do not find sufficient reason why the true translation, indeed, the one which the Church commonly uses, should not be accepted and that that is the literal translation is evident from the verse of the hymn (Passion Sunday hymn Vespers 3 v.): *Fulfilled are the things which (David) sings,* etc. Still, two reasons are assigned for not accepting such themes from an unknown translation: (1) in the first place one who proposes such an unknown theme seems to seek human praise, as if he himself knew unknown things, nor does he preserve the order of learning in which one proceeds from the known to the unknown; (2) if this procedure were allowed, liars, heretics, and ignorant men could make themes as they pleased and devise an unknown translation, of which the exemplar could not easily be found, and there would be a great occasion for error. Therefore, it is better here to follow the common method, that of taking a known theme or one from a known translation. That is why it is said that Christ did not change the theme which His precursor, John, before Him frequently had taken and preached.

## CHAPTER XVII

Sometimes, however, we may omit and pass over some parts of speech which are in the Bible, for instance, conjunctions which join sentences. For example the theme: *Let us put away the works of darkness,* is well taken, although literally it is: *Therefore let us put away,* etc. Likewise, literally, *For now our salvation is nearer,* etc.; and yet in the theme the word *for* can well be omitted and we can say: *Now our salvation,* etc. So also I say about the word *however* as in *now however you are converted.* One can say: *now you are converted.* Similarly a copulative conjunction can be omitted as long as the sentence is complete. For example, if from some saint is taken the theme: *Heal me, O Lord, and I will be healed.* For it is fitting to add the word *and.* And so for the others. Other conjunctions which make the propositions conditional, on which the sen-

tence of the propositions depends, cannot be omitted. Such conjunctions are: *while, since, if, because, or,* and their equivalents,
whether they go before or are placed in the middle.

An interjection also that precedes can be omitted, as long as the
sentence stays complete. Hence in war, to arouse one's side against
the adversary this can be accepted as a theme: *I will comfort myself
over my adversaries;* however, literally it is: *Ah! I will comfort myself over my adversaries.* Therefore the interjection may in this
way be omitted. Sometimes, however, if it is left out the sentence
will remain incomplete. If in a sermon to contemplatives one should
take as his theme: *woe is me because my sojourn has been prolonged,* one cannot leave out the interjection on account of the
meaning of the sentence. The same must be held about interjections even in the middle of a proposition, for example, the word
*also.* The other parts of speech can in no way be skipped nor left
out because the omission would change the sentence. For example
if on Pentecost would be accepted this theme: *the Spirit of wisdom
came.* This would not be valid because the literal sense is: *The Spirit
of wisdom came upon me.* However, if it were taken as: *The Spirit
came upon me,* and without anything more it would not be incorrect, because, although the words *of wisdom* are missing, the sentence is not changed much.

Nor is it allowed to change one tense of a verb to another tense.
Hence the theme which some take on the Ascension: *He ascended
opening the way before them,* is incorrect since the Bible literally
has: *he will ascend opening the way before,* etc.

<h2 style="text-align:center">CHAPTER XVIII</h2>

Sometimes it happens that the text of the Bible is not changed,
yet is perverted; as, if one giving a sermon to contemplatives should
take as his theme: *you will believe if I speak of heavenly things.*
This seems to me to be a perversion of the letter and sense of Scripture; for Christ in the Gospel uttered this interrogatively and in a
negative sense, as if to say: *you will not at all believe.* Therefore
it is a perversion if it draws to the opposite of this meaning.

The same perversion occurs when a thing is attributed to someone with whom there is no comparison, for example if a theme is

taken from Easter: *Triphon arose.* There is no agreement there; Triphon is the worst of all; Christ, the best.

Likewise it is perversion to transfer a noun from the meaning in Scripture; for example if one should take as a theme on Palm Sunday: *I know O Lord, thy judgments are equity,* and should explain it as referring to his equitation on an ass, when the Scripture speaks of his *equity* which is a noun.

In the case of authorities it is likewise faulty if, for example, for St. Edmund the king this theme should be taken: *the sinners have bent their bow,* and then in the course of the sermon one should adduce an authority of another meaning for *bent* as (bend) *hearken to my voice,* and: *O God,* (bend) *come to my assistance.*

Similarly there is perversion when an incomplete part of a preceding clause is taken together with the beginning of the following clause, if for example in a sermon to penitents would be taken the theme: *Be sorry/offer up the sacrifice of justice* (Ps. 4 end v. 5 & begin v. 6).

A theme, then, is perverted by shortening, by too great a disagreement, and by too violent a transfer from its proper meaning.

Some shortening, however, is allowable, as is some disagreement, some transfer, as long as it is not excessive. On the first Sunday of Lent this theme may well be taken: *May you receive the grace of God;* and yet the authority is shortened and what is there negatively is taken affirmatively. For in that locus is said: *Do not receive the Grace of God in vain,* and it is evidently negative. But it must be said that the Apostle urges two things here, that they receive grace, and that they do not receive in vain. For they would receive it in vain if they did not retain it, because it would not minister to them. Therefore, because either is in the intention of the Apostle, either member of the complete construction can be accepted for a theme.

Likewise on Easter Sunday may be accepted for a theme: *The man arose and opened the gate;* or on the Ascension what literally is said in Judges (19–20) about the Levite who divided his wife into twelve parts, between whom and Christ there is a very great disparity; but nevertheless tolerable and not too excessive. And thus also about Nicholas is taken: *the boy grew,* which literally is said about Samson.

Likewise in as far as a transfer can be made from the literal signification to the moral the theme can be taken about St. Paul or Peter, martyr: *He struck the rock and waters flowed forth.* Literally *rock* here means that stone which Moses struck with his rod, and *waters* means those natural waters and that striking was the action of Moses, who was a good man. And conversely, here the striking was that of an evil man. But certainly *rock* can morally mean a heart solid in faith, *water*, doctrine, and *striking* permissively can be God's; and thus it is well accepted.

## CHAPTER XIX

Further, in this method of preaching only three statements, or the equivalent of three, are used in the theme—either from respect to the Trinity, or because a threefold cord is not easily broken, or because this method is mostly followed by Bernard, or, as I think more likely, because it is more convenient for the set time of the sermon. A preacher can follow up just so many members without tiring his hearers; and if he should mention fewer, he would occupy too little time.

The reason why a theme may be the equivalent of three statements is that it can happen that some words which cannot be divided and should not be may fall into a theme. Of such kind are prepositions and conjunctions, and also a general word which is included in every other word. Hence if the theme were: *the just is delivered out of distress,* no division would fall upon *out of* nor upon *is.*

Hence, a division ought not to be made on the word *is* when it is placed thus. Yet sometimes it can. Sometimes it does not stand generally but gives its action to one particular only, as: *who is he who sent me,* and again: *you are the selfsame.* And then because it stands attributively, division can be made of it, so that one may say that identity, stability, uniformity, or the like is noted in it.

No matter how many statements there may be, as long as I can divide them into three, I have a sufficient proposition. Posit that the theme on the Annunciation, on the vigil of Nativity, or on the day, and on the first Sunday within the octave of the Nativity, and on the day of Circumcision: *God sent His Son made of a woman,*

*made under the law, that He might redeem them who were under
the law.* Here are seventeen words; [6] yet the whole can be divided
into three so that it may be said that in these words three things are
touched upon: (1) There is noted in the doctor a generously-
expended sublimity because it says *God sent His Son.* (2) There is
shown how virtuously-shown humility heals because it says *made
of a woman, made under the law.* (3) There is shown how fruit-
fully-extended utility is derived, because it says *that he might redeem them who were under the law.*

But when the theme is thus divided, one must see that the dividing parts correspond with the parts of that which is divided. For
example, here is said that in the doctor is noted a sublimity, etc.
when is said *God sent* etc. Notice the correspondence, because *God:*
sublimity; because *He sent:* expended; because *His Son:* generously.
And thus about the rest. There is no lack of artistry if these three
things can be confirmed by one authority in which verbally there
are the three: *God, sent,* and *Son* and that in the sentence such great
nobility is communicated to us. But because such authorities are
difficult to find, themes of so many words are not commonly
accepted.

Sometimes it happens that there are only two words in the theme
which can be turned into three: for example let the division be into
three concerning St. Nicholas: *the boy grew,* that it may be said:
"In these words St. Nicholas is commended for his state of purity,
because it says *boy,* for his advance in dignity because it says *grew,*
and in both for his reward of happiness, because it says *the boy
grew.*" And then it is right that this third member should have
authority in which each is used vocally with the sentence of division. It is therefore clear what it is to take three statements for the
theme or statements convertible into three because this can happen
whether there are more or less than three.

## Chapter XX

Those who follow this opinion say that if a theme is taken to be
divided into four parts, the subdivision ought also to be divided into

6. That is, it has 17 words in the Latin: *Misit Deus filium suum factum ex muliere,
factum sub lege, ut eos qui sub lege erant redimeret.*

four, and if the theme is to be divided into five, then the subdivision ought also be divided into five parts, and it should so correspond and follow that the end should agree with the beginning and that there should be at least some evidence of art. With this I also agree, save that he who takes too long a theme and divides it into too many parts seems to show that he is rather incompetent. Yet one may immediately divide his theme into twelve parts or less and follow up with something about each, so that he does not make many divisions. For example, suppose the following theme on the Apostles: *there are twelve hours of the day*. Then immediately one would continue thus: The first hour of the day we may well call St. Peter, and so on with the rest. This method St. Bernard uses frequently. But this method is foreign to the artistic one of which there now is talk.

I have also heard a capable man use the following theme as a whole in a sermon to a synod: *Ask the lord of the harvest to send laborers into his vineyard. Go.* This fellow was a grand master in theology and a great prelate who was expert in problems as well as sermons, yet his theme was generally condemned by all intelligent men especially for the addition of the word *Go*. On this word alone there could be quite an artistic and useful sermon. And according to the Philosopher, it is inconvenient to do with more what equally and conveniently can be done with fewer words.

## Chapter XXI

It is incidental to my plan to consider here whether there can be a sermon on one statement. It seems to me that there can be a sermon on one explicit statement, but which implies another statement or more, namely by discussing a word used in exhortation, saying: *understand ye, preach* or *preach ye, go ye, walk ye,* and the like. But this method is almost totally unknown. And therefore it pleases me, insofar as I am able, at this place to insert an example of such a sermon.

Let those, however, who intend to imitate this method know that it is incorrect to take only one word of which a full understanding is not aroused. For example, if one were to take as his theme on the Purification: *Simeon;* that would be wrong, no matter how interesting the continuation would be.

But that this unknown incidence be made known, let the theme be taken on Peter the martyr of the order of Preachers which is written in the epistle of that feast: *understand ye* (Tim. 2). Just as St. Gregory in his homily *If anyone love* [7] uses as an antetheme: *no one rightly attributes to a man teaching that he understands from the mouth of the teacher, for unless there is one who teaches interiorly, the tongue labors in vain exteriorly,* etc. From this authority it is evident that in fruitful preaching there are three things necessarily required: the supreme teacher, God, teaching the intellect, the listener obeying the words of the teacher, and the teaching itself, useful and advantageous. And these three the Gospel of Luke 24:45 equally embraces. *He opened,* he says *their understanding that they might understand the scriptures. He opened their understanding,* behold the master teaching, He *who opens and no one closes, who closes and no one opens* (in the Apoc.). For sacred Scripture is closed by the mysteries of secrets, but opened through the ministries of preachers, because *the declaration of the word of God illumines and gives understanding to the little ones.* Secondly, there is required the obeying listener, otherwise there is no understanding. Therefore it says: *that they might understand.* Hence in Eccles. 5:13: *Be meek to hear the word that thou mayest understand.* Thirdly, it is required that the teaching itself be useful and advantageous. And this is the last word: *Scriptures,* it says not *trifles,* of which there is written in Timothy: *All scripture inspired of God is profitable for teaching;* Gloss: first, the ignorant; secondly, to persuade the negligent; thirdly, to reprove those insisting on vain things.

But, as I have said, I doubt whether I can have this of myself; rather it is from the Lord of whom is written, Wis. of Sol. 3:9, *They that trust in the Lord will understand the truth.* Therefore let us ask in the accustomed manner *that he open for us the door of his word,* Col. 4:3, as long as *I sing thus and understand,* Ps. 100:1, for his and his saint's honor, that, as the Scripture says, *rivers of living water,* John 7:38, i.e. graces flow from us indeed, into us. Since this is so, anyone may say to him, at least mentally, *Give me understanding that I may know your testimonies.* Ps. 118:125.

Already there is evident in this antetheme sufficient subtlety because first, it is introduced with an original authority with which

7. Migne *P.L.* 76:1222.

the authority of Scripture harmonizes; secondly, the authority of Scripture is divided according to the original and each part is so confirmed that it voices the statement about which there is preaching; thirdly, the third authority includes at the same time itself and the two preceding authorities; fourthly, for asking grace, the parts of the first authority are laid down in order, e.g. against *He opened their understanding* there is placed *may he open for us the door of His word*. And so for the rest.

Later on, further development of this will be shown; now, there is only talk about the antetheme.

Although, in Chapter XV, I said that for the good invention of a theme three statements or statements convertible to three are necessary, and afterwards, in Chapter XIX, that a theme may contain only two statements, and here, only one explicitly is needed, I have not contradicted myself, for the first represents the opinion of those who follow it as a principal method. Considering this fact it happens that another method may be good enough. It is also evident how two statements can be converted into three. I say that they are converted into three when there can be a continuation in the same manner as if there were three statements, and this can happen even if there are twelve statements, or only two, as was shown, or only one, as will be shown later.

## Chapter XXII

It is well stated in Chapter XV that in the beginning care must be taken to provide verbal concordance for the statements of the theme, because there are enough such in every language for presenting the proposition and avoiding contradictions. Otherwise the preacher will be rightly considered ignorant, for the Scriptures are definitely extensive enough in themselves so that what is necessary may be quickly and promptly found, once the beginning of a sermon has been well chosen. His ignorance, therefore, is greater because he binds and limits himself where it is not necessary to do so.

Next is found where the agreement of words is, rather than whether it is only real and not verbal. Although the learned Gregory and others do not follow this procedure closely, nevertheless they always observe it in principle. I say "in principle" for this

reason: concordances can be well expressed and divided accidentally, just as long as enough is said about the essential division. For
example, if the theme established is: *walk ye*, one can say that a
road is threefold: straight, level, clear. Concerning the straight,
which is the way of commands, it is written: *make straight the paths
of our God*. Certainly this is the way, *walk ye* on it to *on the right*,
etc., and so also concerning the other members. It is evident that
what is said about the way is not a verbal concordance for *walk ye*,
but nevertheless the division is concluded through one authority in
which *walk ye* is included and this suffices.

But, say that one must preach in English and does not use as his
theme: *walk ye*. Could he without fault choose as the main authority one in which there would not be *walk ye* but its convertible
*to go?* For example if one would say: one must walk first, freely on
the way of God because of definite and just reward; hence the Lord
also says *Go ye also into my vineyard and I will give you what is
just?* It seems to me yes. Nor is there any difference in English
between one or the other, and I see nothing to prevent this unless
there be some learned men who note the authorities in their sermons
because in Scripture the difference between *to walk* and *to go* is
immediately evident but the unlearned do not know how to discern it.

To avoid all difficulty, and to make a sermon serve all languages
and all to whom one preaches, it is better to use verbal agreements
a little, in the way described. For example, in the theme: *walk ye*,
it is permitted to take an authority in which is contained any deriva-
tive of this word. If seven verbal agreements on any statement can
be found for the purpose, that is sufficient, and at least so many are
required. But it is difficult to find so many that apply to novelty
which one strives to attain unless the agreements are very many
indeed.

## Chapter XXIII

In the aforementioned Chapter XV, it is well stated that in select-
ing a theme, the antetheme and theme should be the same. In former times some preachers used to select one theme for themselves,
and then took an authority dealing with some word of the theme

in place of an antetheme; that is observable in the sermons of
Guido [8] and many others. Take, for example, the theme: *see how
you walk*. Immediately they would add one authority which contained the words *to see* or *to walk*, saying *what I saw I will tell you*,
or: *He walked with me in peace and truth and turned many from
iniquity*. And then they would follow the second authority for an
antetheme, and the first for the theme. I see no need for this unless
the second authority is more properly and immediately suited to
the preacher of God's word, or to the hearer, or to the word itself,
or to all three at the same time, or to two of the three.

But here it must be carefully noted that it is not right to divide
the antetheme so thinly that the three members of the division in
the authority which is used instead of the antetheme are always
explained. It is sufficient to mention the three members on the basis
of which allusion is made to the parts of the authority, which is
taken as an antetheme. For example, if the theme were: *The just
man is delivered from distress*, one way the antetheme could be is:

As St. Gregory says, Christ taught truth and goodness yet
he suffered evil; but *a helper in due time in tribulation* com-
forted him. Thus it is also with those who imitate him, the
preachers of God's word. Hence in the preceding words a
threefold condition of a preacher is noted namely, gravity of
teaching, ferocity of pressure, and proximity of redress. 1. The
gravity of teaching, so that about him can be said, Prov. 10:21,
*The lips of the just teach many. The just man shall correct me*,
says the Psalmist (140:5), *and shall reprove me. But let not
the oil of the sinner fatten my head*, i.e. the fawning of a flatterer will not fatten my head, or, he will not overreach my
reason, etc. 2. There follows with many the ferocity of pressure. Hence, in Job, according to the exposition of St. Gregory, a good preacher is called a lamp, despised in the thoughts
of the rich; a lamp, because of true and lucid teaching; despised, because of the frequently brought-on assault. But, as is
written for this one and the former: Wisdom 5:1, *the just
shall stand with great constancy against those that have*

8. The identity of Guido is not known. (Could it be Guido Arezzo, whose scale
is used on page 203?)

*afflicted them.* The reason is that the use and action of these evils of which I now speak is against the Lord who is able to overcome His adversaries and is kind in helping His own. Therefore, no matter how much the pressure of persecution rages there always abounds the redress of consolations which is number three. To this the Psalmist (33:18) attests when he says: *The just cried, and the Lord heard them: and delivered them out of all their troubles.* Therefore, let the just cry through sincere teaching, which is first; and from all tribulations of those raging with pressure, which is second, God will deliver them through his assisting grace, which is third. Let us cry, therefore, in the accustomed manner for gaining that grace, and without a doubt the Lord will hear us, who, as the Psalmist attests (33:18), heard those praying, and will deliver them from all tribulations.

It is now evident that this antetheme is artistic enough, and yet there is only an allusion from the members of the division to the statements of the theme. Proof. It is certain that in the capacity of this word *just* there is not included the gravity of doctrine, because one can be quite just without teaching anything; and, on the contrary, one can teach right things and yet not be just. And yet the authority which corresponds to this first member includes teaching and explains verbally that statement to which there is an allusion, and this suffices. In the second member the chosen authority does not express that preachers hear distress, nor does it imply this, but merley states it. It also places one authority which alludes to the second statement, as is evident, and this is less than in the first. Yet this suffices. Similarly the third authority does not touch upon preachers more than others, but still with a unique dexterity and subtlety is applied to them because of the connection with the preceding authorities.

## Chapter XXIV

Now that we have treated in general the first ornament of preaching, to wit, the Invention of the Theme, the second ornament follows, namely the Winning-over of the Audience. The preacher, as far as he can do so according to God, ought to attract the mind of the listeners in such a way as to render them willing to hear and retain. This can be done in many ways. One way is to place at the beginning something subtle and interesting, as some authentic marvel which can be fittingly drawn in for the purpose of the theme. For instance, suppose that the theme is concerned with the Ascension or the Assumption: *a spring rose from the earth*. One could adduce that marvel which Gerald narrates in his book, *De mirabilibus Hiberniae* [9] about the spring in Scicilia: if anyone approaches it dressed in red clothing, immediately water gushes from the place of the spring though none appeared there before, while it remains unmoved in the presence of all other colors. That spring is Christ, about Whom it is written in Eccles. 1: *the word of God is the fountain of wisdom*, to Whom he 'approaches dressed in red' who, devoutly suffering with Him and as it were incarnadined with the blood of His Passion, intently and inwardly revolves the thought (of Him), and considers the saying of Isaiah: *why is Thy apparel red?* Such a one approaching finds living water, viz. graces, because His blood was of such virtue that, when it was shed, the earth quaked and the rocks were torn asunder. Much more ought our hearts to quake and be torn by the cry of God's word, unless they be drier than the earth and harder than rocks.

Likewise if an unknown cause of some saying is used, it is reducible to the same category, for example if a cause is given to explain why the eye does not have a determined color; because if it did have a definite color, it would perceive only that color and there would have to be as many senses as there are colors; and this may be applied to sinners, especially the avaricious and clever ones who do not perceive the word of God or its effect because they are totally determined by its opposite.

Another way is to frighten them by some terrifying tale or example, in the way that Jacques de Vitry talks about some one who never willingly wanted to hear the word of God; finally when he died and was brought to the church, and the priest in the presence of the parish began the eulogy which is wont to be spoken over the body of the dead, the image of Christ standing between the choir and the church tore away and pulled His hands from the nails

9. Giraldus Cambrensis, *Topographica hibernica* dist. II, cap, 8. In *Opera* V. p. 90.

piercing them and from the wood to which they were fixed, and plugged His ears, as if to intimate that He did not wish to hear the prayer for him who once spurned to listen to Him in His preachers.[10]

Likewise, pertinent to the same topic are the different stories which teach how Christ appeared to some hardened sinners, extending His palm full of blood taken from His side, saying: This blood which you so obdurately contemn will bear witness against you on the day of judgment. After they lived awhile it was frequently disclosed that the blood could not be washed away and they were buried with it. Some repented and confessed and then easily enough, as it were, it disappeared.

This second example I myself have come upon, in connection with an infamous woman hardened to all sermons. Christ appeared to her and took the woman's hand, putting it into the wound in His side, saying, as she herself had said: the blood which you reject will adhere to you for evil, unless you correct yourself. It is well known that she confessed; still it adhered to her and could not be washed away till finally in some way she confessed a great hidden sin and immediately after that it disappeared. Such terrifying stories have great value in the beginning of a sermon.

The third way is to show by an example or story that the devil always tries to hinder the word of God and the hearing of it.

The fourth way is to show that to hear the word of God is a great sign of predestination. To this are reduced those ways which show that other benefits, earthly or heavenly, such as the fertility of the earth, the disposition to penitence, and the like, accrue to those who listen willingly.

The fifth way is to show that the preacher intends only to convert them, and not immediately after that to start begging. He should draw them to the love of God, to the fear of evil, to the honor of God, lest, if it is a principal feast, it may lack due honor. Then he should put the hearers into the right disposition for the Indulgence, which is granted to those who listen to the word of

10. Jacques de Vitry was the compiler of a popular collection of such *exempla*. See *The Exempla or Illustrative Stories from the Sermones Vulgares of Jacques de Vitry*. Ed. Thomas F. Crane. Publications of the Folk-Lore Society, vol. 26. London, 1890.

God, and preach like things by which he rightly deems to win over the hearers according to their condition.

Zeal will teach him who does not have an evil intention about these and other methods. If someone should make it his goal to attract hearers in order that glory may follow for himself, he rather repels than attracts. Therefore some who are about to speak with mouth and heart say in the beginning—although beneath their breath lest it be ascribed to hypocrisy—*Not to us, O Lord, not to us,* etc.


## CHAPTER XXV


In the beginning it is also customary to offer a prayer, and that is well, because as Plato says in the *Timaeus:* divine help should be implored in the smallest things. Since even the smallest things cannot occur without its influence, how much more should it be implored in the greatest? Hence Boethius, *De Consolatione: I feel that God must be called upon, without whom no beginning is duly established.*[11]

But some were wont to do this immediately, even before the theme, for example St. Francis, as we read in his life. In the beginning of his sermon he always wished peace to his hearers, saying: *peace to you,* imitating in this his master, Christ, who appeared frequently to His disciples, almost always in the beginning wishing them peace, and thus taught his disciples who were about to preach. Luke 9 (Matt. 10): *Into whatsoever house you enter, first say: peace be to this house,* etc. *If the son of peace be there,* etc. In like manner the Lord commanded the sons of Israel that when they came to cities to destroy them, they should first offer them peace. Therefore, preachers who undertake to destroy the cities and dwellings of sinners ought to do thus. Likewise, St. Augustine, *De Doctrina Christiana,*[12] urges that a preacher be first a man of prayer before a talker, for himself and for them from whom he receives, i.e. learns.

11. Boethius, *Cons.* 3.
12. Augustine, *De doctrina christiana* IV. 15.32. For an excellent modern translation of this important treatise on rhetoric in preaching, see *Saint Augustine On Christian Doctrine.* Trans. D. W. Robertson. Library of Liberal Arts No. 80. New York, 1958.

But the three things here touched upon are not commonly observed, namely (1) that peace be wished or offered, if only mentally, before the theme is set up; (2) that even immediately after the theme has been proposed it is not touched upon, but reference is had to grace, thus: *the grace of God be with us*, or some such thing; (3) that we are not accustomed in the beginning to pray for those from whom we have learned, but only for ourselves who preach and for our hearers.

To me it seems better to propose the theme, and immediately to make a prayer about it, and to invoke both peace and grace as Paul did in his Epistles: *Grace*, he said, *and peace to you, etc.* For example, suppose the theme to be: *a spring arose from the earth*; immediately there should be added: may His peace and grace be with us, from Whose side and heart flowed the fount of grace for making peace between God and mankind and between man and man. Then in the words *with us* can be included at least mentally both those from whom the preacher has learned and those whom he teaches, and even himself. Thus he fulfills all the points mentioned above.

I have not seen it mentioned in any authentic author that such a prayer ought to be said before the theme, yet I have frequently seen it done. It is proper, whether before or immediately after the theme, because both theme and prayer ought to be said in the beginning. The authorities wish no more than that in the beginning they invoke divine help, yet many do not observe the rule at all in Latin sermons. This I consider incorrect. And yet they say that it is enough in the beginning to place the prayer before the execution of the theme. Though they put the prayer before the execution of the theme, they always put it at the end of the antetheme. Still, I consider it safe either way.

It should also be noted here that the prayer which is at the end of the antetheme ought always to depend on what has preceded, so that it contains something which pertains to the prayer, and at the same time contains a word of the theme, even vocally, and especially that word on which depends the persuasion to prayer. For example, if the theme is: *make straight (dirigite) the way of the Lord*, it could, in the process of the antetheme, form a prayer on the word *make straight (dirigite)*, thus: Let us direct (*dirigamus*) our prayers to God because we are thus instructed, Eccles. 37,°

*above all these things pray to the most High that He may direct thy way in truth.* And the cause is designated, Jeremiah 10:23, as *the way of a man is not his, neither is it in a man to walk, and to direct his steps.* This is the method of the Oxonians.

The method of the Parisians is different: Through experience you observe that when a red rose is sprayed with sulphur fumes it immediately loses its color and beauty and pales or blanches. And again if it is sprayed with incense smoke, it regains its former beauty. Sulphur smoke is the smell of sin, especially luxury. Therefore the Lord rains sulphur upon such, who immediately lose their beauty of soul. *Fire,* says the Prophet, *has devoured the beauty of Jacob.* But the smoke of incense, i.e. of devout prayer, restores their beauty; for you know that the smoke of incense rises not at the sides but straight up, and spreads. If it went out at the side, it would not go upwards so quickly. So it is with prayer. Hence the Psalmist: *let my prayer be directed as incense in Thy sight.* Such uncommon and interesting things are very acceptable and moving to some persons (i.e. in the audience).

## CHAPTER XXVI

Now must be eliminated the error of those who say that themes must be selected from the following sources: the four Gospels, the Psalms, the Epistles of St. Paul, and the Books of Solomon. Because all of Scripture depends on the Holy Ghost as the author, Who can neither lie nor err, Who has no greater authority in one Book than in another, but in fact inserts statements of great motivation in every book, as long as there is a person to understand. I, therefore, safely say that it does not matter radically from what authentic book of Scripture the theme is taken, provided it meets with the other conditions.

There are many other books which are called bibles, but they are not thus made genuine, because it is not quite evident that their authors were inspired. In fact, sometimes there is doubt about their authors and sometimes about many things said in such books. From whom they are, which they are, and what these books are can be seen in the *Prologue* of Jerome, and others.

It must be understood that all the books commonly found in the Bible are authentic except the 3rd and 4th of Esdras, because the

1st of Esdras is authentic, and likewise the 2nd which is called by some Nehemias, although incorrectly, for no book should be titled thus.

Likewise in some bibles there is a Psalm of David which they say he composed when he was snatched from the wild beasts and on the acceptance of his kingdom, and one book which is titled *Of the Pastor,* and one Epistle of Paul to the Laodiceans; none of these is authentic.

Likewise the authors of Ecclesiasticus and the book which canonically is called Jude are uncertain, although now they are commonly accepted. Likewise some have doubts about the Prayer of Manasses, and the Prayer of Jeremias. Judith and Tobias are thought by some to be apocryphal books. So too, the book of Wisdom and the two books of Maccabees are doubtful to some because it is clearly evident that they breathe more Greek or Latin than Hebrew eloquence. Yet Jerome in his defensive *Prologue* says that he found the first book of Maccabees in Hebrew.

Likewise Ecclesiasticus, also Sidrach, the son of Jesu, the Wisdom of Philo, and the Canonica of Jude the Apostle, who is said to have been called Thaddeus. Daniel from the 13th chapter inclusive to the end is considered totally apocryphal.

There is no doubt about the whole of the rest, nor is there any confusion. In fact, a theme is taken from it freely in these days, and what is more, on account of their antiquity all the above-mentioned books are accepted except for the 3rd and 4th books of Esdras, that unknown psalm of David, the book of the Pastor, and the letter to the Laodiceans.

It is safe to take a theme from the certain and canonical Scriptures, especially when one must preach on solemn occasions or before persons of excellence.

It will be clear to one perusing the *Moralia* of Gregory, that when he takes something written in Ecclesiasticus he does not state that it is Ecclesiasticus but that it is some wise man who says so.

## Chapter XXVII

For the sake of what I have already said, I must exemplify in particular how these things can be done better and more easily. Some are wont to take their theme from only the Gospel or Epistle of the feast on which they preach. It is a praiseworthy thing if it so happens; if otherwise, it is not wrong if done in the way that we have mentioned.

Therefore, following what has been said, very little may be specified about very many things on how themes can be chosen according to fitness with a day. At any time, when the season is considered, the themes can be: *Prepare your hearts unto the Lord,* I Kings, 7. . . .

[*Here, and in the following three chapters. Basevorn lists a number of sample themes taken from Scripture. Omissions are noted by ellipsis signs (. . . .).*]

### Chapter XXVIII

We must now see what themes in particular can be adduced for the more famous saints. On the feast of St. Andrew: *And running before, he climbed up into a tree,* etc. (Luke 19.)

### Chapter XXIX

It is also always useful to have a few prepared sermons which can provide for every saint and for the Dedication (of a church), because it frequently happens that the church or place where the preacher happens to be preaching solemnizes a saint or dedication of which he has not even a thought. Therefore, the theme for any saint and even the dedication can be: *Wisdom built for herself a house, truly the Lord is in that place,* etc. The same can be said about a male or female saint, or saints.

. . . Notice also that feasts on which one must preach, other than the specified ones, frequently concur. Sometimes there coincides on a Sunday a feast which is not celebrated by the Church on that day, but it is considered proper by the people and is solemnly held; for example, when the feast of St. Andrew falls on the first Sunday of Advent, or when the feast of St. Nicholas falls on the second or third, etc. On such a concurrence it is a mark of diligence to take the theme from the Sunday and briefly to touch upon something from the Sunday, and to treat more diffusely the theme from such a saint whose feast is commonly considered more solemn. For example: if the theme should be from the first Sunday of Advent and the feast of St. Andrew: *Blessed is he who comes in the name of the Lord*, it could easily, as is evident, fit St. Andrew. Again . . .

. . . and so concerning the rest. Notice here, however, that in Easter or Pentecost week, one must speak of and touch upon the saint but briefly, and likewise during the octave of Corpus Christi; speak diffusely, however, about the feasts themselves.

Sometimes different vigils fall on a Sunday. Then, as it seems to me, it is more useful and more elegant to take the theme from the Sunday and briefly to touch upon some things which prepare the mind for the feast to come, and to handle the Sunday material more diffusely. To others it seems that the theme should be taken from that which is the Sunday's principal Mass, whether it be the vigil or the Sunday. This is probable, and doubtless true, when the greater part of those to whom one preaches is learned. Therefore certain themes must be specified for such concurrences . . .

Sometimes it happens that there is a certain principal feast, as a Sunday or a saint's day, and only a commemoration or three second-nocturne lessons of another saint or saints, just as when a feast of three lessons falls on a Sunday or the feast of Sts. Cornelius and Cyprian on the Exaltation of the Holy Cross. Then the theme and handling will be on the principal feast; on the one which is considered superficially, as it were, some narration or brief example according to a proposition from the principal feast should be adduced.

## Chapter XXX

It is now appropriate to specify what themes can be taken for incidental material, as on visitations, at elections, in synods, in processions, (at meetings), in disaster, on solemnities, and at times similar to these . . . to different states of life, as to the Pope and Cardinals, . . . at a Council. . . . to Carthusians and solitaries, to the white monks or canons, . . . to the black monks or canons . . . to the gray monks, . . . to the Brother Preachers . . . to the Friars Minor . . . to the hermits of St. Augustine and the Carmelites . . . to any Religious . . . to the sick, sorrowing, and suffering . . . to merchants . . .

Indeed I do not consider him a totally perfect preacher who does not know how to apply to these incidental sermons a theme appropriate for any Sunday or feast. Therefore it is better to take a theme from the feast of a saint if it be on the day on which he is to preach, and then to apply it to the incidental material. For example if the theme be of a saint: *behold the true Israelite in whom there is no guile*, one can easily, indeed very easily, pass over to the frauds of merchants; or if the theme be of the season: *no guile was found on his lips*. And so it can be said about the rest.

I also consider it expedient that whenever a sermon is to be given with deliberation about some material, that the four chapters immediately preceding be perused in order that a theme better adapted to the imagination and talent of the one about to preach may be found.

## Chapter XXXI

And now, according to the order set out in Chapter XIV, having considered somewhat the three ornaments of the antetheme, we shall consider the ornaments of the theme, of which the first is Introduction, and which in the whole is the fourth ornament.

Concerning this ornament it must be known that after the prayer the same theme must be resumed and the book and chapter must be quoted. This ought to be done in the beginning in the antetheme, and, following the modern method, nothing must be quoted regarding the chapters.

It is allowable to quote the books to everybody in every authority, so that the quotation is said to be written in the first book of Kings or the second, or in the first canonical Epistle of Peter, and so for the rest.

In the same manner, concerning original quotations anyone is allowed to quote the books, even if they are expository of another book. One can quote this: Just as Gregory says in his first, or second book, *Moralium*, on Job: *There was where he*, etc.

It is allowable for the teachers and professors of Sacred Theology, indeed it behooves them, to quote everything accurately, because in this aspect others defer to them on account of their testimony of their teaching excellence, on account of humility in those who so defer to them, and on account of dignity, rank and honor.

Another thing must be kept in mind, namely that in resuming the theme after the prayer, it is considered faulty to quote thus: "as before," although the quotation was previously spoken in the antetheme; but it must be stated explicitly as it was expressed in the antetheme, on account of some who by accident, as frequently happens, were not present for the antetheme. And even if they were, it is safer to quote explicitly. It suffices, however, just as it befits anyone writing sermons on Scripture itself, to quote the chapters. But he is too simple who alludes to all Scripture, saying for everything: *as it is written.*

In the third place comes the Introduction, which can be formed in three ways: by authority, by argument, or by both at the same time. Through authority, as was mentioned in Chapter XXI, is a method which is more commonly used in the antetheme than afterward in the development. No other Introduction must be made in the antetheme for fear of prolixity. Such an Introduction is commonly very short, indeed it is not wrong if no Introduction is placed in the antetheme but the statement is immediately made: "three things are necessary for a preacher as a learned man." Therefore Introduction is not postulated as an ornament of the antetheme, because the antetheme can be wtihout it; and yet one is artistic if one has an Introduction and that a short one.

The authority for an Introduction can come from something original, from a philosopher, a poet, or someone with authority, as long as it is not from the Bible or from another book, which, though apocryphal, is contained in the Bible and of which kind I have made mention in Chapter XXVI.

The second method of Introduction is through argument, and it is appropriate to form the Introduction in as many ways as there are ways for arguments. These are by induction, by example, by syllogism, by enthymeme.

By induction, as follows: let the theme be: *to them that love God all things work together unto good.* Whatever exists in the world is either favorable or unfavorable. But if one loves God, the favorable things cause in him fear of the present life, the unfavorable, desire for the celestial life or love. Therefore, *all things work together* for those loving God.

By example, in a threefold manner: through examples in nature, in art, in history. By examples in nature, as follows: you see that a father naturally provides for his son as much as he can, that he may have everything that can accrue to his use or advantage. Hence, if desire and ability were equal in him he would make all things useful for himself. But God is our father who can do all He desires. A loving son is a good son. It follows then that *to them that love God all things work together*, etc. A bare example, not extended nor applied, is not valid in this case; as if one should say: Just as a good father provides everything as best he can for the advantage of his son, so God provides for those who love him, and we can well say that *to them that love God all things*, etc. This method, as I have noted, is not valid in this case.

By example in art, as follows: In art you see that a doctor, approaching a sick man to heal him, first of all establishes as far as possible in the invalid a firm confidence that he can be healed and can be healed by him. Thus through this confidence, when his attitude towards the doctor has been changed for the better, the doctor cures him easily, for everything the patient takes aids him on account of that attitude. Christ is the doctor; we, the sick. If, therefore, we have the proper confidence in Him and proper attitude towards Him, immediately all things will avail us for the healing of sin which is spiritual infirmity. And this is what the Apostle says: *to them that love God*, etc.

By a historical example, as follows: Valerius tells in Book 4 of his *De Gestis Memorabilibus* [13] a story about two friends, Damon and Phintias, one of whom, when Dionysius the tyrant wished to kill him, asked time to return home and set his affairs in order. He could not obtain the request unless the other gave himself as surety for his return. This he did not hesitate to do. When the appointed day approached and his friend as yet had not returned, all condemned him for his foolish surety, but he answered that he had no fear about his friend's constancy. At the very hour fixed by the tyrant, the other returned. The tyrant, admiring their constancy and friendship, remitted the punishment, and asked that they receive him as the third party of the group. Thus the love of friendship obtained a remission of death, mitigated tyranny, gave life, equalized them with a king, brought to light famous men, so that all things cooperate for those who love each other. Therefore much more do *all things work together for them who love God*.

13. Valerius Maximus. *De Gestis Memorabilibus*, ch. 7.

An Introduction can be formed by a third method of argument, syllogism, thus: All things that befall right reason, according to its judgment, and the appetite conforming to reason cooperate for their own good. But all things befall those loving God according to the judgment of right reason and the appetite conforming to it. Therefore, *to them that love God*, etc.

In this manner of Introduction, the major premise having been posited, it ought to be proved immediately if it is not self-evident. Then the minor premise must be given with its proof. If the proofs be too extended, after the proof of the minor, the major and minor must be restated and the theme immediately concluded by stating: it has already been proved that all things that befall reason, etc.; second, it has been proved that all things befall those loving God, etc. Therefore, it follows what has been asserted for the theme, that *to them that love God*, etc.

It must also be recognized here that in just as many ways as a good syllogism can occur—one that does not err in matter by using some false statement, nor in form by proceeding according to some fallacy—in the same number of ways we can form an Introduction of this kind. And so, he who uses this method of Introduction must take great care in which way or according to which form he argues lest he err in form, and clearly to prove, if necessary, his premises lest he err in matter.

The fourth method of Introduction by argument is by enthymeme; for example, if one were to say: to them that hate God all things work together for evil. Therefore, *to them that love God all things work together for good*. Granted that the antecedent is evident of itself, and the consequence likewise, this is a good way of forming an Introduction. Lacking evidence, first the consequence, and secondly the antecedent must be proven immediately after if there be whatsoever any doubt about them. Then it must be restated as follows: It has been proved that if to them that hate God, etc., that to them that love God, etc.

Here it must also be realized that just as there are many ways of making an enthymeme a "compelling" enthymeme, so there are the same number of ways of varying this type of Introduction. It is even allowable in this type to use commonplaces which have a greater probability. The "compelling" enthymeme is one that is reduced to an impeccable syllogism through a single necessary middle term. Therefore, he who desires to know the various methods necessary to form a syllogism and "compelling" enthymeme can find them in the book *The Prior Analytics*, and the probable methods in Boethius' book *The Topics*, which cannot be enumerated here on account of their number.

It must also be seen that the method of the Oxonians, which I have mentioned and which is used throughout England, makes use of the seven ways of forming an Introduction already mentioned.

The eighth method, and a better one, which is that of the Parisians, is that no matter what kind of argument they use for the Introduction, all parts are confirmed with the authority of Holy Writ. For example, it was stated above in the inductive method of forming an Introduction that whatever is in the world is either favorable or unfavorable. The Parisians would immediately add some figure with great artistic value in the case, or at least the testimony of Scripture, which is not considered of great value by them. Hence they would say: Whatever is in the world is favorable or unfavorable. According to this figure God divided the whole of time into day and night, into the day of favor and the night of disfavor, or something similar. If the application be some saint's it would be more elegant to say: as such and such a saint explains in such and such a place. Thus also are the other parts confirmed.

It should, moreover, be known that anyone may use all these methods of forming an Introduction in themes that are comprised of two statements or more. But when a theme is made up only of one explicit statement, it is not fitting to use all these methods indiscriminately.

## CHAPTER XXXII

Following the schedule of promise in Chapter XXI, I think a more elegant mode of forming an Introduction of such a theme occurs if the theme is introduced at first by an authority, so that from the authority three members which correspond to the feast and the theme can be immediately drawn. For example, suppose the theme is as in Chapter XXI: *understand*. It can be introduced as follows: as Plato says in the *Timaeus*, God is very good; and envy is far distant from the very good. Therefore as a consequence He wants to make all things like Himself, insofar as the nature of anything is capable of beatitude, so that just as He Himself is good, so all other things will be good. And just as He Himself is intelligent, so all other things will be intelligent in the manner in which it is fitting for them to be. Hence there is something which understands all things in essence, and this is God alone. There is something else which understands all things in species and nothing in essense, and this is the human soul. There is another thing which understands all things, some by species, others by essence, and this is an angel.

Since more ways of understanding, or more intellectual natures, do not exist, although Aristotle seems to make the heavens animate, therefore, as a certain philosopher says, the eternal ruler resides ruling as it were from a tower of a human city and from Him there eternally comes forth an edict that the knowledge of each thing be written into the book of His providence. After Him in a lower heaven, and sometimes in the air as though in the middle of a city, an army of angels fighting with a vicarious administration diligently applies its protection to man. Man as a foreigner living in the suburb of the world does not refuse to give obedience to the angelic army. Therefore in this city God rules; the angel works with Him; man obeys. God disposes by His authority; the angel adjusts himself by action; man obeys, submitting himself to His will. God rules by the dominion of authority; the angel cooperates by the ministry of action; but man obeys by the submission of will. All these aforesaid things fit one statement.

St. Peter fully obeyed the command because he was totally changed over to the divine intellect by the truth of doctrine; he was marvelously placed on the same level with the angelic intellect by the purity of life; in a measure he was singly raised above the human intellect by the harshness of suffering. Thus Peter glows with the grace of doctrine, is strong with the greatest purity, is distinguished by the victory of suffering. Thus in three ways he efficaciously fulfilled what simply was commanded in one statement: *understand*. Thus is made clear a very artistic method.

Still other methods can serve here, although not so elegantly. For example, if the theme be: *walk ye,* the Introduction could be:

It is necessary that one progress or retrogress, because it is impossible to stay on the same level of good for a length of time. But to retrogress is dangerous, because those who walk thus, quickly fall and do not foresee the place of their fall. To progress is fruitful, because the place to which one progresses becomes one's own. *Every place*, says the Lord, *that your foot will tread upon will be yours.* Therefore *walk ye.* And this way is reduced to the second.

It is therefore right to use other methods, but those who use the first method will find it easy to proceed according to Correspondences and Circuitous Developments which the others will not.

## Chapter XXXIII

It is desirable now, according to what I said in Chapter XIV, to to treat of Division, which is the fifth ornament. Concerning Division it should be known that the following principles ought to be observed. Though not expressed, the force of a word should be considered first. For example, if the theme should be on a synod or about a learned man: *the intelligent minister is acceptable to the king,* and it should so be divided that in these words three things were touched upon—namely, intellectual perfection, because of *intelligent*, ministerial humility, because of *minister*, a fraternal acceptance, because of *acceptable to the king*—the Division in all its members would be faulty, because in sound the words "intelligent" and "intellectual," "ministerial" and "minister," "acceptance" and "acceptable" are too much alike. If, however, the same idea should be spoken in other words, there would be no fault in the Division if it were, for example, formed as follows: In these words three things are touched upon, mental perfection, spiritual humility, and brotherly kindness. It is clear that this is materially the same Division as that made above. It is also evident that in every word of the theme the dividing member is included in the divided. For example, intelligent connotes mental perfection, and so with the rest. A Division that leads thus to the force of the words is more real.

Hence ought to be noted a precaution that may be very useful in Division. It sometimes happens that an authority which fits the force of a word cannot occur. There must then be added another determinant which the authority will fit. For example, suppose that I cannot find an authority proving that intelligent things include mental perfection. I must then add another determinant by means of some adjectives, or in some other way, so that it may be stated thus: first, rational perfection is shown to be severely punished in those abusing it. Hence, Wisdom 6: 2–6, *Hear therefore, ye kings, and understand: learn ye that are judges of the ends of the earth. Give ear, you that rule the people, and that please yourselves in multitudes of nations: For power is given you by the Lord, and strength by the most High, who will examine your works, and search out your thoughts: Because being ministers of His kingdom you have not judged rightly, nor kept the law of justice, nor walked according to the will of God. Horribly and speedily will he appear to you, etc.*

Moreover provision must be made that one statement is not placed before another indifferently, and that the division of the second word of the theme is not placed before the division of the first. The division ought either to occur according to the thing done or to be done, or according to the order of the constitution, or according to the order of the delivery. This last method is less artistic than the others, that is, the first and second, unless perhaps other conditions concur with it. Of the first two methods I consider that one more elegant which fits the theme better. But it is very artistic if both concur, that is, if by a single division Division is according to the order of construction and at the same time according to the order of the material.

An example of these. Such is the order of a thing that the knowledge of doing good precedes, there follows suitable conversation, and finally from these will follow gratifying remuneration. And according to this the division first falls upon the word: *Intelligent,* and secondly upon the word: *minister,* and thirdly upon the words *is acceptable to the king.*

Concerning the second: according to the Rabbi Moses, purity of life is a proximate disposition to knowledge and prophecy, and likewise to grace, according to the saints. And according to this as well as according to the order of construction there is put before as an antecedent necessity. 1. innocence of life: *minister*, 2. the concomitant knowledge: *intelligent*, 3. gratifying satisfaction: *acceptable to the king*.

Concerning the third, namely the order of delivery: as St. Augustine teaches, grace precedes all good works, good will follows to will efficaciously, and finally from both sometimes, as the saints say, the perfection of knowledge is communicated. Hinting at this order the Psalmist, 118: 66, says: *goodness*, namely of precedent or prevenient grace, and *discipline* of obedient humility, *and knowledge* of perfect truth *teach me*. And these three are included in the theme according to the order of delivery.

CHAPTER XXXIV

Conveniently following this kind of division is the sixth ornament, the Declaration of Parts, which ought to be such that it shows the distinction of parts either in a way by which the parts of a virtual whole are distinguished, or also of an universal whole, or in some other way which clearly shows some distinction of parts. It is difficult, however, to find another distinction of parts which would not be reduced to the above-mentioned triple distinction, either according to the parts or to the whole.

For example, after the division of the theme: *the intelligent minister is acceptable to the king*, etc., a statement can be added to accord to the order of the material which pertains to the parts of a virtual whole, as if one should say: There comes first, therefore, the splendor of truth by which one is celebrated in the power of vision; next, the course of purity by which one lives with affection, which provides us with hope for the sweetness of charity by which one is actually rewarded. It is evident that the power of vision and feeling, that is reason and will, are parts of a virtual whole, the soul.

Another way is the following. Faith disposes for the first, that is, the knowledge of truth; by the second, that is, a life of pruity, hope adds certitude; by the third, that is, a reward of eternity, charity makes an end. It is also clear that a theological virtue is some universal whole, that is, a genus containing Faith, Hope, and Charity, as parts of an universal whole.

A third way is the following: The knowledge of truth, because it is first, is, as it were, a foundation from which doing good begins; the cleanliness of purity is, as it were, a wall or medium by which a spiritual edifice grows; and the satisfaction of sincerity is, as it were, a roof or the completion by which eternal reward is perfected.

To exemplify more specifically, the statement can be made by means of different parts of speech, nouns, verbs, adverbs, participles, prepositions. Pronouns, however, conjunctions, and interjections, cannot ordinarily minister to this purpose. This can be done especially by means of a substantive, through its two accidents, comparison and case, and in a third way by means of adjectives without comparison.

Through comparison, as follows: good, better, best, and then the reason for each ought to be given.

Through case, as follows: in the first place we tell what kind of a man an ecclesiastic ought of himself to be: *intelligent;* what he should do to others: *minister;* whom he should please by this; *is acceptable to the king.* This method was customarily used in ancient orations by means of the categories who, what, why, and the like.

Through adjectives, as follows: I mean in the first place honorable excellence; in the second, compensative patience; in the third, ineffable friendship; and the use of adjectives such as *favorable, fruitful, glorious.*

The statement can, as I have said, use common nouns and other accidents, but these are simply useless in this method.

The statement can be made by means of the properties of nouns or attributes. By the first there is a likeness to the wisdom of the Son; by the second, to the clemency of the Holy Ghost; by the third, to the power of the Father. Or as follows: *intelligent,* not learning or refusing to learn; *minister,* not master; *is acceptable,* not rejected.

Declaration may occur thus in the theme; *I will cover the sun with a cloud.* (Ezra 32:7). First the sun shines alone with the gravity of law and judges; but later it comes under the cloud by the kindness of the Incarnation; and finally at the judgment it is covered with the equity of the sentence, because it does not respect the person of man. And thus: 1. the sun was in the sign of Leo, 2. passed through the sign of Virgo, and 3, came to Libra.

The Declaration may occur through verbs thus: the first perfects one self as oneself, the second draws the love of others, the third makes one happy with God. And so concerning the others. Many do thus in sermons especially about the saints: the first commands the beginning by which there is a start, the second, the middle by which there is progress, and the third, the end by which there is exit.

In as many ways as there can be Declaration through verbs, in so many can there be Declaration through their participles, such as beginning, progressing, etc. Also through verbal nouns, such as a beginning, a progrssing, etc. And so about the rest.

Declaration can be made through the accidents of a verb, for example through genus. Let the theme be for the Nativity: *He sent his word and healed them, and delivered them from their destructions.* This could be the Declaration: *The word*, I say, which was active with the Father in the creation of things, the same Father *sent* that the word be passive in assuming our nature, and *healed them* while the word was dead (neuter) in the flow of water and blood from His side, *and delivered them* while the word was laid in the grave (deponent) in the release of the patriarchs from limbo, *from their destructions* by which the word will be common in the severity of judgment. Still it is better that such artistry be placed in the beginning of the last member of the development. For example, granted that the theme is of the Nativity: *Let us see this word.* Here there is persuasion to the act: *let us see*, to the object: *word* and thirdly it suggests a particular perfection of the object: *this*. Then in the development the object is subdivided thus: this object was pleasant for meditation in the Incarnation, painful to see the hearts of the sympathizers in the Passion, but in the judgment both pleasant to hear for the good, and painful for the bad. And after coming to the development of that third member, immediately after *painful for the bad* one should begin thus: for the same word which first was active in the creation of things, passive in the redemption of its own, etc.

In the same way there can be Declaration through other accidents of the verb—namely, tense, mood, person. Through tense thus:

*would that they knew* the past, *understood* the present and *foresaw* the last things concerning the future. Through mood thus: This word (verb) was indicative in the assumption of a visible nature, imperative in teaching and preaching, and so on. Through person: as if on the Purification the theme would be in the person of the blessed Virgin speaking to Simeon about her son: *I will show you every good.* After the division one can make this declaration: at first the kindness of communication is shown in the first person: *I will show;* second the aptitude of disposition is suggested in the second person: *you;* but third the fertility of fruition is necessarily concluded in the third person: *every good.*

The verbs which some use in such Declarations are many: it is demonstrated, noted, designated, implied, explained, repeated, preached, commended, praised, persuaded, (exhorted), taught, suggested, expressed, shown, described, touched upon, furnished, set forth, converted, concluded, taught, defended, defined, and many like verbs.

Since whatever a participle has, it has from the noun or the verb, once having established how a Declaration may be made through a noun and verb, it is evident how it can be made through a participle. However one more thing can be said. Say the theme is about the Magdalen: *Mary has chosen the better part.* In the development of declaration could be: Mary was a participle in the state of sin, taking part from the noun, while losing the proper noun *sinner;* and a part from the verb when in the beginning of her repentance, approaching the Word, the Son of God, she heard: *Your sins are forgiven you;* and a part from both while for thirty years she bewailed a life named for evil, and at times was joined to the word of God and raised by angels' hands in contemplation.

Applied to morals thus: Most of what a participle has is from the verb because it is immediately derived from it; yet it is no part of the verb, however like it. Thus some men are participles of the world. A part they have from the noun when gaping at riches, pleasures, and honors *they call their names on their lands;* a part they have from the verb (*verbum*) i.e. God—though derived from Him through creation and thus similar to Him, externally they often so behave according to his image and likeness that they seem to be a part of the verb, i.e. worshippers of God; and yet in truth they are not because a participle never turns into a verb. But it does turn well into a noun as one who loves Him.

Note: Declaration can be made through adverbs in the same way as through the nouns, and especially the adjectives from which they are derived.

Declaration can be made through prepositions, as Hugo, in *Super Ecclesione*,[14] declares the authority: *Vanity of vanities and all is vanity*. He says: He shows all things subject to vanity namely also those which were made for man, in those which were made by man, and in those which were made in man.

Sometimes this is done through many parts at the same time and follows in the same quotation: those things made for man are the vanity of mutability: behold vanity; in those which were made by man is the vanity of curiosity: behold vanity; in those which were made in man is the vanity of mortality: and all is vanity. Thus there is a triple approach, into man, to man, against man. And then: the first is the cause of sin, the second is sin, the third is punishment for sin. Traditionally themes are wont to be declared and divided this way: who, what, and how, as seen in this theme: Ps. 140: 5, *the just man shall correct me in mercy*. Noted is who ought to be the ecclesiastical judge: *the just man;* what he ought to do: *shall correct me;* how he ought to correct: *in mercy*. And this is now called more elegant: these words describe him 1. as a subject, 2. as an act, 3. as mood. As a subject, what sort he ought show himself; as an act, whom he ought exercise; as mood whom he should hold to.

In like manner the statement is made diversely according to different sciences. Grammatically it has been shown how. Likewise logically it is shown according to parts variously taken from the whole; physically, as in the theme: *I leave the world and go to the Father*, by using three parts. In motion there are three things concurrent or needed: a point from which, a point to which, and a mobility of form between the two points. Concerning the point-from-which He says: *I leave the world;* concerning the mobility of form or changing form: *I go;* concerning the point-to-which: *Father*. And so according to other sciences there are other methods of statement than those here specified, but they can definitely be and should be reduced to these.

14. Migne, P.L. 175:116.

## Chapter XXXV

The seventh ornament, Proof of Parts, follows immediately after the preceding, because it is complementary to the things mentioned before. Proof is variously effected by different men.

At the present, the Parisians, after the division of the theme, make a single statement of the parts and at the same time add a confirmation of the parts. This is done in such a way that they verify the first part of the statement immediately, sometimes with a Biblical authority alone, and sometimes with both an original and a Biblical authority. Then, concerning the first part, a Biblical authority of such a kind is used which can be divided simply into three parts in the manner in which it is done in the main theme. This way is rather easy, since it is nothing else but division into four themes, namely a main theme and three authorities which must be divided in the same way over all.

Some, however, divide the first authority of verification into three parts; the second, into two; and the third they leave undivided, and briefly explain it. This way also is easy, yet formal and reasonable.

Those who use the third method take such an authority for verification as can be divided into three parts, so that these three parts also divide the statement treated into sentences.

An example is the following: Suppose that this theme is introduced: *The just is delivered out of distress*, and it is so divided that we indicate the holiness preserved in John: *just;* the senseless evil in his adversary: *out of distress;* in the gracious God infinite goodness: *is delivered.* The Parisians immediately add one statement more, as follows: in the first, sanctity, shines forth his exemplary life. Then they verify this with such an authority as I have described, as follows: hence are described those like him (Prov. 4): *the path of the just as a shining light goes foreward.* Next they introduce the authority of both the first and second parts by some example, whether in nature or in art, in the manner mentioned above. Some insert this Introduction before they express their authority, some after; both come to the same thing. They also observe this rule carefully, that the Introduction which is used for the word *just* does not differ from but agrees with the division, as if explaining it, and this is done in a fitting manner. Then they divide this authority into any three parts they want, as long as the first authority alludes to that which is *light*, the second, *shining*, the third, *goes forward*.

A third group, more artistic than the foregoing in the present connection, adds that these three parts also divide the statement in which there is a division, so that what the three parts, *light*, *shining*, and *goes forward* mean, indicate in sense a threefold part of justice.

Over and above this, a fourth group adds something verbally, at least by way of allusion, and I shall discuss this later. If I gave an example of this method, it would be clear that the preceding methods are easier. This can happen so that it may be said that in that authority three parts of justice or sanctity are noted, and in them consists the whole form of justice as St. Augustine says: *De Mirabilibus Sacrae Scripturae* [15] in the chapter on Abel. There he says Abel was universally just because he was a virgin, a priest whose duty it is to preach, and a martyr; so that who exercises those parts of justice as he should, is universally just, etc. This that saint did because there shone in him exemplary conversation with the candor of virginal modesty, so that his path is rightly compared to light, because *the path of the just is as light*. Light, as is held by Ambrose, *In Hexameron*,[16] is pure in its essence, beautiful in its comeliness, gladdening in its presence. Such also is virginal purity, as each one who has it experiences in himself. Such was St. John, to whom, as St. Jerome says in his prologue concerning John, there attests a double testimony of virginity in his Gospel, etc., so that it can rightly be said of him: *Light is risen to the just*.

Secondly, he was just by the sweetness of spiritual teaching so that his way is rightly called splendor as follows in the authority: *the path of the just as a shining light*. Thus we read among the Hebrews: *But they that are learned shall shine as the brightness of the firmament; and they that instruct many to justice, as stars for all eternity*. Dan. 12: 3.

Thirdly, his singular sanctity is evident from the special fervor of his martyrdom, to which he went because of the magnitude of love that was in him, so that thus *because of truth, and meekness, and justice, he would set out, proceed prosperously, and reign*.

15. Migne, *P.L.* 25:2155.
16. Migne, *P.L.* 14:154.

In this way consummate artistry is evident: 1. because the division which falls on the first member and on that word *just* confirms by a vocal and real authority, and at the same time divides the three, the division, the member, and the authority. This indeed is great artistry and the first. 2. in this that further division, which shoud be called subdivision, which will be treated later, is taken from an original source. 3. in this that the proposition is confirmed by a corresponding vocal authority, either through allusion, or explicitly. This is seen because the development is about the word *just,* and the first part of the authority deals with the light of virginal justice, and he brings in an authority in which *light* and *just* are used at the same time as is seen in the authority: *Light is risen to the just.* But since that authority: *Light is risen to the just,* does not expressily talk about virginity, it is therefore adduced through allusion and not expression. But, in the second part of the authority when is quoted: *shining* there is a correspondence through expression because there is a real and verbal concordance between *just,* which is the word around which is the main development, and the second part of justice, which is the justice of teaching, and between the second part of the authority used which is the word *shining,* because the authority used contains those three verbally and really, justice, teaching, splendor, and a mutual connection, when is said: *they that were learned,* etc.

From among all the devices I think this one the greatest and most difficult, and therefore few are capable of using it as they should.

The fourth device of this kind is verification by means of the original sayings of the saints. This occurred in the first member, though briefly, where we read: *To whom a double testimony,* as says St. Jerome, etc.

## CHAPTER XXXVI

Having dispatched the rather elegant method of the Parisians, it is only right to give a specific example of this method much used by them, and which operates mostly by means of examples. Let the theme be: *the just is delivered out of distress.* There is a common proverb that says: he swims safely whose chin is supported by another person. This is true if the one supporting is strong enough for the task, knows how, and is willing. And so, Peter was rebuked by the Lord and considered of little faith, because walking upon the water he began to sink and fear *with a fear where there was no fear* although He was present who carried him over the water. From this he knew that He was able, knew how, and was willing. He should have believed that one should finish what one has begun. And this is what Isaiah says: *when thou shalt pass through the waters, I will be with thee, and the rivers will not cover thee; fear not, for I am the Lord thy God,* that is, able, (know how and am willing, and at the same time *thy Savior*).

Now in a way the world is a sea, as it is said in the Psalms: *this sea is great, which stretches wide its arms,* whose bitter waters are tribulations. In these tribulations it does not behoove him who preaches the correct things and lives accordingly, to fear anyone, because God who has greater strength and knowledge than all his tormentors stands by supporting him. In the same way God, sending Jeremiah to preach, told him:

> *thou shalt go to all that I shall send thee, and whatsoever I shall command thee thou shalt speak. Be not afraid at their presence for I am with thee to deliver thee.*

Thus also is verified what is asserted about the good preacher: *the just is delivered out of distress.*

In these words the preacher is described, what sort of man he should be in himself: *just;* what to bear from others: *distress;* what to expect from God: *deliverance. The just,* he says, *is delivered from out of distress.*

Just as he who bows to me and slaps me dishonors me more than he who slaps me only, as in the case of the insults to Christ, so, as it seems, does he dishonor God more who praises Him with his tongue and dishonors Him with deeds, than if he dishonor Him with deeds only. Hence he dishonors Him in just that which seems to pertain to honor. And so, the Psalm says: *God said to the sinner why dost thou declare my justice and take my covenant in thy mouth.* Then because the same justice which such a one exercises and asserts by his mouth is truly evil, He adds, *your mouth abounds with evil.* Therefore it is maintained that the same justice which he asserts ought to be called evil by his own mouth. And so it is said (Prov.10) that: *the mouth of the just is a vein of life and the mouth of the wicked covereth iniquity.* The first thing required of a preacher, therefore, is innocence of lif in action, so that he may teach by word and example; as is said: *the lips of the just teach many.*

In tribulation patience is needed. The disciple is unfit, even inordinately proud, who strives to surpass a good and unerring master; as the Lord says: *the disciple is not above his master.* Christ our Lord is the master as He Himself says: *you call me lord and master and you say it well, for I am.* He, however, bore evil while teaching truth and goodness, as He Himself says: *it was right that Christ suffer,* etc. Likewise He says: *if they have persecuted me they will also persecute you.* Therefore His followers, taking heed of this, no matter how much they were troubled, bore it lightly as if they did not suffer at all; as the *flower of preachers* says of himself and those likc him (2 Cor. 4): *we have tribulation, but are not distressed.* And rightly so, because of God's presence is communicated in consolation. Who can be dejected under so good a physician; who can be in tribulation under so strong a protector; or who can be overcome? No one; unless he despair. Therefore it is said to a preacher (Jer. 1):

> *I have made thee this day a fortified city, and a pillar of iron, and a wall of brass, over all the land, the kings, to the princes, to the priests and to the whole people.*

Observe that a preacher should spare no one.

> *And they shall fight against thee and shall not prevail: for I am with thee, saith the Lord, to deliver thee.*

In whatever field of battle a man may be, the Lord if called upon is immediately present. This is something no other general can do for his soldiers. Hence He claims that singular privilege for Himself, saying: *you have called upon me in tribulation and I have delivered thee.* And, as it were, he adds the cause: *I heard thee in the secret place of the tempest.* Therefore let us cry to Him at the beginning, etc.

Whoever understands this method, understands the more famous methods used at Paris with respect to antethemes. He understands how there is a short Introduction with an example for the sense; how that example is verified by Scripture; how both the example and the verification are concluded by one atuhority which agrees with both; how every theme agrees with the three aforementioned things; how the theme is easily and, for those understanding, intelligently divided; how all parts are stated with sensible examples and verified with agreeing authorities; how the last authority agrees with the first, that is, the authority of the Introduction; how one proceeds from this authority to the prayer. All of these things are clear in their respective places, being nine especially famous observances for antethemes.

## Chapter XXXVII

For those wanting to know the manner of execution of the same [Parisians] it must be known that they have the same manner of Introduction which was exemplified in the chapter immediately preceding. In addition to it some put the Introduction not only to introduce the theme but indeed the division of the theme. Say the theme were as before: *the just, etc.* You see and know that he is not quite sincere nor at peace, who lets one enemy continually molesting go undefeated, no matter how many he has overcome. This is evident in nature. For anyone who is deaf, dumb, and devil-possessed, although cured of the first two, remains without any peace or security if not cured of the third. Christ, therefore, about to cure the man, considering it no cure if it were not a full cure, cured him completely of all.

The same is evident in art. If three adversaries attack to kill you, and after you overcome two the third continually attacks, you have not won completely. You still have something to fear and you can not boast victory, as is said in the book of Kings: *Let not (the girded) boast himself as the ungirded,* i.e. He who should be girded to be prepared for battle is not equal with him who ungirds his sword as total victor. Hence Augustine says, in *The City of God,* that at Rome there was a certain fight between three twin-brothers on one side and three of like condition on the other. The first three killed two of their adversaries not being hurt in any way. Then there remained only the one. And yet, since he alone was left, he overcame all three with boldness and cunning.[17]

Now, my beloved, we have three enemies: the devil, the world, and the flesh, and this saint had them too. These enemies are typified by the sons of Enath (Judges 1: 20), whose name interpreted means *terrible*, i.e. sinner, under whom anyone oppressed must say: *Your terrors have troubled me.* These, Caleph—which interpreted means *whole heart* and marks him who can say: *With my whole heart I sought after thee*—erased from the city of Hebron, namely the soul, given to him by the Lord. From this, as has been proved, there is no victory as long as there remains an undefeated enemy.

Just as all of us, St. John had these same enemies, as has been shown above. It follows therefore that it was fitting for him, as it is for us, to triumph over all if a total victory was to be attained. Therefore St. John fought and overcame, with the means of grace, the devil by driving him from the heart of others through his teaching; he overcame the world by patiently bearing tribulations; he overcame the flesh, by virtuously repressing his inborn passions. By the things proposed in these words he is implicitly commended: 1. by the most excellent action of his rational faculty which is preaching of truth; 2. by the most excellent action of his irascible faculty which is patient endurance of suffering; 3. by the most excellent action of his concupiscent faculty which is the preservation of virginal chastity.

The preaching of truth, by which the devil is expelled, ought to be done by the one who is blameless, and with due control, as St. John did it. This is seen in his epistles when he sweetly calls those his sons whom he scolds, and first shows by deed in himself rather than by the word of the doctrine which he taught. For you sensibly perceive that if there be a blot on some eye or clothing which you would try to remove or erase with dirty hands, or pitch, or something like this, you would dirty it more than clean, because, *he that touches pitch, etc.* And although your hands would be very clean pressing hard upon an eye or clothing you would be more injurious than helpful because, *he that violently blows his nose, etc.* This is the way it is if you try to scold others or to teach and

17. Book III, Section 14.

your life is filthy and shameful. You rather hurt because the evil is twofold. First, men are moved to do things as you do, saying, why can't I do as he, etc. Secondly, you cause the word of God to be blasphemed. Hence the Lord says in the Gospel: *Hypocrite, cast first the beam out of thy own eye; and then shalt thou see clearly to take out the mote from thy brother's eye.*

No matter how holy or clean a man may be he may so harshly scold that he might rather subvert than convert. Therefore, the Psalmist shows us how St. John exercised that duty, and how we ought to do it when he says: *The just man shall correct me in mercy.* In this authority he shows three things which were in St. John and that they belong in anyone who tries for the aureola of a learned man, namely, the beginning to be set forth, the office to be exercised, the judgment to be used.

The beginning to be set forth is proper purity, by which he is *just.* No one will wear an aureola who does not wear an aurea because the aureola is a certain accidental joy superadded to the essential joy which is called the aurea. And so, just as it is great folly to wish to build a house and not start with the foundation, it is thus folly to wish to obtain the aureola without a foundation, i. e. the purity of life. Therefore it is written: Prov. 10: 25 *But the just (man) is as an everlasting foundation.* Likewise it is foolish to clean the outside of a cup unless it is first cleaned inside because this is more necessary, as the Lord says in the Gospel. So certainly he who tries too hard to cleanse others extrinsically, having neglected himself, is foolish and lacks the judgment of reason. Against such the Psalmist says: Ps. 36: 30, *The mouth of the just shall meditate wisdom, and his tongue,* etc. This, then, is the duty of a wise man: first to do what is first and especially necessary and then the other things, as the Lord says: Matt. 6:33, *Seek ye first the kingdom of God and His justice.* This, then, is the beginning to be set forth, namely, internal purity by which one is *just.*

Secondly, there follows the office to be exercised when is said, *shall correct me.* If a watchman sitting in a high tower sees a hostile army approaching and near enough for the city to be captured, and because of his silence it is captured, he is guilty of the death of all killed and lost there. Likewise the prelates and learned of the church are put on a higher plane that they provide for and fortify the others. Ezech. 3: 17 *I have made thee a watchman for the house of Israel.* And therefore, if they keep silent, they are guilty of all those things which happen because of their negligence. Hence it follows there, Ezech. 3: 18 *If, when I say to the wicked, thou shalt surely die: thou declare it not to him . . . the same wicked man will die in his iniquity. But I will require his blood at thy hand.* But alas! *His watchmen are all blind.* Isa. 56: 10.

Because they themselves are blind, in vision through ignorance and in affection through evil, they therefore do not foresee their own or the ruin of others. Typically it is said of them as of Heli the priest, I Kings 4: 15, *his eyes were dim, and he could not see.* Of him the Lord said when talking to Samuel: I Kings 3: 11. *Behold I do a thing in Israel: and whosoever shall hear it, both his ears shall tingle. In that day I will raise up against Heli all the things I have spoken concerning his house: I will begin, and I will make an end. For I have foretold unto him, that I will judge his house for ever, for iniquity, because he knew that his sons did wickedly, and did not chastise them. Therefore have I sworn to the house of Heli, that the (iniquity) of his house shall not be expiated with victims nor offerings for ever.* This, how it began to be fulfilled, is told in the following chapter: I Kings 4: 17 : *Israel has fled before the Philistines, and there has been a great slaughter of the people: moreover thy sons, Oplini and Phinees, are dead, and the ark of God is taken.* When Heli heard that the ark of God was taken, *he fell from his stool backwards by the door, and broke neck, and died.* Hence is said: Ecclus 19: 13 *reprove a friend, lest he may not have understood, and say: I did it not: or if he did it, that he may do it no more.*

And yet God adds: *Admonish thy neighbor before thou threaten him. And give place to the fear of the most High,* showing that this should be done with moderation.

This office therefore must be exercised because necessity forces it. But judgment must be used, i.e. discretion, that a due may be conserved, namely, that it be in mercy: *The just,* it says, *shall correct me in mercy.* If the fear of the Lord always attends correction one will hardly err in correction by doing too little, or by exceding much. It is less dangerous to pity from compassion than to excede from anger. Aristotle says in Book 9 of *Concerning Animals* that a pregnant ewe separated from the flock aborts if it hears thunder. The ewe is the human soul. Hence in the Psalms: *we are his people and the sheep of his hand.*

This ewe is pregnant when it conceives of a good proposed by the Holy Spirit. Isa. 26:17: *As a woman with child, when she draweth near the time of her delivery, is in pain, and crieth out in her pangs: so are we become in thy presence, O Lord. We have conceived and been as it were in labor, and have brought forth (the spirit of salvation).* This ewe is separated from the flock when its life does not conform to the holy life of the others. As a sign of this we have Luke 18:13: *the publican afar off prayed within himself.* The thunder which sounds horribly is the hard and harsh voice of the one who corrects. Hence in the Psalms 103:7: *at the voice of thy thunder they shall fear.*

This ewe then aborts as it were when she does not effect the proposition of this kind or the beginning of charity. In an abortion, that perishes which was expected. So here that vanishes which was expected. Lam. 3:18: *My end and my hope is perished.*

Therefore this abortion occurs when a prelate, a preacher, or a confessor hurls his hand and harsh sermon against one who is simple and only beginning—not advanced—in good. The type and the very deed is shown in 3 Kings 12:13 where is said: *the king answered the people roughly.* And then follows 3 Kings 12:19: *And Israel revolted from the house of David, unto this day.* This agrees with what the Lord says through Ezekiel, Ezech. 34:4: *you ruled over them with rigour, and with a high hand. And my sheep were scattered.* So just as you wish to be heard by the Lord, as you cry to Him: Lord, rebuke me not in thy indignation, etc. Have mercy on me, etc., so it behooves you, Matt. 18:33: *to have compassion on your fellow servant* as you wish him to have compassion on you. Therefore he who was such as St. John, in whom all these things concur, truly and justly merits the aureola of a learned man, because he is just in life, teaching, circumstance, i.e. in the way; because of such a one is verified that statement of Isaiah's 53:11: *by his knowledge shall this my just servant justify many,* by expelling the devil from their heart and by illuminating them with sound teaching whom he himself tries to blind. And it is plain that so brave a struggle, so special and laudable a victory especially merits to be crowned and to be privileged with a singular splendor. Hence: Dan. 12:3 *they that are learned shall shine as the brightness of the firmament: and they that instruct many to justice, as stars.*

This could be the end. But you see that when someone defeats one great leader, the faithful soldier of that leader tries to avenge what his lord has suffered and he lies in wait to know how to cause hurt. A type for this is in the Book of Machabees 9:36, taken from the wedding of Medelia (Madaba) when John, one of the seven Machabees, was captured, imprisoned, and killed. When the sons of Jambri, by whom this was done, celebrated the wedding as if there was nothing to fear, Jonathan and his brother Simon, 1 Mach. 9:38, *remembered the blood of John their brother: and they went up, and hid themselves under the covert of the mountain;* and when the sons of Jambri came, *they rose up from the place of ambush and slew them.*

Now, the devil is the prince of this world, i.e. of those loving the world, as the Lord attests in the Gospel. Therefore, although he may be overcome, there is no security unless the world, which is faithful to him and a vigorous aide, is overcome. Therefore it is right, if a victory is to be total and security prevail, to triumph over the world also. Martyrs overcome the world most powerfully through bearing the final suffering, which is the second principle: *from distress. The just,* it says, *from distress, etc.* And this merits a second aureola, which belongs to martyrs.

You know that a child would nurse too long unless something bitter were put over the nipple or something to withdraw it. Thus childish men would totally adhere to the world and consequently would not conquer, unless it was filled with the bitterness of distress, as Augustine and Gregory teach, and as the prophet says: Isa. 26:16 *Lord, they have sought after you in distress.* From this is learned that so necessary and useful a distress ought to be joyfully accepted by one who understands rightly, especially since the Lord of majesty *ought to have suffered these things, and so enter into his glory* himself saying: *narrow is the gate and straight is the way that leadeth to life.* And therefore the Apostle says: 2 Cor. 12:10: *I please myself in my infirmities,* i.e. I rejoice, *in reproaches,* i.e. of words, *in necessities,* i.e. needs of sustenance, *in persecutions,* i.e. of evil men, *in distresses for Christ.*

In this authority he posits three things which made St. John, and anyone having them, worthy of a martyr's aureola. For martyrdom does not deserve a reward according to what is inflicted exteriorly, but according to what is voluntarily borne, because we do not merit except by things within us and not outside of us. However, by how much it is more difficult to bear voluntarily what one does bear voluntarily, by so much does the will which bears this for Christ stand more firmly fixed in Christ. And therefore a more excellent reward is due it. Hence the three things which the Apostle mentions are needed: a free will, for which he says: *I please myself;* the pain borne, which he numbers: *in many infirmities, reproaches, necessities, persecutions, in distress;* the necessary cause, therefore he says: *for Christ.* He sets forth the will assenting with grace as a root of good when he says: *I please myself, etc.*

Those who use this method develop the second member in the same way, as was explained for the first; they also introduce a third, as was exemplified for the introduction of the second; and the third they commonly terminate with some word which touches upon the joy of heaven by wishing for it, or the pains of hell by cursing them. They do this by saying concerning the former: *to which may he lead us who lives and reigns without end,* and concerning the latter: *from which in his love may he protect us who lives, etc.* These do not care about any more ornaments.

## Chapter XXXVIII

Some preachers, especially in England, do not follow this method of developing the parts but multiply the statement in such a way that they add to the division of the theme a double statement of the parts without authorities, and afterwards a third statement of the parts and an expression of the words of the theme, and then immediately add to this third statement of parts a brief verification of the parts.

For example suppose the theme to be the same as above.[18] It can

18. *The just man is delivered from out of distress.*

be divided, stated, and verified according to them in the following way: In these words three things are proposed for the praise of St. John, namely, protected sanctity, foolish malice, and infinite goodness. The first statement goes as follows: In John the innocence of sanctity is denoted; in Domitian, the vehemence of malice; in the viewer of both, the meekness of piety. The second statement goes as follows: In his sanctity his life is to be imitated; in the king's cruelty, John's rewardable toleration; in God's piety is denoted the admirable care of His own. The third statement with its verification goes as follows: As I have said, his exemplary life is shown in his sanctity, because (he is) just. For it is said in Proverbs that *the path of the just proceeds as a shining light.* From the king's impiety is added John's extraordinary tribulation: *from distress,* so that the saying of Job seems to be fulfilled in him:

> *He knows that in his hands is made the day of darkness. Tribulation will terrify him and hardship will surround him;*

but finally in the piety of God is concluded the familiar love by which *he was delivered* as St. Paul says with his fellow apostle (2 Tim. 4:1):

> *... was delivered out of the mouth of the lion. The Lord hath delivered me from every evil work: and will preserve me unto His heavenly kingdom.*

Therefore this *just man was delivered from out of distress.*

Some add to this mode, after a verification by Biblical authority, verification by an original authority, and this is elegant if it agrees with and explains the authority to which it is added. For example if the authority, *the path of the just, etc.,* is used, I would use an original statement that as light draws to itself sight for the admiration of its beauty, so the shining life of a just man draws to itself the will of others for its imitation. The reason why they pass over this ornament so briefly is that they use the remaining ornaments which demand much time.

In this ornament one must be aware that there be no division between at least one statement and its verification, i.e., one must make sure that the authority of the verification should never be added unless another statement immediately precedes. They do the contrary who assert their authorities as follows: *In the first place it is written,* and so on. For example suppose that the following is said: In his sanctity his exemplary life comes first when it is said: *just;* in the impiety of the king, extraordinary tribulation: *from distress;* in the piety of God, familiar love by which he was *delivered.* For the first part it is written in Proverbs: *the path of the just,* etc. For the second part in Job *he knows that,* etc. For the third part one can quote from the saying from 2 Tim., *I have been delivered,* etc. To verify in this way is incorrect. When one says *in the first place,* it may happen that the listener already has forgotten what was the first part, and therefore it must be expressed.

## Chapter XXXIX

We must now see, following the plan set forth in Chapter XIV, with what variety the eighth ornament, called Amplification is used. There are eight main species or methods of forming this ornament. The first is by proposing to discuss a noun as it occurs in definitions or classifications. For example, *the Lord led the just man,* etc., or *the just man as the palm,* etc. The just man is defined as he who renders to everyone his due; to his superior, God; to his equal, for example, to himself; to his inferior, for example, to his neighbor.

When, however, something is defined or described, the preacher can conveniently make transference to the opposite, because the definition is valid for defining the other. Having described justice he can go on to any other virtue, and show, for example, how prudence is used in discerning good from evil, and likewise the greater evil from the lesser. Prudence is the discrimination between good and bad things. And so about the other virtues. Thus we use Amplification by proposing to discuss a noun, not only by noting what is in the theme but also other things on account of it.

When, however, we wish to amplify by means of interpretation, we must consider the different interpretations, and that one must be selected which best fits the proposition. This method is important in the first division of the theme discussed above.

The second method of Amplification is by division. As Porphyry says, one who divides must consider a multitude of things. For example, suppose that the word *head* is present in the theme. Christ, a prelate, a man, is called a *head*. Yet not all division is to be used in preaching. For it does not pertain to laymen to know the multiplicity of some noun, because division of a word into meanings must be used in lectures to solve contrarieties and in disputations to solve paralogisms—because to know how many ways it is used is useful for paralogizing and not be paralogized, as is evident in the *Topica*. In preaching we can use other divisions also, namely, that of genus into species, of superior into inferior, or of a whole into its integral parts.

One must, however, avoid too great a division of parts, for division is the better the less of it there is. But once a division has been made there can be subdivisions. For example, if the theme is: *power, when it is tried, reproveth the unwise*. One proceeds thus: of virtues, some are theological by which we are directly moved towards God, as faith, hope, charity; some are social, by which we are indirectly moved towards God, as prudence, fortitude, temperance, justice. By Faith we believe in God, by Hope we hope in God, by Charity we love God. The social moves indirectly because prudence is the discretion of good and evil things on account of God. And so about the rest. Or, the members must be noted, by explaining or defining, as Boethius teaches in *Divisiones*, and the first helps the second method. A division once made, it is quite right to give an authority for each part. This should be done especially after the statement of parts, that is, a division of the statement which is being treated. This division is commonly called a subdivision.

The third method of Amplification is by reasoning or argumentation, which in preaching occurs especially in three ways. One, when the reasoning deals with two contraries, the one proving, the other disproving. For example if one tries to prove that continence should be maintained he should speak thus: Luxury destroys money, the body and soul, and one's good name. Therefore continence should be preserved. Another way is to reason with hidden enthymemes and by asking the listeners to draw the conclusion. For example: Would he not be foolish who would weave or make a rope with which his enemy would hang him? Such a one is he who commits sin by which he is damned. Prov. 5:22: *Each one is fast bound with the ropes of his own sins.* Nathan used this method with David, and the Lord in His parables used it about the farmer. By this method a sinner is entirely confounded and secretly condemns himself. The third way of reasoning is by example; this avails much with lay people who are pleased with examples. The Apostles and other saints passed to the kingdom of God through many tribulations, therefore we ought to also.

The fourth method is by concordances, and this may vary in a threefold manner. One way is when authorities having different meanings come together in one statement. *Blessed is the man that endureth temptation, Blessed is the man that shall continue in wisdom.* Of this man this is in Job: *Gird up thy loins like a man.* Another way is when the authorities come together in the meaning but not in the expression. v. g. *Faith without works is dead;* the same is in Genesis: Rachel said to Jacob: *Give me children, otherwise I shall die.* In Rachel, which means seeing the beginning, is understood Faith; in children, deeds done in charity. The third way is when one authority speaks fully and another even more fully by additions. For example, *So run that you may obtain.* How one must run is determined in the psalms: *without iniquity have I run,* etc.

The fifth way is through those things which agree in essence, although they have other differences, as by adding the superlative to the positive and comparative. For example: *gird thy sword,* etc. Some are girded powerfully as the married, others more powerfully as the continent, others most powerfully as virgins. Or, *Be inebriated, my dearly (most) beloved.* Dear ones are imperfect in charity; more dear are those who can suffer for themselves or Him, although uneasily; most dear are those who as drunk laugh among reproaches. Or, *Take away the tarnish from silver, and there shall come forth a most pure vessel.* Pure vessels are the laity, more pure the clergy, most pure the prelates, who above all should be clean and washed. To this method pertains that dilation which occurs by descending through various compositions. v.g. *Seek ye His face evermore.* God is sought (*queritur*) in Baptism, needed (*requiritur*) in Penance, examined (*inquiritur*) by meditating on the divine law, searched out (*exquiritur*) by doing well, and thus finally happily acquired (*acquiritur*) in our native land.

The sixth way is by devising metaphors through the properties of a thing, for example, *The just man will flourish as the lily*. The just man is rightfully compared to a lily, for the white and odoriferous lily blooms close to water. Thus the just man is white with chastity, odoriferous with a good name, and he progresses or grows in the waters of tribulation or grace.

In this method of Amplification one must avoid a sudden change of metaphor. The discourse, however, may proceed conveniently to the parts, universal or integral. For example, suppose the theme were: *I am a flower of the field*. The sermon could rightly be about a rose, a lily, a violet—that is, could point out how Christ was a lily in His birth, a rose in His passion, a violet in His burial. However it is not fitting to show in that same sermon how He was a shepherd or a rock.

The seventh way is to expound the theme in various ways: historically, allegorically, morally, anagogically. For example, *Jerusalem which is built as a city* may be taken historically about the Church on earth; allegorically about the Church militant; morally about any faithful soul; anagogically, about the Church triumphant.

An allegorical exposition occurs when one part is understood by another. For example, by the fact that David slew Goliath it is understood that Christ overcame the devil. A moral exposition occurs when one deed that must be done by us is understood through another, as the fact that David conquered Goliath signifies that every believer ought to overcome the devil. An anagogical exposition is one in which by some deed on earth is understood another that must be done in heaven or in the Church triumphant. This is seen in many mysteries concerning the temple, by which is meant the triumphant Church as the Church militant is understood by the tabernacle. Anagoge is derived from *ana* and *goge,* the former meaning "up" and the latter, "leading," as if *leading up*.

Faith is built by allegory; morals are formed by tropology; the contemplatives are raised by anagoge.

Not all allegories are about Christ, but also about the Church and her parts: Gentiles, Jews, Apostles, the blessed Virgin or some saint.

In tropology it is right that words be elicited with gravity so that one consider why this is rather than that, why thus and not otherwise. v.g. *Thou art my son, this day have I begotten thee.* Well does it say: *I*, as if there is no other; well does it say: *begotten*, as if I have not created or made; well does it say: today, not yesterday, not tomorrow, not at night; well does it say: *you*, not yours.

The eighth way is by causes and effects, giving the necessary or essential causes. And one can make transference in speaking about a cause to the effect and vice versa. For example suppose the theme were: *be ye humbled under the strong hand of God.* One could make a transference to the causes of humiliation which are the imperfection of body and soul, another perfection, the better life of another, the poverty and Passion of Christ. Afterwards one may give the effects of humility: it illumines, preserves, affects, exalts, holds man in his proper place, provides an easy approach to Scripture, and expedites prayer.

## CHAPTER XL

Because the method of the Oxonians is more commonly used we must illustrate it more specifically. This method consists in adding a division, called subdivision, immediately after the verification of the parts of the theme once the theme has been divided and the parts stated. As was said before, first one must make sure to see what the statement is which is described, and then the division which is called subdivision ought to divide both the statement itself and the description of it. For example in the proposition, *just*, there is the first statement in the theme: *the just man is delivered from tribulation.* In it there is a description of the exemplary sanctity of St. John. Then, after full verification has been made, one ought to render it as follows: Concerning the first item, namely the exemplary sanctity of his life, for which he is called just, one should know that we can see a triple sanctity in him according to which he was triply just. For as St. Augustine says, *De Gratia et Libero Arbitrio*, one is a saint if he has a holy desire, and holy love, and does holy deeds, for sanctity consists of justice and actions.

This just man, therefore, was a saint by a triple sanctity; (1) by giving his superior his due, namely holy desire in the fervour of contemplation; (2) by giving his neighbor his due, namely love in the sweetness of compassion; (3) in giving himself his due, namely, holy action, in the beauty of clean living.

His holy desire in the fervour of contemplation is evident when, as says St. Peter Damian,[19] with sharpness of mind he attains to that place after which no prophet, no patriarch, and finally no one in the flesh, from the beginning of the world, is known to have aspired. This is clear when in the beginning of his Gospel he exclaims: *in the beginning was the Word* so that it can be said of him alone (Prov. 10), *the tongue of the just is as choice silver.* Nor is it surprising that, as is said in the same place, *the mouth of the just begets wisdom.* And this came about in an extraordinary way, since he obtained it from the source of wisdom, when at the last supper, as one more beloved than the others, he rested on the resting-place of His heart. Woe to us if we do not follow the doctrine of such a great teacher, and unless by adhering to God *we serve Him in justice and sanctity before His face.* Secondly, he was just in the holy love of his neighbor. Hence his story is full of love. In the Gospel: *God so loved the world. This I command you that you love one another,* and the like. His prophecy is full of love. In the Apocalypse: *He loved us and cleansed us,* and the rest. His doctrine is full of love. In the Epistles: *He who loves his brother remains in the light,* and so forth. Again he says: *let us not love by word but by deed and truth.* In this way, as he says there, *everyone who has hope in God, sanctifies himself, as He himself is holy* and who does justice is just as He is just.

Thirdly, he was just in holy action through the preservation of purity, following, and teaching others to follow, the maxim of his fellow Apostle (Rom. 6), *yield your members to serve justice, unto sanctification,* etc. This St. John certainly did, and as I believe, to a degree worthy of the angels, because as a sign of most chaste virginity he was chosen as son and guardian of the incomparable chastity of the Virgin Mother of God. Thus, in a way, he was put above the Mother of God because he was her guardian, and in a way equal to God and the Son of God because he was substituted as another son.

Now we must see how in the above-mentioned subdivision the idea of sanctity is as well divided as that of the just man in whom the sanctity is implied, and how the three authorities verifying the subdivision include verbally and implicitly in the thought the sanctity and justice treated. This method is very artistic. It should suffice,

19. *Sermo de S. Joanne.* Migne, *P.L.* 144:859.

however, to include the idea of sanctity, so that it could agree as a genus, or in some way as a major premise, with all species of sub-divided justice. The best provision for those using this method of preaching is to make sure that when they divide themes they make a general description of the first divisions. And from this descrip-tion one can in the subdivision descend, as it were, from genus to species or from some whole to its parts. But still another thing must be realized—that those who use this method must see to it that the authorities used include verbally a statement which they treat. Hence, in the proposition, if an authority is used in which *holiness* is expressed, and which is treated in the sermon, there should be nothing about the holiness of doctrine and only implicitly *justice*.

## Chapter XLI

Digression, which is equivalent to Transition, is the ninth orna-ment. It occurs when one proceeds artistically from one part to another, that is, from one original member to another. One who looks at the *Rhetoric* of Cicero can see that this is improperly called Digression. For Digression, properly speaking, occurs when one says or declares something incidental and outside the main proposi-tion. If we consider Digression in this way, it is not properly an orna-ment having a definite place in a sermon. It can be used anywhere in the sermon for any reason as long as it is not too remote from the proposition nor too prolonged. It can be used extensively when one teaches or discusses. Hence, as Gregory wishes in his prologue to the *Moralium*,[20] we have: as the water of a stream wherever it finds low places flows into them, so sometimes authority must be twisted so that useful things be said even on the side. But in a sermon, a Digression must be brief.

The digression mentioned above is not the Digression with which we are chiefly dealing now. The Digression we are considering is a certain skillful connecting of two principal statements, namely a transition from one principal statement to another by verbal and real concordance. For example, after the words that another was substituted as son, in the preceding chapter, one can add: Woe

20. Migne, *P.L.* 75:415.

therefore to the person having so many examples of purity who is not at least in expected purity if not virginity, when in almost every church there is placed in a high spot to see and imitate Christ, a virgin, on His right His mother, a virgin, and on His left John, a virgin. Woe to him who after so true, so valid, so manifest examples has spurned the angelic life, neglected the human condition, and is involved wallowing in the filth of unclean flesh. He can only expect certain and eternal damnation, and even a sudden one, because Prov. 12:13 says: *ruin draws nigh to the evil man.* The certainty of this he cannot even avoid in the present, without foretasting a bit through remorse of conscience, bitterness, and tension what he will drink in eternal damnation, because as Boethius says: all desire has this that it drives with stimuli its own satisfaction. Against this remorse he can escape with St. John, having with him the aforesaid purity within himself, true friendship for his neighbor, the fervor of love for God, as is verified about both in Prov. 12:13, *the just shall escape out of distress,* [*The just man,* I say, which is the first principal, through exemplary living *shall escape out of distress,* which is the second principal.] *The just,* it says, *out of distress,* wherein is implied a singular tribulation being suffered which he bore in three ways, namely in the heat of the oil, the labor of the exile, and horror of the poison. This we can more easily admire than imitate.

Then in the same way this must be confirmed by three authorities. And thus one passes to the third principal part by the ornament which is properly called Transition, which can be through 1 Macc. 2:53 *Joseph in the time of distress kept the commandment,* and 1 Macc. 2:60 *Daniel in his innocence was delivered.* Hence this ornament alone is put twice in a sermon.

Some, however, use this ornament only implicitly, tying the second to the first principal in some way, so that the transition is compact and connected, as if the Transition were: But because St. Augustine says that in this life it is the lot of the good, or just, to do good and suffer evil, then after the virtuous life of St. John, since he is called *just,* there follows his painful passion, since it says: *from distress.*

The first method is more elegant, the second more obvious, and therefore, more useful. There is no place for the first method when a sermon concerns only one statement, but the second method may well be used in such a case.

## Chapter XLII

The tenth ornament, called Correspondence, is the express agreement of parts among themselves, as when the first principal part is divided into *a b c,* the second into *d e f,* the third into *g h i.* Then, according to this ornament, there must be agreement among *a d g, b e h,* and *c f i.*

This can occur in two ways: I. some say: (1) the first principal part is divided into three parts without another authority of the Bible; (2) the second principal part is immediately divided in the same way, and then (3) the third in the same way. After this is done, one says: And these correspond with each other. Then is posited the first part of the first division, the first of the second division, namely *a* and *d,* and the first part of the third division, namely *g.* Each part is immediately confirmed by an authority of the Bible. Take, for example, in particular: if after the division of the theme, declaration and confirmation of the parts, one would say: *The just man,* I say, by a triple justice in which is all justice from a triple *distress was* triply *delivered.* For, 1. he was just with the purity of virginal modesty, with the teaching of spiritual sweetness, and with the privilege of special love. Because evil is against the good, his distress was threefold: the heat of burning oil, the rigor of a prostrating exile, the horror of a destroying dangerous cup. But, *because many are the afflictions of the just, but out of them all will the Lord deliver them,* he was freed with power, with wisdom, with clemency.

And these correspond with each other; thus, 1. *the just man* with the candor of virginal merit, as is verified about him: Ps. ? *the just man shall grow like a lily, from the distress* of burning oil, which can be explained by Job 15:24: *distress shall surround him, was delivered* through the power of his Protector, and thus became one such of whom 1 Macc. 2:59 says: *believing were delivered out of the flame.*

Here one must be aware that some, immediately after the words *through the power of his Protector* put the eleventh ornament, called the Congruence of Correspondence, of which there will be talk later.

2. the *just man* by the glory of his spiritual teaching of which Prov. 10:31 says: *The mouth of the just shall bring forth wisdom, from the distress* of the squalor of an oppressing exile, of which Isa. 49:20 could say: *the place is too strait for me, was delivered* through the wisdom of the Savior. Thus this wisdom *delivered the just man who fled* from the wicked that were perishing, as is noted in Wisdom 10:6.

3. *the just man* by the love of his special acceptance by which *the Lord is just, and has loved justice* Ps. 10:8 *from the distress* of the terror of a destroying cup of which could be said, Job 6:7: *the things which before my soul would not touch now through anguish are my meats, was delivered* through the clemency of the Creator, so that giving him thanks he may say: *Thou hast delivered me, according to the multitude of the mercy of thy name.* Ecclus. 51:4.

II. Others develop the first principal part totally of itself, and then the second totally, and then, having made an artificial transition to the third principal member, they immediately add the correspondences, saying: this is the third principal member and it corresponds harmoniously with the first two, because *the just man* by strength of purity *from distress* of burning oil *was delivered,* through the power of His Protector. They then add the Congruence of Correspondence, and bring forth authority which is confirmation only of the third member, by saying: For him one can uniquely say: *You have become a helper and protector for me, and you have delivered my body.*

## Chapter XLIII

Here is a good place to treat the eleventh ornament, because it is the completion of the former and is called, I have said above, the Congruence of Correspondence. It is a clause or statement expressing the substance of the connection made between the parts of the principal statements. This is uniformly assigned by those who use the first method and those who use the second, so far as position is concerned, but diversely with respect to the finesse applied. The less elegant form a simple congruence which they can easily in-

vent, and the more elegant form none except one which they can
verify by a figure. Both, however, put this ornament after the correspondence has been established. For example, in reference to St.
John the Evangelist: *he is just* by virtue of the glow of virginal
merit. Then, whether an authority is added or not, the proposition
is the same: from *distress* of boiling or heated oil, *he is delivered*
through the power of his Protector, Who commended to him, a
virgin, the Virgin. Then a simple congruence follows: Indeed it
was very appropriate that tormenting flames did not burn him who
had extinguished the flames of vice within himself, and that he who
was free from the corruption of the flesh was thus made a stranger
to the pain of death, as St. Jerome says.

Other preachers, more elegant, add a figure, as follows: according to this example the young men, Ananias, Azarias, and Misael,
noble and pure, fleeing the contaminations of the gentiles, were
freed from fire (1 Macc. 2). This procedure holds also for the
other members.

It must be noted also that after the Congruence of Correspondence has been carried out to the full, insofar as the material and
the form are concerned, it is then most appropriate to inveigh
against vices, to say something which appertains to morals or to
devotion, because then the development is not interrupted nor
impeded.

In this way an invective can arise from any statement in the
correspondence about the first item, justice, or the second, distress,
or the third, divine liberation. It is commendable to place some such
thing in three places in the sermon, for nothing better than this can
be offered for helping the memory.

## Chapter XLIV

To the preceding ornaments some add a twelfth, which is called
Circuitous Development. It is nothing beyond Correspondence than
an artificial linking of the first part of the last principal statement
to the second part of the first principal statement, namely, *g* to *b*,
and again the linking of the second part of the last principal statement, namely *h*, to the third part of the first principal statement,
namely *c*. This double connection of the last to the first is

called Circuitous Development, so that if either connection is lacking there is no encirclement. It is called Circuitous Development in the image of extending a circle where the end and the beginning are the same.

The difference, however, lies in this: that in extending a circle, the beginning and the end are of the same line. But this is not done absolutely; only relatively, according to the words. For example, the first correspondence is: *the just man* by virtue of virginal purity *from* the *distress* of smelly oil *was delivered* powerfully by the Lord of purity, etc., confirming the parts as before and forming a congruence. Then, for the purpose of Circuitous Development, one can say: thus is evident the truth of the saying of Solomon in Prov. 11:6: *the justice of the upright will deliver them.* This is true materially, because it is the material cause of their deliverance. Then we add Prov. 11:9: *the just will be delivered by knowledge.* And so, secondly, St. John was just by virtue of the knowledge of spiritual doctrine, etc.; by executing as before the second parts of the principal statements, and then when that has been done by making a similar connection between the second and the third parts of the principal statements, i.e., the third part of the first staement.

Some doubt the usefulness of this ornament. I know that it is more decorative than useful. I generally do not use it even if it presents itself, because it dulls the mind of the listener by making an unsolvable labyrinth, unless the listener is very subtle. It can be effected simply without authority, as I said when discussing the Congruence of Correspondence, and then less confusion of mind will result.

## Chapter XLV

There follows the thirteenth ornament, which is called Convolution; it adds something over and above Correspondence, because in Correspondence determined parts correspond to determined parts, as the first part of the first principal statement to the first part of the second principal statement and to the first part of the third principal statement. Again, the second parts correspond to each other and to the third part of the third principal statement. In this ornament, however, any part corresponds to every other part, so that the first part of the first principal statement corresponds to every part of the second and all parts of the third. In the same way, the second part of the first principal statement corresponds to all the above-mentioned parts, and again the third part of the first principal statement or member, which is the same, corresponds to each of the same parts. It is called Convolution, because there is not a determined application of one part to one part only, but an application of single parts to single parts and of all parts to all parts at the same time.

On account of its prolixity, especially when the theme consists of three statements, no one can easily and explicitly use this ornament unless he omits something. It can be used more easily when the theme consists of two statements, and most easily when it consists of one. In order the better to see this, an example is given of one statement.

Let the theme be as used above in Chapter 33: *Understand.* Having made the division which is there, the development can be as follows. He was, I say, transformed triply through the preaching of truth in the divine intellect which is three in persons, as if the Lord had preached the same about him through Isaias: *Behold my servant shall understand, he shall be exalted, and extolled, and shall be exceeding high.* Behold he posits three proclamations which accompany intelligence, elevation, exaltation, sublimation, so that they may be joined thus: Behold he will understand and will be elevated, he will understand and will be exalted, he will understand and will be sublimated. Nor should one use a diversity of words unless to signify the different grades of good.

St. Peter was elevated by resisting [*repugnans*] the artificial life of the heretics with the sincerity of holy living; he was exalted by attacking [*impugnans*] wisely the falsehood of errors and stupidity; but he was sublimated by conquering [*expugnans*] powerfully the deeds of faithless and manifest malice. Hence we sing of him: A fervent preacher, a zealot for the Faith; this the first. He traveled about an undaunted damner of heresies; this the second. Always a stern conqueror of vices; this the third.

Of him St. Augustine [21] says beautifully: *The things pertaining to the Catholic Faith, since they are stirred by the clever distur-*

21. *City of God* (L.b zvi cap I).

bance of the heretics, and that then can be a defense against them, are considered by the intelligent, are understood more clearly, and preached more earnestly. Therefore, he was elevated resisting the falsehoods of the heretics with the sincerity of a good life, and through this he is transformed into the Holy Spirit who flees the falsehood of teaching. For thus does the Lord, Jer. 51:16, *lift up the clouds from the ends of the earth*, i.e. the soul of the just man which was light and mobile as a cloud through obedience, moist through devotion, elevated through contemplation from this miserable and terrestrial life. *Understand these things, you that forget God*, you who, given to the earthly, seize [*rapitis*] foreign things, *lest he snatch* [*rapiat*] *you away* who snatches [*rapit*] the devil, and *there be none to deliver* [*eripiat*] *you*.

There follows: and he will be exalted by wisely attacking the errors of the unwise. And in this he is similar to the Son who is the wisdom of the Father. For thus *did wisdom exalt his head*. Ecclus. 11:1. For an example of this: Understand, *ye senseless among the people*.

Thirdly, there follows: And he will be sublime, conquering the evils of the faithless. And in this he is in a way compared to the Father, to whom is appropriated power. Of him Isa. 57:15 has: the Lord (is) *High and Eminent (that) inhabits eternity*, to which sublime men will go. But alas! Man does not know when he can attain that honor. Not so this saint, for he inhabits eternity with Him, first, eminent with the Spirit; secondly, exalted with the Son; thirdly, sublime with the Father.

All of the preceding pertains to the first principal member. And now, if it can occur, would be made the artistic transition to the second. In this case, however, it can be done no better than by insinuation, through which is understood that a transition is being made by saying: *I now go to the second;* or *now, the transition* and immediately is added: Secondly, he was made equal in intelligence to an angel through the purity of his life, because virginity, according to Jerome is known to the angels. Hence of him we sing that *his mind was angelic*. For he understands what Prov. 14:8 says: *the wisdom of a discreet man is to know his way. A wise man declines from evil*, Prov. 14:16, and *a wise servant is acceptable to the king*. Prov. 14:35.

And here is closely joined the triple hierarchic act of the angelic intellect. The hierarchic acts, according to Dionysius, are purgation, illumination, perfection or consummation. But in St. Peter there was the purgative act while, grace intervening, he preserved himself from the filth of all mortal concupiscence. Therefore it is said in the authority: *the wise man declines from evil.* But now, *who is wise, and will keep these things; and will understand the mercies of the Lord?*

Secondly, there was in him the illuminative act while he brightly adorned himself with the purity of virginal decency, because as the wise man he knew his way. Concerning the way as if by comparison (?) [22] the wise man says: *who is the man that can understand his own way?* Alas! *They have not known nor understood;* because *they walk on in darkness* of concupiscence.

Thirdly, there was in him the perfective act while he consummated his life with the firmness of final perseverance. And therefore *as a wise servant was acceptable to the king,* as if the Lord had promised him, in the Ps., *Understand: I will give thee understanding,* by 1. purging the appearance of your mind; *and I will instruct thee,* by 2. illuminating its love; *and I will fix my eyes upon thee,* by 3. leading it to perfection through martyrdom.

I now pass over to the last, by which he was uniquely exalted beyond human intellect through sustaining death. And he would well say with St. Bernard in one of his sermons: [23] *Above all my enemies you have made me prudent,* and this is pleasing; *above all my teachers I have learned,* and this is more pleasing; *above the elders I have been wise,* and this is most pleasing. But why? *Is it because you have dressed me in purple and linen?* Or, because I have abounded with more magnificent meals? Or because I have known the subtleties of Plato, the cleverness of Aristotle; or that I have labored to be wise? Forbid! But because I have sought out your testimonies. These testimonies St. Peter sought until his death, held to his whole life, and attained with death itself. Thus then is fulfilled in him the saying of the wise man, Prov. 17:8: *The expectation of him that expecteth is a most acceptable jewel: withersoever he turneth himself, he understandeth wisely.* And this author-

22. MS. reads codo[do].
23. Migne, *P.L.* 183:332.

ity, since he was prudent, comprehends three parts of the human intellect, which according to Tullius,[24] are memory, intelligence, and prudence. Memory, he says, is that through which the soul recalls the things that were; intelligence, through which it sees the things that are; and prudence, through which voluntarily it is aware of the things that will be.

Therefore, St. Peter is well called a most pleasing gem, because wherever he turned himself, he prudently understood the past, present, and future things. He was a pleasing gem remembering the fragility of his origin. But the fool will not understand these things, because sinners arose as grass. He was a gem more pleasing than the rest, because he understood the brevity of the present life. Concerning it there is verified the saying, 1 Cor. 2:14: *The sensual man perceiveth not.* He was a most pleasing gem, because he foresaw the severity of future judgment of which severity of judgment, and the fear of those to be judged, he was able to say with the Psalmist: *I will understand concerning their last ends.*

And now certainly it will appear evident how all things correspond to all, each to each, all to each, and each to all, because having a deiform intellect, and through purity of life conformed with the Holy Spirit, he is sufficiently disposed according to the triple hierarchic act of the angelic intellect, to understand all things, present, past, future, which the prudence of the human intellect requires, having been purged, illumined, and perfected—indeed purging, illuminating and perfecting. In the same way he was conformed with the intelligence of the Son and the power of the Father.

Still, as it seems to me, it is not fit to express these things, but easily and lightly to insinuate a correspondence by saying in addition, after stating the last authority which was *I will understand,* etc.: And these three correspond to the preceding ternaries. As can be elicited from Augustine, *De Trinitate,* and Dionysius, *De Angelica Hierarchia,* these ternaries correspond most appropriately among themselves, namely, the Holy Spirit, the purgative act, and the will or prudence. Again, the Son, the illuminative act and intelligence; the Father, the perfective act and memory. Just as each person is in

24. Marcus Tullius Cicero. *De inventione.* Ed. & trans. H M. Hubbell. (Cambridge, Mass.: Loeb Classical Library, 1949), II.53.160.

the other by circumincession, namely the Father in the Son, both in the Holy Spirit, and the Holy Spirit in each of them and at the same time in both, and just as no hierarchical act is perfected to the exclusion of another, so the human intellect is not prudent which needs the comprehension of the difference of time. And thus according to necessity all are interlaced, so that all and each correspond to each and all and thus interlaced enclose each other.

Yet some do not express as much as has been stated, but more simply say: And all of these things and each correspond to all and each, which to express more diffusely would be a sign of too much prolixity and vanity. To do this pleases me more.

Other third groups, most vain, add a confirmation of the parts of the interlacing with authorities of Scripture. But, as I believe, this can happen for some parts, never for all. Therefore, there would be error in such Convolution. Therefore, I counsel that no one use this method, because it is simply useless, and in the whole, as I think, impossible.

## Chapter XLVI

The procedure set forth in Chapter XIV now demands a treatment of the fourteenth ornament, which is called Unification. Unification is a period or *clausula* which contains in a unit what has been said separately in the development. This is formed sometimes according to both substance and verbal expression with respect to the whole, sometimes in accordance with substance with respect to the whole and verbally with respect to the part. It cannot be formed in other ways except incorrectly.

An example of the first type is the following. After a Convolution is formed (if it must be formed), or if a Convolution is not formed after Circuitous Development, and further, if not after it then after the Correspondence, some authority should be given which verbally contains all the statements treated in the sermon. Then, whether it be about these statements or those added in the authority, there can be educed the execution used before. For example, because in fewer things the way is greater, Unification can be mentioned thus in the theme immediately before. After saying:

thus interlaced enclose each other, unification is added thus: thus for all the aforesaid the saint fulfilled that desire: *O that they would be wise and would understand, and would provide for their last end.* For he understood the things that are with God, in as far as the first principal part is concerned; he knew the things of purity that are with the angels, as far as the second principal is concerned; he foresaw the last things which are the means of humility with men, as far as the third principal is concerned.

A Unification of this sort is sufficient. Some, however, develop the Unification rather diffusely, adding thus: He knew the power of the Father, understood the wisdom of the Son, and finally provided the clemency of the Holy Spirit, concerning the parts of the first principal part. Likewise he knew being clean of whatever filth, he understood being illumined with the honesty of knowledge, concerning the parts of the second principal part. He knew the fragility of human origin, understood the brevity of the present life, finally he foresaw the last things, namely, the severity of future judgment. And so concerning the rest.

An example of the second is when there is no verbal Unification according to the whole, although there may be sentential Unification, as in the preceding theme: *The just man from distress*, etc. There can be unison by a saying from Proverbs 11:4: *Justice shall deliver from death*, because the words *just* and *justice* there is enough literal or verbal concordance, as well as between *delivered* and *will deliver*. But between the two *from distress* and *from death* there is a real concordance, i.e. sufficient for the purpose. Or more acceptable for the purpose could be Psalms 33:20: *Many are the afflictions of the just; but out of them all will the Lord deliver them*, because the real agreement between affliction and distress is greater than between death and distress.

One must also be aware that some use this ornament partially in some places, although considering the whole it cannot occur except in this place, because in the development of the principal parts, when they divide and also when they subdivide, they always bring forth a third authority expressing itself, i.e. the purpose for which it is brought forth, and including the two preceding ones. An example of this was shown above in Chapter XXIV.

CHAPTER XLVII

Finally, no matter how a theme is divided or used, and no matter how the development is carried out, a Conclusion must follow. Conclusion is a prayer ending the sermon and directing the mind to God as towards an end. This is effected in three ways. Sometimes by way of praise, as when the last authority contains something which appertains to the divine excellence or goodness, as follows: *many are the tribulations of the just, and from all of them the Lord will deliver them*. The Conclusion may be formed as follows: to whom may there be honor and glory, etc. Sometimes by way of dispraise, as when the last part of the last authority concerns some horrible evil whether of sin or punishment, as if, for example, the last authority of the Unification should be: *justice will deliver from death*, and this should be interpreted either as the death of mortal sin or as the death of eternal damnation. Then by way of dispraise the Conclusion would be: from that death may God, who alone can do so, deliver us, lest we fall into so great and endless an evil. Amen.

Sometimes a Conclusion is formed by a desire for completeness, which can be effected in three ways. Sometimes a Conclusion can occur anywhere in the sermon, whatever be the statement of any authority; for example, if it touched on vice or punishment: May God grant us so to avoid or beware of these vices that we can finally come to Him; or if a cardinal or theological virtue is touched upon: May God grant us to approach this good and hold it, that, etc. The preacher should always have this method ready so that he can use it at his pleasure.

Over and above this, some add that the Conclusion depends on the last authority as a whole, or in such a way that it verbally contains the statement of the theme concerning which the last authority was adduced, or at least some other statement of the theme, for example in the former theme: *Understand* after the unison made by the authority: *O that they would be wise and would understand*, etc. the conclusion could be: Of these Bernard says well in one of his letters: [25] *O would that you knew, and understood, and foresaw the last things; knew the things of God, understood the things of*

25. Migne, *P.L.* 182:498.

the world, foresaw the things of hell. *Then you would abhor the infernal, strive for the supernal, and contemn the things at hand.* Thus Bernard: this wisdom, this understanding, this foresight may God deign to grant us, that, as the Apostle wishes: *you may be filled with the knowledge of His will, in all wisdom and understanding.* Amen.

An example of the second. Positing the theme as before: *The just man from distress,* etc. because the development finally will be about delivering an artistic conclusion and could be brought about through an authority in which there would be nothing about any statements of the theme except deliverance alone, such as is the saying of the Apostle: *Being made free from sin, and become servants to God, you have your fruit,* which may He grant us, etc. Amen.

An example of the third would be if the conclusion occurred through this authority: *The just man is taken away from before the face of evil, [that] peace come to him and [that] he rest in his bed, namely of eternal security and delight, to which,* etc.

A third very tasteful group makes the whole theme a Conclusion collecting together certain preceding things, and beautifully stated, as if one should conclude: (Isa. 57), *the just man is taken away from before the face of evil that peace may come to him and that he may rest in his bed. That peace may come to him,* that is, wonderful tranquillity, *that he may rest* quietly in delightful pleasantness, *in his bed* of endless eternity, where there is nothing lacking to those who fear God, where may He lead us, by His prayer who is there at the head of all the just, where every *just man is delivered from distress.* Amen.

This ornament is very reasonable and artistic, because, according to the Philosopher, art imitates nature as much as it can. But nature, insofar as it seems (through violence and human industry) to depart from the principles naturally within it, always returns to them as much as it can. It is as with a lion. No matter how tame he is, if his mouth be whetted with blood, he immediately returns to his natural savagery, and forgetting his tameness, does not spare even his own trainer—indeed kills him first.

Likewise it is as with a bird. No matter how delicately it is handled in its cage, if taken to a forest with the window of the cage open, it forgets its former training and flees into the forest as to its natural habitat. And the bough of a tree, bent to the ground by force, if the force is withdrawn, raises its height to the sky, swiftly returning to the natural principles. Therefore, just as the animate vegetative soul and the animate sensitive soul return to their natural principles, so man, animated by a vegetative, sensitive, and intellective soul, using the art which imitates as far as possible, ought to return at the end to the beginning of an artistic process. Hence Boethius in *Consolations* [26] after the three forementioned examples, thus concludes universally: *all seek their own retreats and no one has a traditional order except that each join beginning to end and make a stable world of its own.* These words in Boethius.

Hence even the tones of a chant end in the last verse in the same way as they end in the first, as is the case with the notes of the sequence, *Laetabundus.* So here, because the beginning was made with a prayer, the end likewise ought to be made with a prayer or something convertible into a prayer, such as praise of God or detestation of evil. Therefore it is evident that their procedure is not artistic who do not use any of the above-mentioned methods in forming a Conclusion.

However, the more the end is like the beginning, so much the more subtly and elegantly does it end. As we see, they who end with a prayer make a more subtle finish than those who do so by praise or detestation. They make a most elegant finish who have the same end and beginning—for His praise who is the self-same, the alpha and omega, the beginning and the end, to Him honor and glory forever. Amen.

## Chapter XLVIII

It seems to me that almost all the procedures can be understood from the preceding, whether the theme be comprised of one statement or of more, or whether the division be into two parts or more. There are various methods and procedures of preaching other than those which have already been mentioned: some of these I shall touch upon briefly, because cursorily.

Sometimes the theme consists of one statement. Then the first,

26. Boethius, *Cons.* 3.

indeed the whole division is made in the beginning, be it into two, three, or more, up to twelve parts inclusively. For example, let the theme be: *have faith*. It is good to have faith. Therefore *have faith*. It is good to have faith for three reasons or for four or for twelve.

Sometimes the theme consists of two statements and the division of the theme is into two parts only. The procedure is such that the subdivision is made in the second statement into two, three, or four parts but not more; or it is made in both statements so that in one there are two or three parts and likewise in the other. For example: *walk ye in love*. The Apostle does two things; he motivates us to progress: *walk ye;* he shows the right path: *in love*. One must walk in two ways; on a threefold path; or there are four things that motivate one to walk. Concerning the second, love: one must walk in love because love has its wings that raise man; or because it includes a triple condition of good: the delightful, useful, and honest; or one must walk in love which ought to be exercised or adhered to in four ways.

This method, with something added, is quite artistic if subdivision is effected after the first division thus: one must walk in love for a fourfold reason. Then in each case the meaning of walking is really indicated and the authorities which are adduced for this subdivision contain both verbally, *to walk* and *love*. As I have said, it is made formal if after the first division into two, it is subdivided into two, as follows: one must walk for a twofold reason in a twofold love.

Sometimes the division of the theme is into three parts, and the execution of each into three parts is carried out without any connection, or correspondence, or any of the aforementioned ornaments. Sometimes, although the first division is into three parts, in the subdivision some statement among those which were divided is taken up and then subdivided into four—and sometimes more—parts, even to a total of seven.

Sometimes the division of the theme is into four parts, which occurs in two ways. At times the first division of the theme is into two parts and then each of these is immediately divided into two parts, and the subdivision indifferently into two, three, or four; for example, *Be ye merciful, as your Father also is merciful*. He exhorts to an act of piety: *Be ye merciful*, and shows an efficacious example: *as your Father*, etc. First, in the noun *mercy* is proposed piety itself, and second in the verb *Be ye* is suggested its stability. In the second part however, is shown God's nearness to us: *as your Father*, etc., and the depth of his love: *is merciful*. Then the subdivision according to the parts must equally be made thus: *He is merciful* in two, or three, or four ways, etc. And in those ways *be ye merciful* so many ways.

At other times the first division is immediately into four parts, and the subdivision is such that any of these is divided into two, three, or four parts at most. It is better to subdivide into two or three parts, as when the theme is on the Trinity: . . . *God sent his mercy and his truth.* Four things are noted here: the power of the Father to be venerated—*God;* the wisdom of the Son to be feared—*truth;* the clemency of the Holy Ghost to be embraced—*mercy;* and the one essence in the three to be believed; *He sent* and *His.* The power of the Father is to be venerated for a twofold or threefold reason given in the Canticle of Moses: *Give ye*, he says, *magnificence to our God.* There follows: *is not He thy Father?* So also for the rest.

Sometimes the division is into five parts and the subdivision into five, as if the theme were from the Passion, Matt. 27:50: *Jesus again crying with a loud voice, yielded up the spirit.* Here are noted the utility of the Passion: *Jesus;* the power of the sufferer: *crying;* the truth of His humanity: *with a loud voice;* the freedom of His suffering: *yielded up;* the pain of separation: *the spirit.* Then it is subdivided thus: There are five vowels, A,E,I,O,U, which make up every word. Thus the five wounds of Christ make every sound whether of sorrow or joy. See in the hands the A and E: (Attraxi) *I have drawn thee, taking pity on thee*, and (Ecce) *Behold, I have graven thee in my hands;* in the side the I: such a sign the wound of the lance imprinted, that is *the door of the Ark* which *in the side,* and (Infer) *Put in thy finger hither . . . and put into my side, and be not faithless*, etc.; in the feet the O and U: (Omnia) *God put all things under His feet.* Therefore as you proceed you may state in deed: (Vestigia) *my foot has followed His steps.*

Sometimes the division is into six parts and the subdivision, likewise, into six, as if the theme were of St. John the Baptist: *I am the voice of one crying in the desert, prepare ye the way of the Lord.* In these words six things are noted: the honor of preceding: *I am the voice;* the fervor of teaching: *one of crying;* the austerity of living: *in the desert;* the excitement of meeting: *prepare ye;* the direction of proceding: *the way;* the reason for doing these things: because *of the Lord.* Concerning these things one must know that this voice cried with six notes which are contained in the first verse of his hymn: ut, re, mi, fa, sol, la;

*ut* queant laxis
*re*sonare fibris
*mi*ra gestorum
*fa*muli tuorum
*sol*ve polluti
*la*bii reatum.

For those six notes he sang, ut: (ut) walk as sons of light; re: (revertere) *return, return, O Sunamitess, that we may behold thee;* mi: (miserere) *Have pity on thy own soul, pleasing God;* fa: (facite) *Bring forth fruits worthy of penance;* sol: (solve) loose *the bonds from off thy neck, O, captive daughter of Sion;* la: (lavamini) wash yourselves, be clean, etc.

Sometimes the entire division is only into six parts, as in the sermon of St. Bernard on the six water jars. Sometimes the division is into two parts, both of which are divided into three so that there are six. At other times the total division is seven, as in the sermon of St. Bernard on the seven mercies of God; at other times into eight, as is seen in the Lord's sermon on the mount. Sometimes immediately into nine, as on the angels: *every stone is thy covering,* etc., when nine stones are compared to the nine orders of angels.

The dividing of a theme into three parts and each of these into three comes to almost the same thing, so that all nine correspond to the statements of the theme . . . as on brother Nicholas Gorham: *Let us cast off the works of darkness, and put on the armour of light, as in the day, let us walk honestly;* the Apostle exhorts us to delightful good in the rejection of evil: *Let us cast off the works of darkness;* to useful good in good work: *and put on the armour of light;* to honored good in honored way of life: *as in the day,* etc. However, he exhorts to reject evil indignantly: *Let us cast off;* totally: *the works;* not only work (wisely): *of darkness.* For the second, *let us put on,* lest we be embarrassed in the public view; *the armour,* lest we be unarmed in battle; *of light,* lest we be blind in danger. For the third he puts an example: *as in the day;* the manner: *honestly;* procedure: *let us walk.* But this way does not please me.

Sometimes the entire division is into ten parts, as when the theme is: *ten were made clean;* or: *if you wish to enter life keep the commandments,* and then immediately comes a sermon on the ten commandments of the Decalogue. There is never, or rarely, a total division, nor even a subdivision, into eleven parts. A division into twelve parts can, as I have said, be made in many ways. Either the first and whole division is into twelve parts, as in the theme: *there are twelve hours of the day,* or there is a division into three parts and each is subdivided into four, making twelve. A first division into more than twelve parts must by no means ever be made.

Sometimes, however, the division is into three parts and each of these is subdivided so that the first is divided into three, the second into two, and the third is not divided, thus making nine. Sometimes the third part is likewise subdivided into two, thus making eleven. Sometimes the subdivision is into four parts, sometimes five, sometimes six, sometimes seven, but not more.

As an example, let the theme concern Magdalen . . . *the stones softened by heat turn to brass.* The triple status of Magdalen is here indicated: the state of perversion, the state of conversion, and the state of perfection. The first state, that of sin, is signified by the stone for a sevenfold reason, because of its seven properties comparable to the seven mortal sins. For a stone is inflexible and thus proud; hard, thus avaricious; fragile, thus luxurious; dry, thus irascible; cold, thus gluttonous; insipid, thus a sinner through envy; weighty, thus a sinner through sloth.

The second state, that of grace, is signified in the softening with heat. When something is turned to something else by conversion it is under opposite qualities. Hence Magdalen, who in her former state was a stone by virtue of the inflexibility of her pride, now softened with heat becomes flexible through her humility, she who was hard through avarice, is turned into a softer generosity. And so for the rest.

The state of perfection or perseverance is signified in that she is likened to brass, whose properties are likewise seven. Brass is shiny, resonant, solid, etc. And thus the division and subdivision in all add up to twenty-four.

This method of preaching provides that one can have invectives against vices at hand whenever he wishes. This can be effected skillfully enough if the state of sin is posited in three things: in riches, which pride and sloth accompany; in vices, which anger and envy accompany; in delights, which consist of gluttony and luxury. The opposite of these are humility, charity, and austerity.

<h2 style="text-align:center">Chapter XLIX</h2>

Of the above-mentioned methods of preaching there remain two other methods, which must be set apart by themselves because they are extraordinary. The first of these is very useful and effective and understandable to the ordinary people in any vulgar idiom. The second is very acceptable in Latin to the very intelligent.

The first method belongs in part to the Parisian method and in part to that of Gregory. This method is one by which they immediately choose three materials which they consider very useful and fitting for their listeners. They divide the theme into these three and prove (1) the first by something evident in nature or art or in both, adducing for their proposition an authority of the Bible which contains an example, actually and verbally a statement from which the first material was chosen. (2) They demonstrate this same thing by some figure of the Old Testament, or at least the Bible. (3) They demonstrate the same by some authentic narrative. This they do with the second material and afterwards with the third so that the whole form of the sermon will consist of three beautiful examples, three figures, and three narratives.

It seems superfluous to me, and incorrect, to handle more than three figures in one sermon, although more can be briefly touched upon, and likewise more adduced than three narratives. And I speak of such narratives one of which contains so much of the literal as does the Psalm.

An example of these. Perhaps I know that the listeners to whom I preach are stained especially with these three vices, pride, cupidity, and luxury; and that perhaps it is the first Sunday of Advent, or Palm Sunday. The theme could be: *Your king comes,* and the development thus: Especially three evils, as John says in his Canon, reign in the world, i.e., in worldly men, namely, pride, concupiscence of the eyes, i.e. avarice, and concupiscence of the flesh, i.e. luxury. Against these, Christ, against whom the world had nothing, is proposed to us in the foresaid words as an example against pride. He is described as preserver of humility against pride, because he is *king* (rex) which comes from *ruling* (regendo). Now no one is better ruled by any virtue than by humility through which a king is seen to differ from a tyrant. This is evident from examples in nature, in figure, in history.

You see in nature that a branch of a tree can grow so high above the other branches that, with a gust of wind, it cannot control itself to stand upright, but is tossed hither and thither and sometimes breaks.

A like example in art is some pinnacle built too high, especially if the base or column supporting it is too slender or weak. Thus anyone who is elevated more than he ought above others, bending to every temptation, finally, with everybody watching, he falls, is broken, and confounded, etc. For the devil himself, upon whom his followers depend, could not sustain and rule with such pride without falling most vilely, damned for his eternity from that happiness which he could have had through humility. And those proud ones go the same way, of whom John speaks in the Apoc. 9:10–11: *And they had over them a king of the bottomless pit, whose name is Exterminans*, i.e. one placing (himself) outside of the due limits of nature and grace. He is the king over all the sons of pride. And the wise man says the same thing, Prov. 20:28, that *mercy and truth preserve the king*, i.e., the words of mercy, *and his throne is strengthened by clemency*. Note the sentence about clemency.

The same thing is evident through the figure (Judges 9:7–15) that the trees wished as king the olive, fig, and vine, which have rather laudable qualities of a king: the olive peace, the fig sweetness, the vine consolation or joy; all of which the humble man holds to and the proud man dissipates. And because the trees, these having refused, made the bramble as king to rule over them, forth from the bramble, spiny, stinging, and generating of itself the fire of pride, envy, and other evils, fire therefore came and destroyed itself and the electors. Thus when some man, who is as a ruined tree having the qualities of such a bramble, is elevated above the others, because he is weak in truth, and the column or foundation on which he depends, namely life or riches, is fragile and perishable, with the coming of a slight breeze he falls, the fire of his iniquity consuming him and others.

The same is proven by that famous and wonderful story of Daniel in the whole of Chapter 4.

And here note diligently that an example is brought forth about the same thing, and there is confirmation by a figure, as is evident, because the example is about a tree, the figure about how trees made themselves a king, the history about how Nabuchodonosor saw himself about to be humiliated under the parable of a tree about to be cut down.

Christ is proposed as communicating his goodness against the avaricious, because one avaricious of anything is always selfish. *All,* says the Apostle, Phil. 2:21, *seek the things that are their own.* Nor is there anything which seems to bring on so many evils, so many dangers to human affairs as these two pronouns, "mine" and "yours", as Seneca says. Because you try to make yours what ought not to be yours but common, from this come greed, envy, quarrels, fights, wars, death, finally hell. And these are proved in the same way as before.

Against the luxurious, Christ is proposed as lover of purity through his advent. Therefore he comes being born of a Virgin, He himself always preserving virginity. But alas! now it can be said with sorrow: *the light is come into the world, and men loved darkness rather than the light.* For you see in nature that without light nothing beautiful is seen, etc., in the way as before.

I must here explain that another story than one from the Bible may be used, for example, some narrative from Augustine, Gregory, or another author, or from Helinandus, Valerius, Seneca, or Macrobius. In this method a tale from Augustine is more acceptable than a story from the Bible, provided it is novel and unusual. One from Helinandus, or from an author rarely considered, is more acceptable than one from Augustine or Ambrose. The reason for this is nothing else but the vain curiosity of men.

## Chapter L

Now we must discuss the second method, which I have already touched upon, the method which is considered elegant. It is not to be used before any but the most intelligent people. The method is such that in the whole sermon not even one authority is brought forth unless it be the theme at the beginning. No division is made and yet many sufficient divisions are virtually included, and the whole sermon is sprinkled with authorities. This type of sermon is very artistic. For example, let the theme be from the Nativity of the Lord: "*Let us see this word.* (Luke 2). The Word of God once heard illuminates the affections as a lamp for the feet and a light for the way, so that *we see* the light in His light; retained, it eliminates errors powerfully as with a sword, so that *let us see* how we may walk more cautiously; preserved, it leads us, a personal companion, that *we may see* the face of the King. Therefore, let us go together to see about this word: *let us see this Word.*

"I, who am about to release my nets in this Word, who seeing my property and who, therefore, ought to speak with supplication, beg each of you to speak for me before the King as each will deem most fit, so that He may speak today to his servant in such a way that *we may see this Word* more fittingly on this feast of His glorious birth.

"Our envious enemy, seeing in our first parents the innocence from which he had fallen, never to be uplifted, offered the woman the fruit of the forbidden tree. Seeing that it was good to eat and beautiful to the sight, she ate of it and gave it to her husband, less with the creditable word of God and too much with the words of a wife. And both of them, wanting to excel in knowledge supreme, presumed the forbidden. Thus the evil one poured the noxious poison of blindness into the woman and the man at the same time. The holy and powerful God, however, even in the very beginning of the world, foreshadowed the prepared remedies by telling the serpent that a future progeny of the woman would crush his head, a prophecy He faithfully fulfilled through the mystery and ministry of the Word Incarnate. Therefore, while we recognize God made visible, let us be drawn by Him to the love of the invisible. For this reason He wisely ordained that we *see this Word.*

"Let us consider, therefore, the fullness of divine mercy by which it was fitting that He should deny to no nature that of which it was capable from the very beginning. Hence, since our nature was so blinded (yet it would be illuminable), He brought it about again for us, as was fitting, that with the return of the original light, we *may see,* etc. This comes first, that anyone might say of himself, *once I was blind, now I see.*

"Secondly, let us consider the steadfastness of divine justice, by whose law it is established that sin be never forgiven without due satisfaction. Therefore, it was fitting that He clothe with human nature Him who could fully satisfy, a thing no pure man could do. And therefore the hand of God did this, which is second: *let us see,* it says, *this.*

"Thirdly, let us consider the due order of divine wisdom, which had to find the most convenient manner of reparation. The most convenient manner, however, is that nature be restored entirely. But if He had restored man by an angel, man would have been always in debt to an angel for his salvation and thus could not be equal to him in happiness. He would have obtained this equality by innocence had he not sinned. This equality man attains even now by grace so that he is as the angels of God in heaven. Therefore He Himself alone restored us who is the wisdom of the Father and the *Word,* which is the third. On account of this *the Word was made flesh.* Therefore, *let us see this word.*

"First let us see, while marveling at this most powerful Word preparing a mother, the resting place of the whole Trinity, that in respect to His Father equality is in some way bestowed, since He Himself is the Father and she the Mother; in respect to Himself, i.e., the Son, she is preferred, since He Himself is the Son, she the Mother; *and He,* says the Scripture, *was subject to them;* in respect to the Holy Ghost the whole immensity is included by whose action she conceived Him Who in heaven has no mother and on earth no father, that thus we might see sitting upon a high throne the venerable Trinity of Whose majesty this earth is full and who liberally gave her fruit, a virgin and at the same time the glorious begetter from whom was born the holy and equally eternal, *for this was in the beginning with God, and in the beginning was the Word.*

"Secondly, let us see while we praise this most pure Word pre-electing the Virgin in whom He humiliated the marks of Deity and who covered God, nursing at her breasts, with the meanness of poor swaddling clothes and by whom infinite Majesty is enclosed in the narrow confines of a rough manger. The Creator of all is born of a mother; virginal dignity is not lost that was typified in the burning bush. If this is above us, let us go up with Moses and see with him. Rightly does one ask: Whence is it that the Word Who remains in heaven, made temporal in my misery, breaks through the heavens and descends for me?

"Third, let us see, while we rejoice, this most holy Word restoring us from ruin by giving us the benefits of salvation, through which light arises for depressed darkness, by whose rising our death dies, the fall of Eve is restored, that thus we, whom He led from this snare according to his word, making goodness for his servants, may see and rejoice. Hinting at this the Scriptures foresee: *tomorrow the Lord will make this word*, for the second and last, *and in the morning you will see his glory* for the first.

"Therefore, my dear people, let us be prepared for the morrow as if we were going to die tomorrow; indeed, for the day which will have no tomorrow, let us turn our entire endeavors to *see this word* and not that we be seen by men whom love or hate have blinded that they see not. Indeed, let us see to it that this be not a scruple for our conscience, if we prefer the word of vanity of a lying man who is all vanity to the word of truth that can not be surpassed. Let us not thus seek such a reward for our labor but so that as a king in his beauty and glory we may *see this word* by which the heavens were made firm. May He confirm this Word that will endure in us, that we who joyfully accepted it about to redeem us may fearlessly *see this Word* about to sit in judgment. Amen."

It is clear to one who understands that what is contained in this sermon is so subtle and so hidden that it scarcely can be examined, so that to a large extent art seems to hide art, as though it would be beneficial to stay hidden. Detected art ought to be modest. Hence it happens that the things which give mental delight within to those who understand and observe the cleverly hidden elements of art rather burden than delight the ears of those who pay no attention, and as if with a confused and inordinate noise beget a wearied boredom for those who listen unwillingly. And we must add that just as this method should be used only with the intelligent, so it should be used only by the intelligent, because an orderly arrangement of words does not become a foolish man, and because a foolish man does not accept the words of prudence. From other methods than the two principal ones proposed it is incidentally evident that we can understand not only from the principal methods but also from other incidental ones still other methods, which have not been touched upon.

In addition to the first methods of the five learned men, two methods of preaching have been mentioned, both primarily and incidentally, namely: one, that of the Oxonians, according to which the theme consists of one statement. This is taught in Chapter XXI, which is concerned with the antetheme, and in Chapter XXXVIII, which deals with the development. The second method, likewise Oxonian, is used when the theme consists of two statements which are convertible into three by means of art. This method is taught in Chapters XIX and XLVIII. The third method is also Oxonian, and is used when the theme consists of three statements and the development is by Correspondence, not by Circuitous Development or Convolution; the fourth method also, when the development is by means of all ornaments. These two methods are taught at length in many chapters. The fifth method is the rather ingenious one of the Parisians, and is taught in Chapter XXXV. Sixteen other common methods are taught incidentally in Chapter XLVIII. Finally the twenty-third, which is in part similar to the methods of the Parisians, is taught in Chapter XLIX. The twenty-fourth and last I have just discussed, in the present Chapter, L.

Thus have been dispatched all fifteen ornaments which directly apply to the form or execution of the sermon. The remaining seven ornaments are more extrinsic, but they serve for beauty. Therefore, something, though very briefly, must be said about them.

Coloration occurs in three ways, either in the number of terminations of the statements, which commonly occurs in the division and subdivision of the theme; or in the cadence, which occurs in pauses or at the ends of clauses; or in some rhetorical color, which can occur anywhere. Of these colors it is sufficient to use those which Cicero puts in the last book of the *Rhetorica Secunda*.[27]

Voice Modulation is the seventeenth ornament, and occurs when

27. That is, the Pseudo-Ciceronian *Rhetorica ad Herennium*. Ed. and trans. Harry Caplan. (Cambridge, Mass.: Loeb Classical Library, 1954). Book four of the *ad Herennium*, which was widely circulated in the middle ages as a work of Cicero, discusses 64 "tropes" and "figures" under the heading of Style.

grand things are spoken grandly, or other things in their own manner, according to Augustine, *De Doctrina Christiana*. Some things must be spoken softly, as, for example, those which provoke the hearer especially to love and supplication; some, with a very sharp accent, as, for example, those things which touch upon fear, namely, judgment, death, hell. Sometimes there must be a change from a subdued accent to a very sharp one because this also changes the mind.

Appropriate Gesture is, as Hugh teaches in *De Institutione Novitiorum*,[28] that a speaker speaks with his mouth only, that he does not extend his arms too much like a disputant, that he does not move his head too much like a mad man, that he does not roll his eyes like an actor, and so forth. Although this frequently happens, it is considered faulty, because it is the method of those who have nothing to say readily.

Opportune Humor, according to Cicero, occurs when we add something jocular which will give pleasure when the listeners are bored, whether it be about something which will provoke laughter, or some story or anecdote. This must be used especially when they begin to sleep. When the *Decretum* prohibits the use of stories, it must be understood that unbecoming ones are indicated. Of this kind are stories about the crimes of Jupiter and the like. This ornament must be used sparingly and at most three times within one sermon.

Allusion is when the Scripture is touched on—not adduced—but not in the same way in which it is written. The person or case is changed, as is evident in the antetheme of the sermon, *let us see this word*.

Firm Impression is when this occurs often in many places, or continually. These colors St. Bernard in particular used. Allusion and Firm Impression are used in other ways, but not to add anything to the proposition.

Reflecting on the Subject Matter is the consideration of who, to whom, what, and how much is to be spoken. If one is preaching to citizens and there is included an invective against jousters, neither *what* nor *to whom* ought to be observed. Likewise one must carefully see to it that everything one says seriously ought to be true.

28. Migne, *P.L.* 176:948.

And it ought to be edifying. It is not right to speak about distant planets and to consider like things, or to say such things as provoke offense, as when one would say to rustics: "It is surprising about you rustics that you are proud, since there is nothing in you of which you should be proud."

Likewise if there is only one king listening to the sermon, one should not inveigh too much against kings. So also for the rest. Likewise it seems to me that I can not inveigh against sermons for profit if my sermons are such; this I discussed in Chapter I after the Prologue.

Fifty chapters besides the Prologue have been completed here. And therefore that I add to these a fiftieth of silence henceforth, the Spirit already says that I cease from this labor, to whom be there honor and glory forever. Amen.

### THE FOLLOWING IS AN ADDITION FOUND IN THE FOUR MOST IMPORTANT MSS

In addition to those already mentioned, there are seven other ornaments which, if used, adorn the sermon. One of these is mentioned in Chapter XIV and is called Coloration, which is the sixteenth of the total number of ornaments.

Coloration is used in many senses. In one way Coloration is the name applied to the like termination of statements, which occurs sometimes according to one syllable only, sometimes according to two in two or three particulars, sometimes according to more. And this method, i.e. one of these methods, is necessary in the division of the antetheme, in the division of the theme, in the declaration of the parts, and in subdivision. For example, sometimes there is like termination according to one syllable only; Let the theme be: *The just man shall correct me in mercy*. The prelate is described concerning his state (statum): *the just man;* concerning his act (actum): *shall correct me;* concerning his way (modum): *in mercy*. It is evident that now these three, state (statum), act (actum), way (modum), have like endings only according to one syllable.

If it be subdivided: There is shown concerning him how the prelate ought show (*exhibere*) himself: *The just man;* what act he ought (*exercere*) exercise: *shall correct me;* what way he should hold to (*tenere*): *in mercy;* then there occurs like termination according to two syllables. And so forth by further multiplication.

It is entirely enough, and most fitting to the artistry of which there is now talk, that that multiplication be not beyond three. And even if there are three, it is a mark of artistry. For example, if the division be thus: three things are touched upon: namely the state prudently to be foretasted (*status prudenter praelibandus*), the act fervently to be frequented (*actus ferventer frequentandus*), the way clemently to be moderated (*modus clementer moderandus*).

Now easily enough is seen how this manner of coloration can be multiplied, by saying: there is set forth the state prudently to be foretasted (*praemittitur status prudenter praelibandus*), there is added the act fervently to be exercised (*adjungitur actus ferventer exercendus*), and there is expressed the way clemently to be moderated (*exprimitur modus clementer moderandus*). Now this is coloration in fours. This manner of coloration is present especially according to a likeness founded on quality.

Another method of Coloration is based on quantity. It consists in a definite measuring of syllables. Generally it is called "cadence" because it rolls well orally. It can have a place anywhere in the sermon where there is a simple pause, which is by some called a *punctus flexus*, or where there is a big pause but not a full one, which some call *medius punctus* or *acutus*, or where there is a full pause, that is, the end of a verse.

This cadence, although used generally by the ancients, and in a variety of ways, is not used extensively in these days except in three ways. One cadence is called dactylic, because it contains two dactyls: *lumbardus origine.* The second cadence is dactylic and simple-spondiac: *natione lumbardus.* The third is dactylic and double-spondiac: *certamine glorioso.*

These are the three cadences. At present the Roman Curia does not use any extensively, and thus the first cadence is never or rarely put at the end of a verse. The second is applied in all three places, but most harmoniously in the middle distinction, which is called the *punctus medius* or the middle point of a verse. The third cadence may be placed anywhere, but is most fittingly placed at the end of a verse. Hence the Roman Curia, although it has frequently put the third cadence in the preceding parts of a clause, nevertheless almost always sees to it that with this third cadence the clause ends.

There are other cadences which the above-mentioned Curia and others use, but not so commonly and thus they are not so solemn. The first among these, the fourth cadence, is called spondaic, since it has three or four spondees, for example *sanctificare noluisti*, or *signa innotescunt*. In general, Ambrose uses this cadence very much.

The fifth cadence occurs when a phrase of three syllables or more precedes, of which the penult is short, and then follow three syllables in another statement, or more than one, of which the penult is lengthened; for example: *fidei defensor* or *in divitiis est parcus*. Although Gregory frequently uses this cadence, it is now the rarest of all. When used, it is placed in an incomplete sentence which must be completed by a more common cadence; for example, *manibus compressum et mortuum*. Hence, to avoid a mark of ignorance it is expedient not to use this cadence because it is unknown.

The sixth cadence is the reverse, and contrary of the fifth.

# Appendix:

Excerpts from Two University Textbooks on Dialectic:
Aristotle's *Topics* and *On Sophistical Refutations*

Students of medieval culture often overlook the fact that the universities provided a considerable treatment of linguistic matters in their elementary training for the dialectical *disputatio*. The discussion of "meaning," "definitions," "ambiguity" and related concepts must surely have helped to make the university student rather sensitive to the complexities of word-use. Indeed it was the dialectical probing of grammatical concepts that led directly to medieval "Speculative Grammar" which questioned the whole semantic basis of language and led ultimately to a distrust of meaning itself.

The medieval student was exposed early in his career to two Aristotelian works dealing with methods of disputing. One, the *Topics*, outlines nearly two hundred "topics" (*loci*) from which arguments might be drawn; Book Eight of the *Topics*, moreover, is devoted exclusively to advice about how to dispute in public. The second textbook, *On Sophistical Refutations*, deals with means of identifying and combatting logical fallacies that might appear in a public dispute. Both works discuss at length the problems created by the use of words and word combinations.

Because such university training has an obvious bearing upon the medieval attitudes toward the uses of language, this brief Appendix includes sample sections indicating the nature of these two textbooks.

# Aristotle:
## *Topics (Topica)* [1]

### Book I

Our treatise proposes to find a line of inquiry whereby we shall be able to reason from opinions that are generally accepted about every problem propounded to us, and also shall ourselves, when standing up to an argument, avoid saying anything that will obstruct us. First, then, we must say what reasoning is, and what its varieties are, in order to grasp dialectical reasoning: for this is the object of our search in the treatise before us.

Now reasoning is an argument in which, certain things being laid down, something other than these necessarily comes about through them. (*a*) It is a "demonstration," when the premisses from which the reasoning starts are true and primary, or are such that our knowledge of them has originally come through premisses which are primary and true; (*b*) reasoning, on the other hand is "dialectical," if it reasons from opinions that are generally accepted. Things are "true" and "primary" which are believed on the strength not of anything else but of themselves: for in regard to the first principles of science it is improper to ask any further for the why and wherefore of them; each of the first principles should command belief in and by itself. On the other hand, those opinions are "generally accepted" which are accepted by everyone or by the majority or by the philosophers—i.e. by all, or by the majority, or

1. Selections from Aristotle's *Topics* and *On Sophistical Refutations* are used, with permission, from *The Works of Aristotle Translated into English*, W. D. Ross, ed. (Oxford, 1928–1956), Vol. 1, 1928. The two works are translated by W. A. Pickard-Cambridge.

by the most notable and illustrious of them. Again (*c*), reasoning is "contentious" if it starts from opinions that seem to be generally accepted, but are not really such, or again if it merely seems to reason from opinions that are or seem to be generally accepted. For not every opinion that seems to be generally accepted actually is generally accepted. For in none of the opinions which we call generally accepted is the illusion entirely on the surface, as happens in the case of the principles of contentious arguments; for the nature of the fallacy in these is obvious immediately, and as a rule even to persons with little power of comprehension. So then, of the contentious reasonings mentioned, the former really deserves to be called "contentious reasoning," but not "reasoning," since it appears to reason, but does not really do so.

Further (*d*), besides all the reasonings we have mentioned there are the mis-reasonings that start from the premisses peculiar to the special sciences, as happens (for example) in the case of geometry and her sister sciences. For this form of reasoning appears to differ from the reasonings mentioned above; the man who draws a false figure reasons from things that are neither true and primary, nor yet generally accepted. For he does not fall within the definition; he does not assume opinions that are received either by everyone or by the majority or by philosophers—that is to say, by all, or by most, or by the most illustrious of them—but he conducts his reasoning upon assumptions which, though appropriate to the science in question, are not true; for he effects his mis-reasoning either by describing the semicircles wrongly or by drawing certain lines in a way in which they could not be drawn.

The foregoing must stand for an outline survey of the species of reasoning. In general, in regard both to all that we have already discussed and to those which we shall discuss later, we may remark that that amount of distinction between them may serve, because it is not our purpose to give the exact definition of any of them; we merely want to describe them in outline; we consider it quite enough from the point of view of the line of inquiry before us to be able to recognize each of them in some sort of way.

Next in order after the foregoing, we must say for how many and for what purposes the treatise is useful. They are three—intellectual training, casual encounters, and the philosophical sciences. That it is useful as a training is obvious on the face of it. The possession of a plan of inquiry will enable us more easily to argue about the subject proposed. For purposes of casual encounters, it is useful because when we have counted up the opinions held by most people, we shall meet them on the ground not of other people's convictions but of their own, while we shift the ground of any argument that they appear to us to state unsoundly. For the study of the philosophical sciences it is useful, because the ability to raise searching difficulties on both sides of a subject will make us detect more easily the truth and error about the several points that arise. It has a further use in relation to the ultimate bases of the principles used in the several sciences. For it is impossible to discuss them at all from the principles proper to the particular science in hand, seeing that the principles are the *prius* of everything else: it is through the opinions generally held on the particular points that these have to be discussed, and this task belongs properly, or most appropriately, to dialectic: for dialectic is a process of criticism wherein lies the path to the principles of all inquiries.

We shall be in perfect possession of the way to proceed when we are in a position like that which we occupy in regard to rhetoric and medicine and faculties of that kind: this means the doing of that which we choose with the materials that are available. For it is not every method that the rhetorician will employ to persuade, or the doctor to heal: still, if he omits none of the available means, we shall say that his grasp of the science is adequate.

First, then, we must see of what parts our inquiry consists. Now if we were to grasp (*a*) with reference to how many, and what kind of, things arguments take place, and with what materials they start, and (*b*) how we are to become well supplied with these, we should have sufficiently won our goal. Now the materials with which arguments start are equal in number, and are identical, with the subjects on which reasonings take place. For arguments start with "propositions," while the subjects on which reasonings take place are "problems." Now every proposition and every problem indicates either a genus or a peculiarity or an accident—for the differentia too, applying as it does to a class ( or genus), should be ranked together with the genus. Since, however, of what is peculiar to anything part signifies its essence, while part does not, let us divide the "peculiar" into both the aforesaid parts, and call that part which indicates the essence a "definition," while of the remainder let us adopt the terminology which is generally current about these things, and speak of it as a "property." What we have said, then, makes it clear that according to our present division, the elements turn out to be four, all told, namely either property or definition or genus or accident. Do not let anyone suppose us to mean that each of these enunciated by itself constitutes a proposition or problem, but only that it is from these that both problems and propositions are formed. The difference between a problem and a proposition is a difference in the turn of the phrase. For if it be put in this way, " 'An animal that walks on two feet' is the definition of man, is it not?" or " 'Animal' is the genus of man, is it not?" the result is a proposition; but if thus, "Is 'an animal that walks on two feet' a definition of man or no? [or "Is 'animal' his genus or no?"] the result is a problem. Similarly too in other cases. Naturally, then, problems and propositions are equal in number: for out of every proposition you will make a problem if you change the turn of the phrase.

\*    \*    \*

## Book VIII

Next there fall to be discussed the problems of arrangement and method in putting questions. Anyone who intends to frame questions must, first of all, select the ground from which he should make his attack; secondly, he must frame them and arrange them one by one to himself; thirdly and lastly, he must proceed actually to put them to the other party. Now so far as the selection of his ground is concerned the problem is one alike for the philosopher and the dialectician; but how to go on to arrange his points and frame his questions concerns the dialectician only: for in every problem of that kind, a reference to another party is involved. Not so with the philosopher, and the man who is investigating by himself: the premises of his reasoning, although true and familiar, may be re-

fused by the answerer because they lie too near the original statement and so he foresees what will follow if he grants them: but for
this the philosopher does not care. Nay, he may possibly be even
anxious to secure axioms as familiar and as near to the question in
hand as possible: for these are the bases on which scientific reasonings are built up.

The best way to secure training and practice in arguments of this
kind is in the first place to get into the habit of converting the arguments. For in this way we shall be better equipped for dealing with
the proposition stated, and after a few attempts we shall know several arguments by heart. For by "conversion" of an argument is
meant the taking the reverse of the conclusion together with the
remaining propositions asked and so demolishing one of those that
were conceded: for it follows necessarily that if the conclusion be
untrue, some one of the premisses is demolished, seeing that, given
all the premisses, the conclusion was bound to follow. Always, in
dealing with any proposition, be on the look-out for a line of argument both pro and con: and on discovering it at once set about
looking for the solution of it: for in this way you will soon find
that you have trained yourself at the same time in both asking
questions and answering them. If we cannot find anyone else to
argue with, we should argue with ourselves. Select, moreover, arguments relating to the same thesis and range them side by side: for
this produces a plentiful supply of arguments for carrying a point
by sheer force, and in refutation also it is of great service, whenever one is well stocked with arguments pro and con: for then you
find yourself on your guard against contrary statements to the one
you wish to secure. Moreover, as contributing to knowledge and to
philosophic wisdom the power of discerning and holding in one
view the results of either of two hypotheses is no mean instrument; for it then only remains to make a right choice of one of
them. For a task of this kind a certain natural ability is required:
in fact real natural ability just is the power rightly to choose the
true and shun the false. Men of natural ability can do this; for by a
right liking or disliking for whatever is proposed to them they
rightly select what is best.

It is best to know by heart arguments upon these questions which
are of most frequent occurrence, and particularly in regard to those

propositions which are ultimate: for in discussing these answerers frequently give up in despair. Moreover, get a good stock of definitions: and have those of familiar and primary ideas at your fingers' ends: for it is through these that reasonings are effected. You should try, moreover, to master the heads under which other arguments mostly tend to fall. For just as in geometry it is useful to be practised in the elements, and in arithmetic to have the multiplication table up to ten at one's fingers' ends—and indeed it makes a great difference in one's knowledge of the multiples of other numbers too—likewise also in arguments it is a great advantage to be well up in regard to first principles, and to have a thorough knowledge of premisses at the tip of one's tongue. For just as in a person with a trained memory, a memory of things themselves is immediately caused by the mere mention of their *loci*, so these habits too will make a man readier in reasoning, because he has his premisses classified before his mind's eye, each under its number. It is better to commit to memory a premiss of general application than an argument: for it is difficult to be even moderately ready with a first principle, or hypothesis.

Moreover, you should get into the habit of turning one argument into several, and conceal your procedure as darkly as you can: this kind of effect is best produced by keeping as far as possible away from topics akin to the subject of the argument. This can be done with arguments that are entirely universal, e. g. the statement that "there cannot be one knowledge of more than one thing": for that is the case with both relative terms and contraries and coordinates.

Records of discussions should be made in a universal form, even though one has argued only some particular case: for this will enable one to turn a single rule into several. A like rule applies in Rhetoric as well to enthymemes. For yourself, however, you should as far as possible avoid universalizing your reasonings. You should, moreover, always examine arguments to see whether they rest on principles of general application: for all particular arguments really reason universally, as well, i.e. a particular demonstration always contains a universal demonstration, because it is impossible to reason at all without using universals.

You should display your training in inductive reasoning against a young man, in deductive against an expert. You should try, more-over, to secure from those skilled in deduction their premisses, from inductive reasoners their parallel cases; for this is the thing in which they are respectively trained. In general, too, from your exercises in argumentation you should try to carry away either a syllogism on some subject or a refutation or a proposition or an objection, or whether someone put his question properly or improperly (whether it was yourself or someone else) and the point which made it the one or the other. For this is what gives one ability, and the whole object of training is to acquire ability, especially in regard to propo-sitions and objections. For it is the skilled propounder and objector who is, speaking generally, a dialectician. To formulate a proposi-tion is to form a number of things into one—for the conclusion to which the argument leads must be taken generally, as a single thing—whereas to formulate an objection is to make one thing into many: for the objector either distinguishes or demolishes, partly granting, partly denying the statements proposed.

Do not argue with everyone, nor practise upon the man in the street: for there are some people with whom any argument is bound to degenerate. For against anyone who is ready to try all means in order to seem not to be beaten, it is indeed fair to try all means of bringing about one's conclusion: but it is not good form. Where-fore the best rule is, not lightly to engage with casual acquaintances, or bad argument is sure to result. For you see how in practising to-gether people cannot refrain from contentious argument.

It is best also to have ready-made arguments relating to those questions in which a very small stock will furnish us with argu-ments serviceable on a vary large number of occasions. These are those that are universal, and those in regard to which it is rather difficult to produce points for ourselves from matters of everyday experience. . . .

# Aristotle:
# *On Sophistical Refutations*
# *(De Sophisticis Elenchis)*

Let us now discuss sophistic refutations, i.e. what appear to be refutations but are really fallacies instead. We wll begin in the natural order with the first.

That some reasonings are genuine, while others seem to be so but are not, is evident. This happens with arguments, as also elsewhere, through a certain likeness between the genuine and the sham. For physically some people are in a vigorous condition, while others merely seem to be so by blowing and rigging themselves out as the tribesmen do their victims for sacrifice; and some people are beautiful thanks to their beauty, while others seem to be so, by dint of embellishing themselves. So it is, too, with inanimate things; for of these, too, some are really silver and others gold, while others are not and merely seem to be such to our sense; e.g. things made of litharge and tin seem to be of silver, while those made of yellow metal look golden. In the same way both reasoning and refutation are sometimes genuine, sometimes not, though inexperience may make them appear so: for inexperienced people obtain only, as it were, a distant view of these things. For reasoning rests on certain statements such that they involve necessarily the assertion of something other than what has been stated, through what has been stated: refutation is reasoning involving the contradictory of the given conclusion. Now some of them do not really achieve this, though they seem to do so for a number of reasons; and of these the most prolific and usual domain is the argument that turns upon names only. It is impossible in a discussion to bring in the actual things discussed: we use their names as symbols instead of them; and therefore we suppose that what follows in the names, follows in the things as well, just as people who calculate suppose in regard to their counters. But the two cases (names and things) are not alike. For names are finite and so is the sum-total of formulae, while things are infinite in number. Inevitably, then, the same formulae, and a single name, have a number of meanings. Accordingly just as, in counting, those who are not clever in manipulating their counters are taken in by the experts, in the same way in arguments too those who are not well acquainted with the force of names misreason both in their own discussions and when they listen to others. For this reason, then, and for others to be mentioned later, there exists both reasoning and refutation that is apparent but not real. Now for some people it is better worth while to seem to be wise, than to be wise without seeming to be (for the art of the sophist is the semblance of wisdom without the reality, and the sophist is one who makes money from an apparent but unreal wisdom); for them, then, it is clearly essential also to seem to accomplish the task of a wise man rather than to accomplish it without seeming to do so. To reduce it to a single point of contrast it is the business of one who knows a thing, himself to avoid fallacies in the subjects which he knows and to be able to show up the man who makes them; and of these accomplishments the one depends on the faculty to render an answer, and the other upon the securing of one. Those, then, who would be sophists are bound to study the class of arguments aforesaid: for it is worth their while: for a faculty of this kind will make a man seem to be wise, and this is the purpose they happen to have in view.

Clearly, then, there exists a class of arguments of this kind, and it is at this kind of ability that those aim whom we call sophists. Let us now go on to discuss how many kinds there are of sophistical arguments, and how many in number are the elements of which this faculty is composed, and how many branches there happen to be of this inquiry, and the other factors that contribute to this art.

Of arguments in dialogue form there are four classes: Didactic, Dialectical, Examination-arguments, and Contentious arguments. Didactic arguments are those that reason from the principles appropriate to each subject and not from the opinions held by the answerer (for the learner should take things on trust): dialectical arguments are those that reason from premisses generally accepted, to the contradictory of a given thesis: examination-arguments are those that reason from premisses which are accepted by the answerer and which anyone who pretends to possess knowledge of the subject is bound to know—in what manner, has been defined in another treatise: contentious arguments are those that reason or appear to reason to a conclusion from premisses that appear to be generally accepted but are not so. The subject, then, of demonstrative arguments has been discussed elsewhere: let us now proceed to speak of the arguments used in competitions and contests.

First we must grasp the number of aims entertained by those who argue as competitors and rivals to the death. These are five in number, refutation, fallacy, paradox, solecism, and fifthly to reduce the opponent in the discussion to babbling—i.e. to constrain him to repeat himself a number of times: or it is to produce the appearance of each of these things without the reality. For they choose if possible plainly to refute the other party, or as the second best to show that he is committing some fallacy, or as a third best to lead him into paradox, or fourthly to reduce him to solecism, i.e. to make the answerer, in consequence of the argument, to use an ungrammatical expression; or, as a last resort, to make him repeat himself.

There are two styles of refutation: for some depend on the language used, while some are independent of language. Those ways of producing the false appearance of an argument which depend on language are six in number: they are ambiguity, amphiboly, combination, division of words, accent, form of expression. Of these we may assure ourselves both by induction, and by syllogistic proof based on this—and it may be on other assumptions as well—that this is the number of ways in which we might fail to mean the same thing by the same names or expressions. . . .

# Bibliography

_____

# A Selected Bibliography

## GENERAL WORKS

Abelson, Paul. *The Seven Liberal Arts*. New York, 1906.

Alcuin. *The Rhetoric of Alcuin and Charlemagne*. Ed. and trans. Wilbur S. Howell. Princeton, 1941.

Atkins, John W. *English Literary Criticism: The Medieval Phase*. New York, 1943.

Augustine, Aurelius. *Saint Augustine On Christian Doctrine*. Trans. D. W. Robertson. Library of Liberal Arts No. 80. New York, 1958.

Baldwin, Charles S. *Medieval Rhetoric and Poetic*. New York, 1928.

Cicero, Marcus Tullius. *De Inventione. De optimo genere oratorum. Topica*. Trans. H. M. Hubbell. Loeb Classical Library. Cambridge, Mass., 1949.

"Cicero" (i.e. Pseudo-Cicero). *Rhetorica ad Herennium*. Ed. and Trans. Harry Caplan. Loeb Classical Library. Cambridge, Mass., 1954.

Curtius, Ernst R. *European Literature of the Latin Middle Ages*. Trans. Willard R. Trask. Bollingen Foundation Series No. 36. New York, 1953.

Farrar, Clarissa P., and Austin P. Evans. *Bibliography of English Translations from Medieval sources*. (Columbia University Records of Civilization 39) New York, 1946.

John of Salisbury. *Metalogicon*. Trans. Daniel D. McGarry. Berkeley, 1955.

Manitius, Maxmilianus. *Geschichte der lateinischen Literatur des mittelalters*. 3 vols. Munchen, 1911–1931.

McKeon, Richard. "Rhetoric in the Middle Ages." *Speculum* 17 (1942): 1–32.

Murphy, James J. *Medieval Rhetoric: A Select Bibliography*. Toronto, 1971.

———. "The Medieval Arts of Discourse: An Introductory Bibliography," *Speech Monographs* 29 (1962): 71–78.

———. "Rhetoric in Fourteenth Century Oxford." *Medium Aevum* 34 (1965): 1–20.

Paetow, L. J. *The Arts Course at Mediaeval Universities with Special Reference to Grammar and Rhetoric*. Urbana, Ill., 1910.

Rashdall, Hastings. *Universities of Europe in the Middle Ages*. 3 vols. New ed. Ed. F. M. Powicke and A. B. Emden. Oxford, 1936.

Robins, R. H. *Ancient and Medieval Grammatical Theory in Europe*. London, 1951.

Thurot, M. Charles. *"Notices et extraits de divers manuscrits Latins pour servir à l'histoire des doctrines grammaticales au moyen âge. Notice et Extraits* 22 (1868): 1–540. (Now reprinted.)

## Anonymous of Bologna
### and the Ars Dictaminis

Alberic of Monte Cassino. *Flores rhetorici.* Ed. D. M. Inguanez and E. H. M. Willard. Monte Cassino, 1938.

Denholm-Young, Noel. "The *Cursus in England.*" *Collected Papers on Medieval Subjects.* Oxford, 1946.

Haskins, Charles H. "The early *artes dictandi* in Italy." *Studies in Mediaeval Culture* (Oxford, 1929): 170–192.

———. "Life of Medieval Students as Seen in Their Letters." *Studies in Mediaeval Culture* (Oxford, 1929): 1–35. [Reprinted from *AHR* 3 (1897): 203–229.]

Kantorowicz, Ernst. "An 'Autobiography' of Guido Faba." *Medieval and Renaissance Studies* I (1941): 253–280.

Leclercq, Jean. "Le genre epistolaire au Moyen age." *Revue de moyen age latin* 2 (1946): 63–70.

Poole, Reginald L. *Lectures on the History of the Papal Chancery.* Cambridge, 1915.

Rockinger, Ludwig. *Briefsteller und Formelbücher des eilften bis vierzehnten Jahrhunderts.* (Quellen und Erorterungen zur bayerischen und deutschen Geschichte, neunter Band.) Munich, 1863. (Now reprinted in two volumes.) Contains texts of:
   a. Anonymous. *Rationes dictandi.*
   b. Alberic. *De dictamine.*
   c. Hugo of Bologna. *Rationes dictandi prosaica.*
   d. Henricus Francigena. *Praecepta dictaminis.*
   e. Anonymous. *Ars dictandi aurelianensis.*
   f. Buoncompagno (summary only).
   g. Guido Faba. *Doctrina ad inveniendas incipiendas et formandas.*
   h. Anonymous. *Prosarum dictaminis.*
   i. Ludolf of Hildesheim. *Summa dictaminum.*
   j. Conrad of Mure. *Summa de arte prosandi.*
   k. "Johannes Anglicus." *De Arte prosayca. . . .*
   l. Dominicus Dominici. *Summa dictaminis.*
   m. Bernoldus of Kaiserheim. *Summa dictaminis.*
   n. "John Bondi" (Lawrence of Aquilegia). *Practica sive usus dictaminis.*
   o. Master Simon. *Summa de arte dictandi.*

Schmale, Franz-Joseph. "Die Bologneser Schule der *ars dictandi.*" *Deutsches Archiv für Erforschung des Mittelalters* 13 (1957): 16–34.

*Adalbertus Samaritanus, Praecepta dictaminum.* (Monumenta Germaniae historiae, Geistesgeschichte des Mittelalters). Ed. Franz-Joseph Schmale. Weimar, 1961.

Toynbee, Paget J. "The Bearing of the Cursus on the text of Dante's *De vulgari eloquentia.*" *Proceedings of the British Academy* II (1923): 359–377.

## Geoffrey of Vinsauf
### and the Ars Poetriae

Baltzell, Jane. "Rhetorical 'Amplification' and 'Abbreviation' and the Structure of Medieval Narrative," *Pacific Coast Philology,* II (1967), 32–40.

Brinkman, Hennig. *Zu Wesen und Form Mittelalterlicher Dichtung.* Halle, 1928.

De Bruyne, Edgar. *Études d'esthetique médiévale.* 3 vols. Bruges, 1946.

Faral, Edmond. *Les Arts poétiques du XIIᵉ et du XIIIᵉ siècle*. Paris, 1924.

——. "Sidoine Apollinaire et la technique littéraire du moyen age," *Miscellanea Giovanni Mercati*, II (1946).

Ghellinck, Jean de. *L'Essor de la littérature latine au XIIᵉ siècle*. 2 vols. Brussels, Paris, 1946.

Kelly, Douglas. "The Scope of the Treatment of Composition in the Twelfth- and Thirteenth-Century Arts of Poetry," *Speculum*, XLI (1966), 261–278.

Murphy, James J. "The Arts of Discourse, 1050–1400, *Medieval Studies*, XXIII (1961), 194–205.

——. "A New Look at Chaucer and the Rhetoricians," *Review of English Studies*, XV (1964), 1–20.

Quadlbauer, Franz. *Die antike Theorie der genera dicendi im lateinischen Mittelalter*. ("Österreichische Akademie der Wissenschaften, Philosophisch-historische Klasse, 241, 2.") Graz, Vienna, Cologne, 1962.

Sedgwick, W. B. "Notes and Emendations on Faral's *Les Arts poétiques*," *Speculum*, II (1927), 331–343.

——. "The Style and Vocabulary of the Latin Arts of Poetry in the Twelfth and Thirteenth Centuries," *Speculum*, III (1928), 349–381.

Sidonius. *Poems and Letters*. Trans. by W. B. Anderson. 2 vols. Loeb Classical Library. Cambridge, Mass., 1963.

## ROBERT OF BASEVORN

### AND THE ARS PRAEDICANDI

Caplan, Harry. "Rhetorical Invention in Some Medieval Tractates on Preaching." *Speculum* 2 (1927): 284–295.

——. "The Four Senses of Scriptural Interpretation and the Medieval Theory of Preaching." *Speculum* 4 (1929): 282–290.

——. "Classical Rhetoric and the Medieval Theory of Preaching." *Classical Philology* 28 (1933): 73–96. [A fundamental statement of the origins of medieval theory.]

——. "A late Medieval Tractate on Preaching." *Studies in Rhetoric and Public Speaking in Honor of J. A. Winans* (New York, 1925): 61–90.

——. "'Henry of Hesse' on the Art of Preaching." *PMLA* 48 (1934): 340–361.

Charland, Th.-M. *Artes Praedicandi: contribution à l'histoire de la rhétorique au moyen âge*. (Publications de l'institut d'études médiévales d'Ottowa, VII.) Paris, 1936. [Now reprinted.]

Dargan, Edwin C. *A History of Preaching*. 2 vols. New York, 1905. [Reprinted in one volume, 1954.]

Gilson, Etienne. "Michel Menot et la technique du sermon médiévale." *Les idées et les lettres* (Paris, 1932): 93–154. [Reprinted from *Revue d'historie franciscaine* 2 (1925).]

Murphy, James J. "Saint Augustine and the Debate about a Christian Rhetoric." *QJS* 46 (1960): 400–410.

Owst, Gerald R. *Preaching in Medieval England: An Introduction to Sermon Manuscripts of the Period, c. 1350–1450*. Cambridge, 1926.

Roth, Dorothea. *Die mittelalterlichen Predigtheorie und das Manuale Curatorum des Johann Ulrich Surgant*. (Basler Beitrage zur Geschichtswissenschaft, Band LVIII.) Basel und Stuttgart, 1956.

Smyth, Charles. *The Art of Preaching, 747–1939*. London, 1940.